Inheritance in America

Carole Shammas
Marylynn Salmon
Michel Dahlin

Inheritance in America From Colonial Times to the Present

Rutgers University Press
New Brunswick and London

Library of Congress Cataloging-in-Publication Data
Shammas, Carole.
  Inheritance in America from colonial times to the present.
  Bibliography: p.
  Includes index.
  1. Inheritance and succession—United States—
History. I. Salmon, Marylynn, 1951–   . II. Dahlin,
Michel. III. Title.
KF753.S53   1987   346.7305'2   86-20409
ISBN 0-8135-1214-X   347.30652
      0-8135-1266-2 (pbk.)

The preparation of this volume was made possible in part by a grant from the Division of Research Programs of the National Endowment for the Humanities, an independent federal agency.

Contents

Figures and Tables

FIGURE

TABLES

Preface

This study originated in a 1982 grant proposal entitled "Inheritance, Family, and the Evolution of Capitalism in America." Before writing the proposal, all the authors, in the course of working on other topics, had come into contact with some aspect of the current research on inheritance: Carole Shammas had worked extensively with probate records while studying colonial consumer behavior; Marylynn Salmon was finishing a book on women and property law in early America; and Michel Dahlin had just completed a dissertation on the elderly in the Progressive era. Our limited exposure to the subject indicated that, although the inheritance process played a crucial role in linking the institution of the family to that of capitalism, the available research raised more questions than it answered about the nature of the relationship and how it had developed over time.

For example, the economics literature on bequests and the problem of capital formation demonstrated the importance of inheritance in the economy and showed ingenuity in devising ways to measure the effects of government policies on the intergenerational transmission of wealth. From our perspective, however, much of the work seemed to be rather ahistorical and monocausal. Most writers assumed parents had, from time immemorial, a "natural desire" to transmit property to the next generation and that little change had occurred until the state began interfering in the twentieth century. Some studied interference in the form of progressive taxation, while others looked at social security. Structural changes in the private sector and in the family, however, did not often enter the picture. Although we were far from sure how all the pieces fit together, we sensed something was missing.

We were also uncomfortable with an extremely functionalist portrayal of seventeenth- and eighteenth-century family relations that was enjoying some popularity among scholars in our own discipline, history. The interpretation went something like this: Yes, it was true that under intestacy laws all daughters and younger sons received smaller shares than the eldest son, that testators could disinherit any or all children in a will, and that married women had only limited inheritance rights, in the form of a one-third share of family realty, and had no will-making powers. But all this was for the good of the family and did not produce much inequality. Disinheritance was rare, and husbands took extraordinary measures to see that their widows were maintained. In addition, the plentifulness of land insured that almost all families owned realty and that most family members got some property. Daughters were established in marriages, and younger sons went off to the frontier. In this interpretation, the family was such a harmonious institution that a reader had difficulty understanding why the system was ever altered. And that was in fact the problem. Nowhere was there evidence of any impetus for change, yet we knew that significant transformations in inheritance had occurred at the end of the eighteenth and during the nineteenth century, when laws giving preferential treatment to eldest sons disappeared and legislators enacted the married women's property acts.

It was puzzles such as these that prompted us to embark upon this study. Given the scope of the project, it would have been impossible to complete our work within a reasonable amount of time had we not received grants from the Law and Social Sciences Program of the National Science Foundation (SES-8208620) and the Basic Research Program of the National Endowment for the Humanities (RO-20466-83). Once the funding had been obtained, we set out to collect the data. We are grateful to Charles Raudenbush Jr. and Kathy Miller in the office of the Register of Wills and Clerk of Orphan's Court, Bucks County; David J. Collins, Civil Processing Division, Los Angeles County Courthouse; "Charles" at the archives of the Los Angeles Hall of Records; and Kai-Yun Chiu, librarian of the Library Company of the Baltimore Bar for their assistance.

The two biggest tasks we faced in this project were the coding of ten sets of probate records and the compilation of inheritance statutes for all the colonies/states at four points in time. Our research assistant, Simon P. Newman, did an excellent job of supervising the coding; and the following students, in addition to Simon, spent long hours in front of the microfilm machines: Mark Angelos, Peter Angelos, Helen Danecki-Hermann, Wendy Henning, Deborah Kitchen, Robert Olwell, and Christine Zienkienicz. Carole Shammas then went through the wills and administrations, checking for inconsistencies and errors. Marylynn Salmon and Michel Dahlin collected most of the statute material appearing in Tables 1.1, 3.1, and Appendixes B and C. Mary Ann Stevanus gathered case and statute materials on nineteenth-century Pennsylvania inheritance law and otherwise served as an able research assistant. Institutional support from the Social Science Research Facility, where the data sets from this study are deposited, the Office of Women's Studies, and the History Department of the University of Wisconsin-Milwaukee speeded the project along.

A number of scholars very generously shared data, provided references, supplied information, and raised questions. We thank Norma Basch, James Brundage, Lois Green Carr, Margo Conk, James Cronin, Jack Crowley, Toby Ditz, Mary Maples Dunn, Cissie Fairchilds, Mark Friedberger, Darryl Holter, Barbara Laslett, Jean Lee, William Newell, Mary Beth Norton, Joseph O'Rourke, Gregory Roeber, Anne Firor Scott, Eileen Spring, Gail Terry, and Lorena Walsh.

Drafts of chapters were presented at the Legal History Summer Seminar, University of Wisconsin–Madison Law School and at the 1985 meetings of the Organization of American Historians and the Social Science History Association. Comments made on those occasions aided us in making revisions. We benefited from a very knowledgeable critique of the entire manuscript by Michael Grossberg. Our biggest debt is to Daniel Scott Smith, both for the numerous letters of support we know he has had to write on behalf of this project and for the insights he has continually provided concerning the dynamics of historical change. Finally, we want to thank Rutgers University Press, and particularly Marlie Wasserman, for offering us a contract when this study was no more than a grant proposal.

Inheritance in America

Introduction

The History of Inheritance in America

The bulk of household wealth in America, perhaps as much as 80 percent of it, is derived from inheritance, not labor force participation.[1] The irony that accident of birth is the prime determinant of one's material situation in a society that considers free market competition to be the most rational and efficient method of making economic decisions has, of course, not gone unnoticed over the years. It was just such a realization that led reformers at the beginning of the twentieth century to push for progressive taxation, and the persistence of poverty has kept a small but dedicated band of researchers busy analyzing the role of inherited wealth in perpetuating inequality.[2]

What invariably has rescued the inheritance system from abolition or more stringent taxation policies has been the fear that these actions would jeopardize capital formation and family organization. Using arguments that date back at least to Ricardo, proponents of the unrestricted transmission of wealth from one generation to the next contend that this accumulation of capital is essential to investment. They point to studies showing that the affluent devote a higher proportion of their lifetime resources to investment and a smaller percentage of it to consumption than do the rest of the population. Progressive taxation, taxing the rich at higher rates than the poor, interferes with this process and, in their opinion, depresses economic growth and employment opportunities. Thus, they maintain, the policy ultimately hurts the very people it was designed to help. Alternative methods of capital accumulation are either not discussed or dismissed as inefficient and inappropriate because they would aggrandize the state. Defenders of the inheritance system also usually bring up, at some point, the danger of meddling with the "natural" desire of parents to leave property to their

3

children, implying that doing so diminishes the industriousness and the cohesiveness of families.[3]

Seldom in the debates about inheritance in America is mention made of the long-term changes in capitalism and the family. In Ricardo's time, after all, family heads not only owned most of the capital in society but also managed the enterprises; death not divorce ended marriages; and married women lacked property rights, to mention but a few of the differences. Many of the codes governing inheritance in the states contain provisions, for example, the spousal thirds, life estates, trusts, and inheritance taxes, originally enacted a century ago or earlier under different conditions. Clearly, to formulate a sound rationale for changing or retaining policies and laws relating to the transmission of wealth requires some knowledge of the social and economic forms prevailing when those policies and laws were instituted. What we need to know, then, is the extent to which the inheritance system we now have reflects the "world we have lost." To figure out that, however, requires knowledge of how American capitalism and the family have evolved over time.

INHERITANCE AND STRUCTURAL TRANSFORMATIONS IN CAPITALISM AND THE FAMILY

When we refer to structural transformations in capitalism, we mean changes in the composition of capital or in who had the right to own, use, and manage it.[4] Was capital mainly in the form of realty (land, buildings, and improvements) or personalty, and was the personalty in tangibles (livestock, equipment, inventory stock, and so forth) or in intangibles (financial assets and cash)? Who had property rights in the wealth—individuals, families, corporations, the state? Obviously any alterations in either composition or rights could affect inheritance.

In the colonial period, one-half or more of wealth tended to be in land and buildings, and almost all property was held by white male heads of families. The absence of financial institutions and private corporations limited financial assets to book debts, mortgages, personal bonds, notes, and bills. In America there were no lords and virtually none of the claims on familial property characteristic of manorial societies. The public sector was also weak, and both monarchy and church had comparatively small accumulations of wealth.

This situation began to change after the Revolution. A rather disparate group of business and institutional studies written in the last few years has improved our understanding of how corporate organization evolved. Despite all the attention lavished upon firms such as the Lowell textile mills, it was not manufacturing concerns that first employed corporate forms most frequently. It was financial institutions, insurance companies, transportation firms, and enterprises concerned with producing energy. These corporations built up the infrastructure in America, beginning after the break with Great Britain. Evolving along with these corporate businesses were family trusts and charitable endowments that, as Peter Dobkin Hall has noted, allowed the wealthy to control, privately, segments of the public sphere. Over the course of the nineteenth century, profit and nonprofit corporations gradually assumed the role of the family in the management of capital. It was not so much that family farms or businesses all became corporations as it was that the existence of financial institutions and stocks made it possible for firms to liquidate and for the patrimony to take the form of financial rather than physical assets.[5]

Another major transformation in capitalism involves the government. Historical research on the growth of the state is only just beginning, so the full contours of its changing influence on not only the economy but family life as well are yet to be explored. It appears, however, that in the nineteenth century the state, primarily through the courts, functioned as an enabler. It permitted corporations, foundations, and trusts to be set up and allowed women and children, in certain circumstances, the right to challenge patriarchal authority. This role has continued into the twentieth century, but it has been joined by the more aggressive forms of government action to which social scientists have drawn attention. Fiscal policy has had a very strong impact on the functioning of the economy and, through estate taxation, has touched inheritance. The expansion of the government's role in assuring the welfare of its citizens—through programs such as social security and Medicare—has purportedly played a part in transforming family relations.[6]

Aside from the possible effects of the state on the family, there are two other structural changes the historical literature indicates are important and perhaps relevant to inheritance. One is the sharp decline in the fertility rate in the nineteenth century. In 1800, women living through their childbearing years gave birth to an average of seven children. By 1900 that number had been halved, and of course the downward trend has continued throughout the twentieth century, interrupted only briefly by the baby boom. Among historical demographers a lively debate rages over the reasons for the drop.[7] It has been tied to a reduction in the availability of land, to literacy, and, most interesting, to what Daniel Scott Smith has referred to as "domestic feminism," an increase in the wife's ability to control household affairs including the size of the family.[8] Whatever the cause, we do know something about the result of the fertility decline. Households had many fewer children, and they were being educated longer and working less.

The notion of a "domestic feminism" operating in the Victorian period has been taken up by other scholars in addition to demographers. Some family and women's historians trace the improvement in the status of wives and mothers back to the late eighteenth century.[9] While, according to this interpretation, domestic ideology may have sharply restricted the behavior and the opportunities of women, it at the same time reduced patriarchal control on the home and altered the structure of authority within the family. If domestic feminism was important to women in any group, it was certainly to those in capitalist households. Part of the improvement in the status of these women was the passage of the marital property acts in the third quarter of the nineteenth century.[10] This legislation altered the common law (the traditional English law adopted with some variations by the original thirteen colonies and most of the states east of the Rockies) to allow women to retain control over their own property after marriage. For wives with capital, the acts greatly increased their economic power within the family. Among other rights, they acquired the power to write a will. Adoption of the community property system (which owes more to Roman law), in place of the common law, by a group of states entering the union in the last half of the nineteenth and early twentieth century conferred even greater rights on wives.[11]

The relationship of the marital property legislation to inheritance law is relatively straightforward, but we do not know how it actually affected the transmission of wealth. The impact of the other transformations is even less understood. Although the history of inheritance has attracted a number of able scholars over the years, most of the research has been clustered in the colonial period and has not dealt directly with changes in economic structure. Instead, the effect of land availability on the disposition of realty has been the primary issue.

The abundance of land in the colonies, so often used as the main determinant of behavior in the New World, was quickly appropriated by legal scholars seeking to explain American departures from the English common law,[12] especially the adoption of the partible inheritance of land and the demise of primogeniture (the practice of devising all land to the eldest son).[13] Local studies of testamentary patterns in early America also have concentrated on the transfer of realty. Their findings support those made by researchers studying inheritance laws. Colonists commonly gave land to more than one son and, in the beginning years of settlement at least, frequently made gifts of realty to daughters and wives.[14]

There is no comparable literature on the growth of financial assets and its possible impact on inheritance. Only a few disparate testamentary studies exist covering the period 1800 to the mid twentieth century, and they do not deal extensively with the effects of changes in the composition and management of capital, although they do record its increased importance.[15] Farm communities and land transfers actually continue to hold their own in the research on testamentary behavior in the modern era, despite the sharp decline in the population living in rural areas and the drop in the proportion of wealth held in realty.[16]

Research on the status of women in the eighteenth- and nineteenth-century family has come to include the study of inheritance. Legal scholars have reevaluated earlier work on colonial intestacy laws and dower rights, the one-third of a man's real estate his widow could claim for her lifetime use. They have investigated, for the first time, the interpretations given those laws by the courts.[17] The idea that America's divergence from English law had provided a golden age for women has been challenged.[18] Improvement in women's ability to bequeath wealth presumably occurred when, in the later nineteenth century, states began passing marital property acts. But some new research concludes that the process began almost a century earlier with the gradual increase in popularity of marriage settlements among the affluent. Equity courts, using the civil law rather than the common law, recognized these agreements, through which married women often received the right to make a will.[19] Complicating the issue further are testamentary studies of early American communities showing that at just the point when marriage settlements gave more autonomy to at least some affluent married women, late eighteenth-century husbands placed more and more restrictions on their wives' ability to control property in their wills.[20] Why this occurred has not been determined, and owing to the limited number of studies for the nineteenth century, we do not know when or to what extent this trend began reversing itself.

Another major structural change in the family, the drop in the number of sons and daughters born to American women, has been linked to inheritance but with the causal arrow pointing in the opposite direction from the one we are considering. One of the most popular theories explaining the nineteenth-century decline in fertility has been put forward by Richard Easterlin. He has contended that land available for bequests to children had a big impact on the number of offspring produced by farm parents. In other words, fertility declined in areas where land had become scarce and expensive and rose where it was plentiful and cheap. The theory has been criticized and alternative explanations offered. No one, however, has explored the reverse problem, how the drop in the number of children affected bequests.[21]

In sum, the existing literature has established certain significant points about the evolution of inheritance in America. Scholars, understanding the importance of land in the New World, have furnished a fairly detailed picture of how its availability altered the laws of distribution. Also the connection between domestic feminism and wives' acquisition of the right to own and will property has been brought out, as has a conflicting trend in the testamentary record of husbands' spousal bequests. Clearly, though, historians have much further to go in explaining the major shifts that have occurred in inheritance practices.

Before much more can be done, moreover, we must fill some of the gaps in our factual knowledge about the history of inheritance law. When the legal history work on primogeniture is put together with the research on women's property rights, the information we have on intestacy laws and dower for the period up to 1820 is extensive and surpasses the scholarship available for any other past era. Inheritance statutes as they intersected with the married women's property acts in the later nineteenth century have also been researched. Aside from that, virtually no substantial historical work has been done on the inheritance law of modern America. There is no place to go, except the contemporary sources, to find out, for example, when states made intestacy laws apply equally to husbands and wives or when lifetime-only restrictions on a widows' dower were eliminated or what widow's rights actually were in the first states adopting community property law. Nor do we know if there has been any change in the rights of collateral heirs to estates or the privileges of charities to inherit.

Most of the research on past testamentary patterns also relates to the colonial period. While not all studies ask the same questions, and some suffer from inadequate sample size, much could be learned by simply putting the pieces of research into a coherent framework. After 1780, however, the work on bequest patterns by historians and legal experts grows too thin to permit any synthetic treatment, and that situation holds true for the periods right up to the mid twentieth century. Consequently, we know next to nothing about the changing behavior of testators toward sons, daughters, spouses, kin and nonkin, and charities during most of the industrial era.

OBJECTIVES AND LIMITS OF THIS STUDY

By necessity a certain portion of this book is descriptive, a historical account of (1) American inheritance laws—those governing intestacy, dower, right to will, and estate taxes—and (2) testamentary behavior—the division of realty and personalty among heirs, restrictions on bequests, the creation of trusts and life estates, and the naming of executors and guardians. We were most interested in what caused these laws and behavior to change. Specifically, we considered how the declining importance of realty and the growth of financial assets, the switch from family to corporate management of capital, the increased role of the state in management decisions and in family welfare, the fall in fertility, and alterations in the power relations within families affected patterns of wealth transmission.

Several issues are involved here. Traditionally, the English and American inheritance system assumed realty was the prime source of wealth. We already discussed briefly the findings of those studying how the plentifulness of land altered intestacy laws and bequest patterns. What has not been much examined is the response to the long-term growth in personalty. In plantation areas, this increase began in the late seventeenth century with the rise in slave importations. A more permanent alteration in the proportion of wealth held in personalty was the proliferation of financial paper. Unless corrected by statutes or wills, the effect of such an expansion would have been to enlarge the proportion of wealth given to widows, daughters, and younger sons, who in most colonies and states received more personality than realty. The question is, were there any reactions to this development? Is that how one explains certain alterations in dower rights and increasing time restrictions on legacies of personalty that historians have noted in the laws and wills of early America?

A related but somewhat grander issue is the assumption that the spread of corporate forms, which separated ownership from management, made it less crucial to settle the majority of an estate upon one male heir.[22] Can we say then that corporate capitalism led to more equality among children and larger legacies for widows? Did it make liquidation more acceptable and dampen dynastic enthusiasm because there was no family business that had to be maintained for the next generation? For example, was there a relationship between the growth of corporate shares and the decline in restricting wives' bequests to a term of years, a trend that has been identified in several studies of testamentary behavior in the late nineteenth and twentieth centuries?[23]

Or was it the government with its progressive estate taxes that led wealthy fathers to abandon all hopes of lineal glory, give up on inheritance strategies, and become depleters? One recent study of affluent twentieth-century decedents shows that the top fifth passed on fewer real dollars to their heirs than they had inherited.[24] Many of the rich, it also appears, do not take full advantage of tax breaks available to those willing to make intervivos transfers to heirs.[25] Yet the trusts and foundations seem more sophisticated and ubiquitous than ever. Do current estate-planning techniques work more efficiently to preserve fortunes for the next generation than earlier testamentary strategies?

Also of interest are the effects on inheritance of changes in household structure and family relations. It is possible to alter the causal pattern suggested above. Perhaps it was not that corporations enabled testators to divide their estates more equitably and set up fewer restrictions on the absolute ownership of property but that the changing dynamics of family life required more equal divisions. Both family capitalism and the patriarchal family, while increasing the power of the household head over his individual unit, cut him off from lineage and community. In certain ways he depended more on nuclear family members, especially the other adult in the family, his wife. In this situation, the esprit de corps of the family proved essential and the loyalty of one's spouse crucial. From the literature on the rise of domesticity, we know that such esprit did in fact develop and with it somewhat more equal relationships among family members. How then could a father easily skimp on dowries or award his wife only dower or less? Familial pressures for a way out may well have been a factor in promoting corporate forms. Whatever the case, the timing of more equitable portions and changes in female status are among the most interesting subjects to address.

Some contemporary debate on the family seems to revolve around the question whether, for most Americans, intergenerational transmission of wealth retains much meaning at all. Legal experts have argued for some time that changing forms of wealth and the current emphasis on the conjugal unit in place of lineal heirs have rendered many intestacy laws and dower provisions obsolete. Wills and surveys reveal that the overwhelming majority of those with spouses desire them to be their *sole* beneficiary, a sentiment in direct contradiction to the one-half, one-third, or less allowed by the states in the absence of a will.[26] In addition, some suggest that lineal heirs today are not only losing out to spouses but also to other relatives or to nonkin.[27] With social insurance enabling more and more widows and widowers to live independent from their children in retirement communities or homes for the elderly, these testators may well be inclined to name heirs other than children and grandchildren.

The effects of long-term structural changes are not the only issues we examine, however. We also investigate the way social and economic characteristics of testators—variables such as wealth, occupation, educational level, ethnicity, gender, age, marital status, and number of children—affect inheritance decisions. For example, studies from disparate periods have indicated that wealthy male testators prefer to leave a smaller proportion of their estate to their widows than do the less affluent.[28] We must never preclude the possibility that these microlevel traits may explain more of the variation in the response of testators than some of the macrolevel transformations we are studying. In addition, we are concerned with the reasons for the differences in inheritance laws among states. Theories ranging from the type of labor system to contrasting ethnolegal traditions (biblical, common or customary, and civil) have been offered as explanations but have not been systematically tested.[29]

Finally, we should mention what is not covered in this book. Throughout American history, most people have not owned sufficient amounts of capital to pass on wealth to heirs. This book focuses upon the propertied, not because they are intrinsically more important than the general population but because they have had a disproportionate influence on the wealth distribution. In this plane of activity, the doings of a Henry Ford or a Howard Hughes are of much greater moment than those of a Mother Teresa or a Martin Luther King, regrettable as that may be. Moreover, our analysis excludes transfers relating to so-called human capital: genes, education, health care, home environment, and so forth. As justification for these decisions, we offer the first sentence of the Introduction.

THE DATA AND PLAN OF THE BOOK

Obviously no single book could cover four centuries of inheritance in what are now fifty states of the union year by year and place by place. Nor would such a study have much coherence or be very helpful in answering the questions we have posed. Because intestacy laws are enacted on the state level and probate is handled by counties, generalizations about the national situation must be combined with intensive investigation of lower jurisdictions. Consequently, we survey the inheritance law of all the colonies/states at four points, each approximately one hundred years apart—1720, 1790, 1890, and 1982—but also study in more depth the law of one old common law state, Pennsylvania, and the most populous community property state, California.

Intestacy statutes and the pertinent case law, however, are not the whole story. By writing a will, a testator could ignore the descent and distribution pattern established by the state. It is necessary, therefore, to examine wills from county records to understand fully the history of inheritance in America. We took will samples from Bucks County, Pennsylvania, for the same four intervals covered in the surveys of intestacy laws. We also sampled Los Angeles County, California, wills in the 1890s and 1980 to chart departures from the inheritance law of a community property state.

We picked Bucks because it had well-preserved probate records going back to the seventeenth century and because of its economic composition. Like most northern communities of early America, Bucks was settled in 1683 mainly by religious dissenters, in this case Quakers, who made a living by farming. It retained its totally rural character until well into the twentieth century; but early on, its proximity to the metropolis of Philadelphia greatly affected its economy. By the 1790s, the period of our second will sample, Bucks farmers were already provisioners for the city.[30] During the nineteenth century, the communities of Bucks never became streetcar suburbs, but developments in rail transportation both helped agriculture and attracted larger numbers of wealthy citizens eager to escape the city environment and set up gracious country homes. Large-scale industry and suburbs came to Bucks County in a major way after World War II, when United States Steel erected the biggest plant ever built on former farmlands in lower Bucks County and the Levitt Corporation selected Bucks as the site for one of its Levittown housing tracts.[31] While Bucks County might not be a good sample of the population of America as a whole, being too much an enclave of affluent WASPS, it shares important characteristics with the nation's *probate* population. Moreover, Bucks County, by being both an agricultural community and a retreat for the rich of industrial America, had a mix of different types of capitalists: small family businessmen (farmers) and rentiers.

Los Angeles County, in the community property state of California, offers some contrasts to nineteenth- and twentieth-century Bucks County. The first California sample covers several years in the 1890s, a time when the recent migration of easterners, midwesterners, and northern Europeans had successfully displaced the native Mexican American population. By the end of the century, those with Spanish surnames constituted less than 20 percent of the population and an even smaller proportion of the propertied elite. Spurred on by the introduction of railroads, the merchandising and professional sectors grew while fruit growing and ranching slowly gave way to land and resource speculation. At the turn of the century, the city of Los Angeles was something of a boom town. Ninety years later, in the 1980s, the county was well on its way to becoming the largest metropolitan

area in the nation, with a majority of its residents members of Hispanic, Asian, or Afro-American minority groups. Minorities are not
well represented in either of the two Los Angeles will samples, however, underscoring the point that testators are a rather special portion
of the general population.[32]

By comparing four periods when different forms of capitalist and
family organization prevailed, we can make some inferences about the
impact of those forms on inheritance. There are logical leaps involved
in doing this, but, in the absence of aggregate data and time series on
such things as testamentary choices, there is little alternative. It is
easier to compare the characteristics of testators in each period with
their testamentary behavior, and the Pennsylvania and California data
enable us to contrast a common law state with a community property one.

While this book presents a historical overview of inheritance in
America from colonial times to the present, its main purpose is to examine how specific economic and familial changes affected the transmission of wealth. It has three parts. The first, "Inheritance under
Family Capitalism," looks at inheritance in America when the family
had a virtual monopoly over both ownership and management of capital,[33] investigates both inheritance statutes and testamentary behavior,
and considers the impact of the Revolution.

Part Two covers inheritance during the nineteenth century as the development of corporate forms began to separate the ownership and the
management of capital, substituting financial assets for physical wealth
and making it less necessary for the family to function as a business
firm. This is also the period that has been characterized by historians
as the era of "the republican mother" and, a bit later, "domestic feminism." The first chapter in Part Two looks at how these changes in
capitalism and the household relate to the transformation in inheritance wrought by the married women's property acts, then compares
testamentary behavior at the beginning of the century with what it had
become a hundred years later.

Part Three treats inheritance in an age when the family still owns
most of the wealth and corporations mainly do the managing, but the
government plays a large role in regulating its distribution. Inheritance
taxes had been around in one form or another since the union was
formed, but the staunchly progressive federal estate tax represented a
quantum leap forward in terms of state intervention and engendered a

large-scale estate-planning industry. One chapter is devoted to the federal estate tax, another to the impact social insurance had on families, and a third to twentieth-century alterations in inheritance laws and how they relate to the changing status of women in America. This part ends with a chapter that analyzes current testamentary behavior.

LONG-TERM TRENDS IN THE COMPOSITION OF THE PROBATE POPULATION AND PROBATE ESTATES

The composition of the American probate population and that population's wealthholdings have of course changed over the four-century period of this study. The question is, how? Was there a strong secular increase in the proportion of decedents who went through probate and who wrote wills as the country grew more literate, urban, and professionalized? When did a sizeable number of women's estates begin to be probated? Did the increase coincide with the passage of the married women's property acts of the later nineteenth century? How much of inherited wealth has been divided according to the principles set down in the intestacy statutes of the state, and how much has been decided by last will and testament? Do estates reflect the late eighteenth- and nineteenth-century growth in corporate forms, or did financial assets continue to represent a smaller share of probated wealth than realty until the twentieth century? Our sample of Bucks County probate records allows us to describe the transformation in at least one county, and this information on trends will give the reader a frame of reference for later discussions of changes in intestacy laws and testamentary behavior.

Tables I.1 and I.2 show that, even in the twentieth century, by no means all adults go through probate or write wills. The figures indicate that over 40 percent of Bucks County decedents in both the 1890s and 1979 escaped court proceedings. Most, presumably, had estates too insignificant to merit probate. Also, to avoid inheritance and estate taxes, those with modest estates now may try to transfer all their property over to their heirs shortly before they die. Only a quarter of decedents at the end of the nineteenth century had wills, while eighty years later the percentage was 36. Comparison with the twentieth-century

TABLE I.1 **PERCENTAGE OF ADULT DECEDENTS**
WITH PROBATED ESTATES AND WITH WILLS,
BUCKS COUNTY, 1751–1979

	Male	Female	Both
Probated estates:			
1751[a]	43.1	2.0	24.1
1791–1801	49.5	11.0	31.4
1891–1893	65.9	39.9	53.5
1979	58.8	59.2	59.0
Probated wills:			
1751	20.0	2.0	12.0
1791–1801	24.7	5.6	11.1
1891–1893	30.3	18.6	24.6
1979	34.2	38.5	36.2

Source: See Appendix A.

[a] Absence of population figures for early colonial Bucks County make it impossible to give estimates for years before 1751.

counties listed in Table I.2 demonstrates that, if anything, Bucks County residents were more likely to be probated and write wills than people living in other localities. It was typical in these places for one in three decedents to be probated and less than one in five to have a will.

In early America, of course, feme covert status, which prohibited wives from owning personalty and devising realty severely restricted female participation in the transmission of property. The married women's property acts, which allowed wives to control wealth they had inherited or earned themselves, swelled the ranks of female probates and testates. Between the 1790s and the 1890s in Bucks County, the proportion of adult female decedents whose estates were probated increased from 11 percent to about 40 percent, and the twentieth century brought a further jump.

The improvement in the probate and testate ratios among men is less dramatic. In the early American period, half of Bucks County adult men went through probate, and nearly a quarter were testates, figures that accord with those from other colonies.[34] Considering the illiteracy, poor transportation, rural nature of the settlements, and comparatively undeveloped state of the legal profession, it is amazing that the estimated proportion of adult male decedents whose estates were probated was only 10–15 percentage points below the modern figures. The importance attached to the filing of probate and the writing of wills suggests, perhaps, the centrality of inheritance to seventeenth- and eighteenth-century communities.

Until the twentieth century, testators of both sexes made up about half or a little less of all decedents who went through probate. In no period did they constitute much more than a third of all adult decedents. The wealth owned by testators, however, tended to be greater than that possessed by those dying intestate. We know the wealth of all decedents whose estates are probated because the executor or admin-

TABLE I.2 **PERCENTAGE OF ADULT DECEDENTS WITH PROBATED ESTATES AND WITH WILLS, SELECT TWENTIETH–CENTURY AMERICAN COUNTIES**

	Male	Female	Both
Probated estates:			
1914–1929, Kings Co., N.Y.	n.a.	n.a.	32.6
1914–1929, New York Co., N.Y.	n.a.	n.a.	30.7
1920–1929, Pulaski Co., Ark.	n.a.	n.a.	22.9
1921, North Carolina counties	n.a.	n.a.	28.4
1921, Camden Co., N.J.	n.a.	n.a.	29.9
1921–1922, Allegheny Co., Pa.	n.a.	n.a.	33.5
1927, North Carolina counties	n.a.	n.a.	26.8
1941, Dane Co., Wis.	59.7	33.3	47.2
1957, Cook Co., Ill.	17.0	13.0	15.2
1963, Washtenaw Co., Mich.	31.7	35.2	33.2
Probated wills:			
1914–1929, Kings Co., N.Y.	n.a.	n.a.	13.0
1914–1929, New York Co., N.Y.	n.a.	n.a.	10.6
1921, North Carolina counties	n.a.	n.a.	9.6
1921, Camden Co., N.J.	n.a.	n.a.	16.2
1921–1922, Allegheny Co., Pa.	n.a.	n.a.	20.1
1927, North Carolina counties	n.a.	n.a.	7.4
1941, Dane Co., Wis.	24.0	15.0	20.0
1957, Cook Co., Ill.	9.0	7.4	8.4
1963, Washtenaw Co., Mich.	15.8	24.2	19.4
1980, Los Angeles Co., Calif.	14.9	23.3	18.9

Sources: Richard R. Powell and Charles Looker, "Decedents' Estates: Illumination from Probate and Tax Records," *Columbia Law Review* 30 (1930):919–953; Edward H. Ward and J. H. Beuscher, "The Inheritance Process in Wisconsin," *Wisconsin Law Review* (1950):393–426; Allison Dunham, "The Method, Process, and Frequency of Wealth Transmission at Death," *University of Chicago Law Review* 30 (1963):241–285; Olin L. Browder, Jr., "Recent Patterns of Testate Succession in the United States and England," *Michigan Law Review* 67 (1969):1303–1360; and Michigan, Department of Public Health, *1970 Health Statistics* (Lansing, 1971). See Appendix A for Los Angeles County.

istrator has to file an inventory and appraisement of the property contained in the estate. In the colonial period, the 1790s, and the 1890s, Bucks County testators owned a little over 60 percent of the inventoried wealth (see Table I.3). In the 1979 probate files, the percentage soared to 92 percent. Estate taxes, increased reliance on attornies, and fewer middle-aged deaths mean that today men and women of property seldom die without a will. The main point, however, is that testators in all periods, even though they might be no more than a quarter or a third of all decedents, owned a disproportionate share of the property, making their behavior well worth studying.[35]

What about the kind of wealth—realty, tangible and intangible (financial assets) forms of personalty—found in the estates of testates and intestates? Does the trend fit our assumptions about the evolution of the American economy? Certainly the percentages in Table I.4 support the notion that stocks and bonds and other forms of financial assets constituted more and more of private wealth and land, buildings and moveables less. In the colonial period, we estimate that over half (56.3 percent) of probated wealth was in realty, one-third in tangible personalty, and 10 percent in cash and financial assets. Part of the reason for the small proportion of wealth in financial assets was, undoubtedly, that America was a colony with so much credit furnished by British sources. In the 1790s the percentage increased over two and a half times, to 28.7 percent. Although some of that rise was owing to the new availability of corporate shares such as bank stocks, most can probably be attributed to greater numbers of mortgages and commercial book debts in the new nation. A tremendous growth in the proportion of wealth held in financial assets occurred in the nineteenth century. This form of property comprised over 68 percent of all Bucks County probated wealth in the 1890s. Moveables had dwindled to 6

TABLE I.3 **TESTATE WEALTH AS A PERCENTAGE OF ALL PROBATED PERSONAL WEALTH, BUCKS COUNTY**

Years	N	Testate wealth
1685–1755	659	61.1
1791–1801	651	61.3
1891–1893	571	62.1
1979	529	92.3

Source: See Appendix A.

TABLE I.4 **COMPOSITION OF PROBATED WEALTH, BUCKS COUNTY**

| Years | N | Percentage in realty | Percentage in personalty | |
			Intangible	Tangible
1685–1755	47	56.3	10.5	33.1
1791–1801	254	53.6	28.7	17.7
1891–1893	516	24.8	68.8	6.4
1979	528	27.7	68.2	4.1

Source: See Appendix A.
Note: Wealth before any liquidation ordered by testator or by the court.

percent, and realty's share had been more than halved.[36] Examination of the estate inventories shows that an increase in the holding of bank accounts and stocks, local bonds, insurance policies, and shares in businesses, especially transportation and energy company issues, were in large part responsible for the growth. The distribution among the three wealth categories did not change much from the 1890s to the 1979 sample. The growth in homeownership apparently made up for the decline in family-owned farms, so that the proportion of wealth held in realty stayed roughly the same. Other studies of twentieth-century probate estates agree with the results from Bucks County.[37] Even though the major asset owned by most people is a home, the financial assets of the rich are so great that, with assets totaled, intangible wealth outweighs realty. Wealth, like inheritance, has a history.

PART ONE

Inheritance under Family Capitalism

Inheritance probably played a more important role in the economy during colonial times than in any other period of American history. Individual family heads had an almost complete monopoly over both the ownership and the management of capital. There were no manorial customs or corporate lineage rules governing the dispersal of an estate and no powerful monarch or church with great accumulations of property. Neither were there financial or industrial corporations nor a large state apparatus to collect and supervise capital. The economy depended on the family firm more or less exclusively, and inheritance determined the distribution of shares among family members. Too wide a scattering of resources and control might jeopardize business operations. Conversion of physical wealth to financial assets was often costly and, in the absence of financial institutions, sometimes impossible. Keeping a firm or farm intact, therefore, had its appeal. But problems of a different sort might accompany too great a concentration of wealth and authority in one heir's hands: dissension among other family "stockholders" and even litigation. The abbreviated lineage system found in the colonies made it especially important that members of the immediate family cooperate with one another.

Chapter One describes the intestacy laws and legal forms that developed in the colonies and the consequences they had for lineal descendants, wives, collateral kin, and the economic order generally. While the colonies, of course, based much of their law on En-

glish precedents, the mother country itself was in the process of transforming its inheritance laws when America was being settled. Adding to the confusion was the presence of many dissenters in the New England and Middle colonies; the existence of a new form of personalty, slaves; and a much higher land-to-person ratio and less developed financial structures than in the Old World.

In some societies, knowing the inheritance laws means knowing how all wealth was transmitted; not in England and America, however, where free adult males and unmarried adult women had nearly complete testamentary freedom. Chapter Two, therefore, explores who benefited and who lost by testators' departures from the intestacy laws in their wills and why testators did what they did.

Much of the American Revolution's reputation as a social movement has rested on a change made in inheritance, specifically, the demise of two practices associated with feudalism and aristocracy: primogeniture and entail. Chapter Three considers just how revolutionary the revised inheritance laws were and how well the legal system was coping with new trends in the economy and the family.

1

English Inheritance Law and Its Transfer to the Colonies

Although the inheritance customs of the peoples who settled America varied considerably, the property laws of one group have from the beginning dominated the transmission of wealth in this country. The economic and military hegemony of seventeenth-century English colonists resulted in the establishment of the common law, which prevailed with little or no challenge until the emergence of the community property system in the later nineteenth century. What that meant, however, merits some investigation because at the time of settlement, English inheritance was a confusing mixture of feudal rights, manorial traditions, ecclesiastical rules, and parliamentary statutes. Probate was changing from a process governed primarily by custom and local lords to one controlled by individual testators and national legislation. To explore how circumstances may have led colonists to alter the rules of the game, it is necessary to establish what the rules actually were.

ENGLISH INHERITANCE

Custom and the Lord

In medieval England, how people's property was distributed among heirs after death largely depended upon what kind of property they owned, their social status, where they lived, and their sex. Theoretically, most people had no testamentary power at all, and those who did could only exercise it over a small proportion of certain kinds of assets. Different inheritance and testamentary rules governed realty (essentially, land, buildings, and improvements) and personalty (all other kinds of property including personal effects, household goods, live-

23

stock, stock-in-trade, equipment, leases, cash, and financial assets such as mortgages and money lent at interest).

The male elite of England—feudal lords and those who had derived their lands from them—had to pass all realty to the eldest son, a practice known as primogeniture. The division of personalty is less clear and apparently varied according to time and place. The Magna Carta stated only that the wife and children were entitled to their "reasonable parts," which apparently in many regions of the country meant one-third each, leaving only a final third available for testamentary disposition. More regulation followed if a man had only minor children. The monarch had the right of wardship over the estate of minor heirs, and the crown received great monetary benefit from this privilege. In larger cities, orphans' courts became the "guardians" of young heirs.[2] The degree of testamentary freedom that did exist was mainly the result of ecclesiastical pressure. The church encouraged the concept, hoping, apparently, to shake loose from the patrilineage, the wife, and the king or lord a piece of personalty for religious or charitable uses.[3]

The bulk of the population was governed by other rules, but testamentary freedom played little role there either. The villager or villein of medieval England was unfree; that is, he owed labor services to a manorial lord in exchange for rights to a copyhold (tenure on a piece of village land) and the privileges accompanying it. While technically the lord was the only possible heir of the villein because he had to give approval and receive a fee when a new tenant took over the copyhold or when personalty passed to the family, in fact manorial custom regulated who was to get what. Manors either had partible or impartible division of a villein's copyhold (i.e., the realty). The former provided for all sons to receive equal portions of land. Impartible succession, prevalent in the regions with the best arable land, meant all went to one son, most often the eldest (primogeniture); but some localities practiced borough-English, or ultimogeniture, where the youngest son received the holding. Daughters could succeed to a copyhold when there were no sons to inherit.[4]

Inheritance rights also differed by sex. England had more of a unilateral or unilineal than a bilateral system of property transmission.[5] Children may have been related to the kin groups of both mother and father, but they inherited primarily from the father. When a woman married, her dowry, the portion given her by her father or obtained in some other manner, immediately fell under the control of her husband, as did any property she subsequently inherited. A married female was a feme covert, covered woman, who no longer had any legal status. Her spouse represented her interests, and he might do what he pleased with the wealth he acquired from her as long as he did not sell or will her realty. Of course, inheritance customs made women less likely to have such absolute rights over realty.

If a woman with realty predeceased her husband and they had children, he could keep all of her land for the rest of his life whether he remarried or not. That was his curtesy. A widow's right in her dead husband's estate, known as dower or, for copyholders, free bench, was different. It could be a "reasonable part" of his personalty (which of course included hers if she brought any to the marriage), often one-third if there were children, one-half if not. Whatever she might get, however, did depend on local custom and, if her husband was a copyholder, the approval of the lord. Her right to realty, usually a third of it, extended for life on some manors and only during widowhood or "as long as she remained chaste" on others. Apparently the lord of the manor sometimes allowed widows to remarry and retain their dower rights when there were suitors willing to pay large entry fees to enjoy their bride's property. These transactions raise the question of whether the demographics of a community determined the widow's tenure. Did a larger-than-normal younger generation lead to pressure on the lord to terminate dower upon remarriage and a bulge in the widow's generation allow her to hold on to it for life?[6]

Examination of manorial court rolls and customals from the mid thirteenth century on shows how villeins, through paying fees, obtained the right to transfer land, make retirement agreements with their children, and even write wills.[7] Because of these devices, younger sons in impartible inheritance areas often received land. These records also reveal the growth of a class of free men and free land not subject to feudal or manorial restrictions but governed by the royal courts. In addition, the "immemorial" custom of a manor could change. There are examples of communities altering succession from primogeniture to ultimogeniture and vice versa.[8] Nonetheless, the family and its head had *comparatively* limited powers under the medieval English inheritance system. So many decisions about use and alienation and transfer were made for the social group, the economic community, or the patrilineage as a whole. Changes only came with the consent, and the paying off, of those with the ultimate or penultimate rights: the monarch, the manorial lords, or some corporate body such as a monastery. The system was very different from that of family capitalism, which came to prevail in early modern England and particularly in colonial America, where almost all capital was held by individual household heads, who had more or less absolute control over it, including nearly complete testamentary freedom.

Testamentary Freedom and National Statutes on Inheritance

In the early modern period, England slowly replaced custom with national testamentary and intestacy laws. By 1500 villeinage had all but disappeared; more and more people held "free" land subject neither to feudal nor manorial restrictions; and wills were commonly written.[9] Yet these testaments were only supposed to bequeath personalty, and local custom prescribed that certain mandatory shares of it be given to widows and children. Most of the amending of legislation occurred in the last half of the seventeenth century, but the first important law was the 1540 Statute of Wills, which permitted testators to devise all of their freehold land and two-thirds of knight service realty to the heirs of their choice. The other third became devisable about 130 years later with the abolition of feudal tenures. Thereafter, only copyhold land had to follow custom rather than a testator's desire, and the amount of realty held in that way was rapidly decreasing. Land was of course still subject to the lifetime claims of the dower third and curtesy.

In 1670 a statute standardized the distribution and descent of personalty in the absence of a will, and the formula established at that time was the basic pattern of intestate division not only in England but in the United States until the latter part of the twentieth century. The state no longer recognized historic claims of monarch, lord, and church to all or part of the estate. Widows received one-third forever, and children inherited the remainder equally. If no children survived, the widow split the personalty with the husband's kin. In the absence of relatives, the property would be escheated to the King. London, Wales, and the north of England had slightly different rules of division that under certain circumstances gave more to the widow and less to the children and the eldest son.[10]

The remaining customary procedure to be overturned by statute was the limit on a testator's freedom to bequeath personalty. In many localities married men with children could only dispose of one-third of their goods by will because one-third had to go to the spouse and one-third to the children. The comments in the 1590 edition of Henry Swinburne's *A Brief Treatise of Testaments and Last Willes* indicate that, as the sixteenth century drew to a close, a controversy raged over the legitimacy of such restraints under the common law. After discussing the custom, Swinburne wrote, "Others (whose opinion hath prevailed)" maintained that testators should have complete testamentary freedom over their personalty and that no mandatory division under the common law existed unless a locality specifically adopted the division. Those advocating testamentary freedom contended that it kept wife and children in line, while those for the customary restraints believed the protection for wife and children was needed.[11]

Statutes at the end of the seventeenth century resolved the issue in favor of testamentary freedom. More provincial areas, the north of England and Wales, as well as the metropolis had kept the customary divisions. In the 1690s, parliamentary statutes mandated testamentary freedom over personalty in the ecclesiastical province of York, the cities of York and Chester, and Wales. Only London retained the old custom, and there it was ultimately overturned in a 1725 statute.[12]

What was the result of these actions? Basically, they meant that men could disinherit whomever they pleased—sons, daughters, and collateral kin. The only claim or "election right" a widow had on her husband's estate was her lifetime third of realty.

Characteristics of the System

The English had a comparatively narrow unilateral system for the descent of property. With primogeniture the default under intestacy and the prevalence of impartible division among copyhold tenures, one son usually inherited a disproportionately large share of an estate, whereas in Europe partible inheritance proved more popular. The English system was also narrow because collateral kin had relatively little claim on the wealthholder's property. Male collateral kin did not take precedence over daughters in the inheriting of land or personalty. Furthermore, there were no corporate lineage rights or assets as there were in some societies.[13]

The system was unilateral too in that, as noted, upon marriage all a woman's property went to her husband, and their children inherited mainly from him. Even what a widowed mother might bequeath had been derived from the portion her husband willed her. The only claim a wife had to the marital assets she had helped form was a lifetime or widow's third of realty. Also, paternal relatives, no matter how distant, were all preferred before any maternal kin in the inheritance of land, another way England differed from most other nations on the continent. Under the civil law, when two lineages joined at marriage, they established a community property fund, and each had a claim on half. In addition, the wife's inherited property was kept separate from the patrilineage. Thus children inherited from both father and mother. While some argue that this practice may have been more for the benefit of the mother's lineage than the mother herself,[14] it did mean Continental husbands had less power over their wives' property than did English husbands.

Theoretically, the new testamentary freedom enjoyed by wealthholders, another notable characteristic of early modern English inheritance, could have opened the whole system up. It gave great power to the individual family head and had the potential to alter greatly the distribution of property within the lineage. What did in fact happen? While studies of English testamentary behavior are still too scarce to draw firm conclusions about the effects of wills, it seems that those who used them, perhaps one-fourth of adult male decedents, liberalized somewhat the distribution among children but had little interest in giving a larger share to collateral kin or wives. Substantial bequests outside the nuclear family by men with children were infrequent, and wills enabled the childless to give to nonkin. The main way the lineage may have been broadened by testamentary freedom was in a more generous dispersal of realty among sons and greater encumbrances on the eldest son's patrimony for the benefit of all the children.

Wills were apparently not widely used to transform the unilateral patrilineage into a more bilateral system either. Evidence seems in fact to point in the opposite direction. Husband's often gave their widows less or limited their ownership over personalty and realty more than the intestacy laws would have. There is some difference of opinion as to whether this tendency was increasing over the course of the early modern period. A couple of studies of wills and dower customs have discovered that in the seventeenth and early eighteenth centuries more widows had remarriage penalties attached to their portions of both realty and personality. This trend is particularly puzzling because remarriage rates among English widows apparently declined between the sixteenth and the nineteenth centuries.[15]

Also, legal instruments were devised for the specific purpose of limiting the originality of testators. At first, dynasts relied on entailing their land so that it could not be alienated but had to pass on to heirs of the body generation after generation. Most often the entail was further restricted to males, giving preference to the eldest.[16] It became increasingly easier to bar entails, however, and so other more effective methods were developed.

An intervivos procedure, the strict family settlement, gained popularity in the seventeenth century because it essentially protected the patrilineage from the wayward patriarch.[17] The great landed families of England employed this device, derived from the civil rather than the common law, at the time of an heir's marriage, using chancery courts, set up by the crown for other reasons, to interpret and enforce the equity law that enabled them to write these agreements. The strict family settlement set out what the groom's wife and any sons or daughters born of the marriage would receive from his estate upon majority, at marriage, and/or at his death. The heir was basically a life tenant or custodian of the family fortune, not its owner. The settlement reassured the patrilineage that, as much as possible, the estate would remain intact and accompany, if there was one, the aristocratic title; it reassured the lineage of the bride, the suppliers of a dowry, that she and any children born of the marriage would be provided for and not be back knocking at the maternal family door. As with wills, reasonable, though still lesser, portions were obtained for younger sons and daughters than intestacy allowed because land formed so important a part of English aristocratic wealth that strict primogeniture would have resulted in grossly unequal shares. The daughters who had no brothers, however, usually did not benefit by these settlements because, like entails, they often removed females from succession to the land and substituted collateral male kin. Furthermore, the portion given the dowager, the jointure, seldom equaled what a widow might have obtained through her right to one-third of the realty for life, and it apparently declined over time. Gradually, the marriage settlement, also an equity law device, was used to ameliorate the situation of wives. These agreements between prospective bride and groom enabled married women to control some or all of their own property and gain a measure of financial independence from their husbands. There is a question, however, as to how frequently couples drew up such contracts.

If the findings of a recent study of the English elite from the mid sixteenth to the end of the nineteenth century are correct, then the strict family settlement seems to have been tremendously successful in maintaining a narrow unilateral system for the descent of property and thus keeping many of the same dynasties on top for centuries.[18]

INHERITANCE LAW IN THE COLONIES

In probate legislation the English colonies founded during the seventeenth century followed one of two patterns. Either they delayed passing any very detailed bill on inheritance, or they continually fiddled with specific provisions, changing distribution statutes three, sometimes four, times. It was settlements dominated by dissenters from the Church of England (mainly Puritans and Quakers) that most often departed from English precedents and where alterations occurred most frequently. Pennsylvania, one of our case study states, is a good example. In 1682, at the time of the colony's founding, the inheritance law provided for widows to receive one-third, for children to divide equally another third, and for the final third to be disposed of by will. When there was no spouse, two-thirds went to the children. This formula followed what was then the custom of London. It severely limited testamentary power, preventing fathers from disinheriting both wife and children. The law was unclear whether the distribution was to apply to personalty only or to both types of property. The next year the assembly passed an intestacy law that gave the eldest son a double portion. There was no indication, however, whether the limitations on testamentary power were to be maintained. In 1688 a statute was enacted that gave testators complete freedom to bequeath their realty but did not make clear how widows' dower rights were to be handled. Five years later, the assembly wrote another law on testacy and intestacy that allowed widows dower in realty only. In 1697 the assembly changed the provision to dower in both personalty and realty. It stayed that way in the laws published in 1701, but the 1706 statute once again restricted dower to realty. This law lasted longer than the earlier ones, but the wording was so ambiguous that it was necessary to pass two more statutes for clarification.[19]

Some of the changes in Pennsylvania laws and in those of the other colonies were of course prompted by the new English legislation slowly replacing regional inheritance customs. Some of the very first New England laws on distribution did not mandate proportions for the heirs but left the determination to the discretion of the local courts and officials.[20] With statutes in flux in some seventeenth-century colonies and totally absent in others, it is difficult to write very authoritatively about general patterns of colonial inheritance much before the second decade of the eighteenth century.

Table 1.1 displays the inheritance laws of colonial America circa 1720. Most of the laws had been formally enacted by the provincial assemblies. In a few cases, most notably those of New York and New Jersey, the provisions originated in proclamations by those governing the settlements.[21] Despite the statutory activity of the Parliament during the early modern period, much of English inheritance continued to depend upon common law precedents. There was no specific statute on primogeniture, dower, the order of succession for collateral kin, or a number of other issues. In the colonies, legislative bodies followed the lead of the mother country and usually passed their own statute of distribution for personalty, and because of the absence of ecclesiastical courts (the bodies that handled probate in England), they invented procedures for probating wills and administrations; but otherwise most relied on the common law. Only when they wanted to alter the customary rules did legislatures go further and pass statutes on the descent of land, kin succession, and limitations on testamentary freedom. In the table, therefore, we distinguish between provisions explicitly mandated by statute and those deriving validity from the common law, the latter appearing in parentheses.

The colonies departed furthest from English statutory and common law practice in their division of the lineal descendants' share of an intestate's wealth. A few colonies also refused to imitate the statutory innovations passed in England at the end of the seventeenth century and grant husbands full testamentary power over personalty. In questions of widowers' inheritance rights and kin succession, however, the colonies showed little originality.

TABLE 1.1 **INHERITANCE LAWS CIRCA 1720 IN THE AMERICAN COLONIES**

| | | When there is no will: | | | |
| | | Division among children | | Widow's share if children | |
Colony	Date of Law[a] (1)	Real. (2)	Pers. (3)	Real. (4)	Pers. (5)
Massachusetts	1710	Eld. share double	Eld. share double	⅓ life	⅓
Connecticut	1702	Eld. share double	Eld. share double	⅓ life	⅓
New Hampshire	1718	Eld. share double	Eld. share double	⅓ life	⅓
Rhode Island	1719	Eld. share double	Eld. share double	⅓ life	⅓
New York	1683	(Eld. share all)[b]	Eld. share double	⅓ life	⅓
New Jersey (West)	1676	(Eld. share all)[b]	N.a.	(⅓ life)	⅓
Pennsylvania	1706	Eld. share double	Eld. share double	⅓ life	⅓
Delaware	1706	Eld. share double	Eld. share double	⅓ life	⅓
Maryland	1715	(Eld. share all)	Equal	⅓ life	⅓
Virginia	1705	(Eld. share all)	Equal	⅓ life	⅓
North Carolina	1715	(Eld. share all)	Equal	(⅓ life)	⅓
South Carolina	1712	(Eld. share all)	Equal	(⅓ life)	⅓

Sources: Massachusetts, *Acts and Laws of His Majesty's Province of Massachusetts* (Boston, 1699); ibid. (Boston, 1714); John D. Cushing, ed., *The Earliest Laws of the New Haven and Connecticut Colonies* (Wilmington, Del.: Glazier, 1977); Connecticut, *Acts and Laws of his Majesty's Colony of Connecticut in New England* (Boston, 1702); John D. Cushing, ed., *Acts and Laws of New Hampshire 1680–1726* (Wilmington, Del.: Glazier, 1978); idem, ed., *The Earliest Acts and Laws of the Colony of Rhode Island and Providence Plantations 1647–1719* (Wilmington, Del.: Glazier, 1977); Charles Z. Lincoln, ed., *The Colonial Laws of New York from the Year 1664 to the Revolution* I (Albany, 1894), vol. 1; "Concessions and Agreements of the Proprietors, Freeholders, and Inhabitants of the Province of West New Jersey in America, 1676," Microfilm Collections of Early State Records, B.1 New Jersey, reel 1; Gail McKnight Beckman, comp., *The Statutes at Large of Pennsylvania in the Time of William Penn 1680 to 1700* (New York: Vantage, 1976); James T. Mitchell and Henry Flanders, eds., *The Statutes at Large of*

Inheritance by Lineal Descendants

In both England and America, children inherited two-thirds of an intestate's estate if there was a widow surviving, the entire estate if there was not. Also, the colonies, like England, gave no inheritance rights to illegitimate children, and with the exception of a short-lived Pennsylvania law, they put no barriers in the way of a testator who wished to disinherit a lineal heir.[22] A majority of settlements, however, as column two and three in Table 1.1 reveal, rejected the English method of dividing that share among the children. The common law dictated primogeniture descent for the land, and the Statute of Distri-

TABLE 1.1 (*continued*)

When there is no will:					When there is a will:	
Widow's share if no children		When widow gets all	Escheat when no		Widow's share if she disregards will	
Real. (6)	Pers. (7)	(8)	Real. (9)	Pers. (10)	Real. (11)	Pers. (12)
⅓ life	½	Never	Next of kin	Next of kin	⅓ life	Use household utensils
⅓ life	½	Never	Next of kin	Next of kin	⅓ life	None
⅓ life	½	Never	Next of kin	Next of kin	⅓ life	None
⅓ life	½	Never	Next of kin	Next of kin	⅓ life	None
⅓ life	N.a.	Never	Descending kin whole blood	N.a.	⅓ life	None
(⅓ life)	½	Never	N.a.	Next of kin	(⅓ life)	N.a.
½ life	½	Never	Descending kin whole blood	Next of kin	⅓ life	None
⅓ life	½	Never	Next of kin	Grandch. of sibs.	⅓ life	None
⅓ life	½	Never	Descending kin whole blood	Next of kin	⅓ life	⅓
⅓ life	½	Never[c]	Descending kin whole blood	Next of kin or wife	⅓ life	Ch. share[d]
(⅓ life)	½	Never	Descending kin whole blood	Next of kin	(⅓ life)	None
(⅓ life)	½	Never	Descending kin whole blood	Next of kin	(⅓ life)	None

Pennsylvania from 1682–1801, 16 vols. Philadelphia, 1896–1911, vols. 1–3; Delaware, *Laws of the State of Delaware* (New-castle, Del., 1797, vol. 2; John D. Cushing, ed., *The Laws of the Province of Maryland* (Wilmington, Del.: Glazier, 1978); William Walter Hening, comp., *The Statutes at Large: Being a Collection of All the Laws of Virginia* (Philadelphia, 1823), vol. 3; John D. Cushing, ed., *The Earliest Printed Laws of North Carolina 1669–1751* (Wilmington, Del.: Glazier, 1977), vol. 1 Nicholas Trott, comp., *The Law of the Province of South Carolina* (Charlestown, N.C., 1736), vol. 1.

[a] Earliest date in which all provisions in the table were in effect.
[b] Parentheses indicate common law provision rather than statute.
[c] Widow got all personalty if no children of brothers or sisters.
[d] Widow got ½ personalty if no children, ⅓ if 1–2 children. Slaves counted as realty, not personalty for dower purposes.

bution specified equal division of the personality. In the dissenter-dominated colonies of Massachusetts, New Hampshire, Connecticut, Rhode Island, Pennsylvania, and Delaware, the eldest son received, instead, a double share of realty and personalty. Younger sons and all daughters received one share. Early New York, perhaps as late as the 1750s, gave a double share of personalty to the oldest son in addition to his right of primogeniture in the land,[23] making it perhaps the least egalitarian spot in the English-speaking world as far as intestacy laws were concerned.

Why the rejection of primogeniture? There are a number of theories. First, it is important to recognize that lawyers in Europe and England during the sixteenth and especially the seventeenth century were continually debating the merits of allowing the eldest son to take all.[24] On the Continent, where primogeniture was less common than in England, civil lawyers argued for its implementation in order to preserve a strong landed elite. In England, where it prevailed, writers criticized the system, pointing out the hardships suffered by younger sons. The dissenter colonies, therefore, opted for the double share in an environment in which the wisdom of primogeniture was being questioned. Clearly, however, economic conditions in the New World made the arguments for a change even more compelling. The New England colonists prefaced their statute of distributions with the following explanation: "Whereas Estates in these Plantations do consist chiefly of lands which have been subdued and brought to improvement by the Industry and labour of the Proprietors, with the Assistance of their Children; the Younger Children generally having been longest, and most servicable unto their Parents in that behalf, who have not personal estate to give out unto them in Portions, or otherwise, to recompence their Labour."[25]

English children often received cash portions. With money of any kind in short supply in America and conversion and alienation expensive, land was not only the most abundant but the most convenient form of wealth to divide up and give, not only to all the sons, but all daughters as well. There was apparently still enough dynastic feeling in these colonists to want the eldest son to be shown preference. Yet, why a *double* share rather than some other proportion? Probably the passion of the Puritans for biblical law is the best explanation. The passage in the book of Deuteronomy that proclaims a double share for eldest sons is, in fact, listed in the margin of one New England intestacy statute.[26] New York adopted the double share under the Duke's Laws of 1665; and Pennsylvania and Delaware, after first trying equal shares, also copied New England practice in the 1680s. In the eighteenth century the royal authorities attempted to get both Massachusetts and Connecticut to conform to the Statute of Distributions and the common law of primogeniture, but the colonies successfully resisted.[27]

The strict family settlement did not develop much of a following among the early colonial elite either. Equity law and chancery courts were viewed with suspicion, for they were associated in many people's minds with the machinations of the Tudor and, especially, the Stuart monarchs to destroy certain common law liberties. The dissenter colonies refused to set up these courts. Although the royal colonies were more receptive, the legal establishment in colonies such as South Carolina, New York, and even Virginia was in a rather rudimentary state during the seventeenth and early eighteenth centuries. What the colonies opted for instead was the use of the common law entail in wills and deeds. Less comprehensive than the strict family settlement and only applicable to land, some colonies attempted to make it an effective dynastic tool by putting obstacles in the way of those who wished to reverse the actions of an ancestor. In 1705 Virginia passed a statute making it impossible to break an entail without obtaining a special act of the assembly.[28] They also redefined slaves as real property so as to allow the entailing of them.

Inheritance Rights of Widows

While the dissenter colonies were the ones who liberalized the inheritance laws relating to children, it was the Chesapeake colonies of Maryland and Virginia who resisted shrinking widows' dower rights to conform to a new standard in the mother country. Parliamentary statutes passed in the 1690s gave English testators complete freedom to will personalty and ended the custom by which a woman was able to claim one-third of her husband's goods forever, if she rejected the share left her in his will.

Of the colonies that have left some record of having inheritance laws prior to 1690—Massachusetts, Connecticut, Virginia, Maryland, Pennsylvania, Delaware, New York, and New Jersey—all except the last two specifically granted widows dower rights in personalty as well as realty.[29] As the seventeenth century progressed and particularly after 1690, however, the laws began to change. Massachusetts reduced the widow's third of personalty to no more than the use of essential household utensils and furniture. Some other colonies did not even go that far. In the end, column twelve in Table 1.1 shows only Virginia and Maryland continuing to grant widows a right to chattel, and the Virginia law making slave men and women count as realty rather than personalty sharply reduced the monetary worth of the dower right.[30] Why this greater generosity toward widows in the Chesapeake? Statutory concern about them was more marked than in England. The Virginia House of Burgesses tacked them on to the succession line for their husbands' and children's personalty to prevent escheat (confiscation by the state).[31] Chesapeake widows also fared relatively well in the wills of their seventeenth-century husbands.

What the Chesapeake laws on dower and succession may actually have reflected was a lively marriage market in widows. We know that women tended to be in short supply in early Virginia and Maryland and that remarriage was frequent.[32] While the dower laws of these two colonies were disadvantageous to the younger generation, they did benefit adult males who might wed widows. We may have here something comparable to the alternation between "for widowhood only" and "for life only" dower in realty that occurred in the customary rights of some English manors. Of course it would be wrong to make too much of these departures from English practice because in most ways the laws of the Cheseapeake colonies and England shared a dreary similarity. For example, in both places, the father could decide to exclude the mother and name an outsider as guardian of his children. Maryland actually went a step further and, after the Glorious Revolution, passed an act permitting the court to remove from their mother's custody the children of a deceased Protestant father if she married a Catholic.[33]

Inheritance Rights of Widowers

The colonies, as best we can discover, closely followed the English common law in respect to the feme covert's loss of property rights and her husband's claim to her realty. Upon marriage, all of a woman's personalty became her spouse's. He also had the right to manage her realty but could not sell it. Upon her death, if a child had been born of the union, her widower received lifetime use of the landed property (curtesy). At his death, it went to her children or, if none survived, to her next of kin. She could only write a will bequeathing personalty if her husband gave his approval, and under the common law she had no power to devise land.

The marriage settlements used in England to remove some of the disabilities of feme covert status by giving wives, usually through a trustee, more control and often testamentary power over assets were apparently used very little in the seventeenth- and early eighteenth-century colonies.[34] Such settlements fell under the supervision of chancery courts rather than common law courts—where the principle of unity of person made the device an anomaly—and these equity courts were unpopular in the New World. Not only did the dissenters refuse to establish them but some initially declined to countenance the settlements themselves. Only later, at the end of the eighteenth and during the early nineteenth century, did the marriage settlement come into its own in America.

Inheritance Rights of Collateral Kin

Inheritance laws of most of the colonies kept silent on the order of succession when no lineal descendants survived. The common law held that in the case of land, only descendants, not ancestors, could inherit, and heirs had to be of the full blood. A father or grandfather could not, himself, take possession of the property. Brothers were preferred to sisters, with the eldest brother inheriting all. If there were no brothers, however, the sisters or their issue took equally with one another. The custom excluded half brothers and sisters entirely. If there were no siblings or issue of siblings, the realty would be inherited by the issue of the decedent's paternal grandfather, the eldest male of the nearest degree succeeding first. All relations on the decedent's father's side were preferred, regardless of how distant, before those on the mother's side.[35]

After 1670, the Statute of Distributions governed the descent of personalty, and the order of succession to this property owed more to the civil law than did the system used for realty.[36] Ascending kin alternated with descending: parents were next in line to inherit if no children of the decedent survived. A law passed by Parliament in the 1680s, however, prevented mothers, if fathers had died, from inheriting all of a child's personalty. Instead they had to share it with the decedent's sisters and brothers. In the absence of parents, or siblings, "grandfathers, uncles or nephews, (and the females of each class respectively), and lastly cousins" fell heir to the goods.[37]

Colonials seemed in no rush to secure the inheritance rights of remote kindred or otherwise conform to the English standard of succession. For example, Maryland in 1642 introduced a law permitting geographical proximity to alter collateral descent by providing that estates should be passed to the nearest kin in the colony rather than just the next of kin. The first laws of the middle colonies cut off succession rather abruptly. New York in 1665 declared a failure in succession and escheat by the King after first cousins, and Pennsylvania throughout the later seventeenth century ended descent with nephews, nieces, and parents.[38]

By 1720, colonial laws on escheat no longer contained any clauses on collaterals that deviated from English law (see Table 1.1, columns 9 and 10), but that may have been because the laws said very little. In fact, we do not really know how often and what collaterals inherited nor how frequently escheats occurred. Did, for instance, colonial officials actually follow the common law and confiscate land from half brothers and half sisters? As late as the 1780s, Pennsylvania authorities comment that no regular course for proceeding with escheats existed.[39]

Interestingly enough, the only explicit deviations from English succession practices involved mothers and spouses, not collaterals. No colony besides Massachusetts and Virginia ever enacted a statute similar to the 1680s English law reducing the rights of mothers inheriting personalty from their children. Moreover, the Virginia law continued to favor mothers to some extent by giving them the entire personal estate if no kin of the father survived. Virginia also put wives in the line of succession to the kin's share of personalty.[40] We can only conclude from all of this that concern about the rights of collaterals was not very great during the colonial period.

ENGLAND AND AMERICA: GREAT SIMILARITIES, TWO NOTABLE DIFFERENCES

According to contemporary sources, American inheritance laws—specifically primogeniture, the testamentary freedom to will property outside of the lineage, and married women's lack of property rights—were among the biggest surprises encountered by immigrants from Europe.[41] Many had come from Old World villages where a customary bilateral system of inheritance prevailed, one which incorporated a broader notion of lineage.

Most of what shocked ousiders about colonial inheritance was English in origin. We should not underestimate the degree to which Anglo settlers replicated the mode of wealth transmission existing in the mother country. The English had a narrow unilateral system with great individual freedom for family heads, and basically, that was what the colonists had as well.

The primary departure from English common law precedents and statutes was in the way the majority of the colonies divided an intestate's estate among lineal descendants. They showed preference for the eldest son by giving him a double share of personalty and realty rather than a single share of personalty and all the realty. The particular wealth mix in the early years of the colonies, with land being abundant and some types of personalty including financial assets less available, seems to be the main reason for this divergence. Dissenters, who had no great reverence for that part of English law they associated with feudal despotism, found it easiest to make this change.

What may be a difference of near-comparable significance was the failure of the elites in the colonies during the early decades to make much use of the strict family settlements allowed by equity law in chancery courts. Thus the colonies may not only have slightly broadened the lineage with the eschewing of primogeniture but also may have abbreviated it. The establishment of a dynasty lasting many generations was more difficult in America. The will took on an added importance because it was the principal tool the elite as well as the average wealthholder had for influencing the transmission of property.

2

Colonial Testamentary Practice
and Family Capitalism

Those who did not like the intestacy provisions of their colony had great leeway in altering the distribution. Through a will, children could all be disinherited; everything could be awarded to one offspring; or portions could be granted for a term of years or for life only. Property could be put in trusts or entailed, preventing it from ever being alienated from the patrilineage. About the only restraint legally enforceable was a wife's claim to dower from the estate of her husband. In most colonies her right of dower or right to elect against her husband's will (what she could claim in place of the legacy he gave) consisted of one-third of realty for life. Although, as we know, in many parts of England and in the first few years of settlement in the colonies, dower had also included ownership of one-third of personalty, by the early eighteenth century the widow's right of election was reduced in most places to just the lifetime land claim.

In the colonial period, anywhere from one-quarter to one-half of those whose estates went through probate wrote wills, and probably a majority of the aggregate wealth in a community was disposed of by this mechanism rather than according to the laws of intestacy (see the Introduction). The question that arises is, how did these testators, 85–90 percent of whom were men, alter the statutory arrangement? Did they opt to increase or decrease the equality among sons and daughters? Did they move to encumber legacies and devises through entails, life estates, mortgages, and so forth so that family members could not alienate or liquidate their shares but would be forced to retain family property for the good of the line or at least keep the "firm" going for a time? Were testators more generous with their wives than were the intestacy statutes, or did they seek further economies in her share for the benefit of the lineage? Moreover, How much control over the estate and its shareholders did the wife retain? Intestacy laws named her as administrator; did testators give her equal authority as executor and guardian?

THE FAMILY "FIRM"

Inequality among Children in Wills

Scholars studying the intergenerational transfer of wealth during the seventeenth and eighteenth centuries have always been impressed that over half the colonies rejected the dominant English tradition of primogeniture in distributing the land of intestates. Some argue, moreover, that even in those colonies with primogeniture, the propertied used wills and deeds to distribute some realty to children other than the eldest son. In multigeniture colonies, intestacy statutes and the courts often directed eldest sons to buy up siblings' shares to create a viable agricultural holding. These adaptations of the laws suggest that the actual difference in land distribution policies between, on the one hand, southern plantation colonies, New York, and New Jersey, which had primogeniture statutes and, on the other hand, more egalitarian northern dissenter colonies, where laws specified only a double share to the eldest male, has probably been overstated.[1]

The distribution of land, however, is really only one part of a larger issue: the degree to which family capitalism required the unequal distribution of all property, both realty and personalty, to heirs. Knowing whether younger sons and daughters received land is primarily important as a clue to whether intergenerational transmission of total wealth was equitable. The intestacy statutes, both those with primogeniture and those with double shares, endorsed some degree of inequality. Is that what wills show as well?

To investigate this issue, we look first at a sample of wills from Bucks County written between 1685, when the county was settled, and 1756, the beginning of the Seven Years' War and the end of the colonial period proper. The county was heavily agricultural, as it was to be for most of the next three centuries, and had a substantial Protestant dissenter population like most of the northern communities of America.

First Quakers, then later Presbyterians, and Baptists moved into the area. Only small numbers of Germans and Dutch (under 5 percent) appear in the sample although they may have existed in larger numbers in the actual population. Unfortunately there is seldom an indication in the wills as to what sect the testator belonged. Testators, who made up half of the probate cases (the rest being intestates), were overwhelmingly male (88 percent), married (two-thirds), and well endowed with children: 75 percent had more than one offspring, and nearly half had more than three.

First, let us consider that popular question of what kind of property male and female heirs (aside from wives) received in bequests. When Bucks County testators divided their estates, they exhibited a strong tendency toward giving women sums of money and reserving the realty and, to a lesser extent, the tangible personalty for the men. Table 2.1 shows the type of property given each sex. Of all testators, 70 percent gave male heirs realty and 71 percent gave tangible personalty, while only half bequeathed tangible assets and less than a quarter devised land to one or more of their female heirs. These figures include land given for life or term of years. Of all testators, 38.1 percent, and of the affluent, 46.0 percent, gave all their bequests to women in cash. In contrast, only 12.3 percent of all testators did this with their male heirs.[2]

This difference in type of property awarded does not however tell us if there was an inequity in the portions left men and women or whether birth order conferred preferential treatment. Table 2.2 compares the portions the prime wealthholders, fathers, gave their sons and daughters in their wills with the intestacy arrangements prescribed in the laws. With sons, it is clear that those fathers having only one son favored preferential treatment for him. Over 70 percent gave the son the double share or more rather than increasing or equalizing the shares given wives, daughters, or other heirs. (Remember, "same as intestacy" in the table means eldest son received a double share of personalty and realty or its equivalent). When there was more than one son, fathers were more inclined to equalize shares among some of them; that is why 40.7 percent are noted as giving some sons more and some less than intestacy. The eldest son got less than his double share, while one or more of the younger sons got more than a single child's share. In only 16.2 percent of the cases did the father opt for the intestacy double share, and even fewer gave male heirs less than the amount specified by the intestacy provisions. In short, fathers were inclined to increase the preferential treatment intestacy laws accorded sons versus other heirs, but among the sons, when there were more than one, there was an attempt to equalize portions among some of them.

With daughters the pattern was different. The number of daughters in a family was relatively inconsequential. Two-thirds of the fathers gave less than intestacy provided. There was also little discrimination among these female heirs, with only 7.3 percent of the testators giving some daughters more than others. Were daughters sacrificed to favor

TABLE 2.1 **TYPE OF PROPERTY WILLED TO MALE AND FEMALE HEIRS, BUCKS COUNTY, 1685–1756**

	Percentage of all legacies to	
Type of property	**Male heirs**	**Female heirs**
All testators		
	(N = 317)	**(N = 294)**
Intangible personalty	12.3	38.1
Tangible personalty	1.3	5.1
Realty	8.2	1.4
Intangible and tangible personalty	12.0	26.5
Intangible personalty and realty	4.1	1.4
Tangible personalty and realty	1.9	1.4
All three types of property	55.8	20.1
Nothing given	4.4	6.1
Affluent testators[a]		
	(N = 96)	**(N = 87)**
Intangible personalty	10.4	46.0
Tangible personalty	1.0	5.7
Realty	10.4	1.1
Intangible and tangible personalty	9.4	29.9
Intangible personalty and realty	3.1	4.6
Tangible personalty and realty	2.1	0.0
All three types of property	61.5	9.2
Nothing given	2.1	3.4

Note: Property includes legacies for life or for term of years.

[a] Affluent refers to those testators in the top third of the will sample, those who had a gross personal estate of £220 Pennsylvania currency or more. Although realty was not routinely listed in the inventories, we found a high correlation between personal and real wealth where the latter was listed. For more on how we arrived at the cutoff points for the wealth groups, see Appendix A.

TABLE 2.2 **FATHERS' TREATMENT OF SONS AND DAUGHTERS IN WILLS COMPARED TO SHARES ALLOWED UNDER INTESTACY LAW, BUCKS COUNTY, 1685–1756**

	Percentage of			
	Just one	**More than one**	**All fathers**	**Affluent fathers**[a]
Son(s), treatment of in comparison to intestacy:				
N	60	167	227	76
More	38.3	28.1	30.0	39.5
Same	33.3	16.2	20.7	13.2
Less	28.3	15.0	18.5	15.8
Some more/less	0.0	40.7	30.8	31.6
Daughter(s), treatment of in comparison to intestacy				
N	63	143	206	73
More	9.6	12.6	10.2	13.7
Same	17.5	15.4	16.0	16.5
Less	73.0	63.6	66.5	65.8
Some more/less	0.0	8.4	7.3	4.1

Note: Because of their small numbers, the categories life estates for more, same, less, or some more/less than intestacy are combined with those categories where the bequest was forever.

[a] Testators with gross personal estates of £220 Pennsylvania currency or more.

sons or to give wives larger portions? When the shares given sons and daughters were compared (Table 2.3), it seems that when daughters got less than intestacy, it was largely because one or more sons got more. In only 27.9 percent of the cases did sons also receive less. On the other hand, two-thirds of the times daughters received more than intestacy, sons did also. The comparable figures (Table 2.4) for mothers who were testators show some bias toward daughters. This preference could not, however, begin to compensate for fatherly discrimination, considering the difference in wealth held by the two sexes. Out of the total personal wealth contained in this sample of testators, 94 percent of it was held by men.[3] Only single women and widows could bequeath property, and the assets they had to distribute were usually small amounts of money, household goods, and apparel.

It might be argued that this inequality is simply the result of inter-vivos gifts. Some children, particularly girls, might have already re-

TABLE 2.3 **SHARES GIVEN SONS AND DAUGHTERS IN WILLS COMPARED, BUCKS COUNTY, 1685–1756**

	Daughters' treatment:				
	More	Same	Less	Some less/ more	N
Sons' treatment:					
N	25	36	136	13	209
More	66.7%	0.0%	32.4%	7.7%	61
Same	0.0%	88.9%	2.9%	15.4%	38
Less	8.3%	0.0%	27.9%	23.1%	43
Some more/less	25.0%	11.1%	36.8%	53.8%	67

ceived their portions at marriage or age of majority, making it incorrect to count them as receiving less. The problem is, in only about 4 percent of the wills was there an indication that undisclosed assets had been given during life.[4] More common was the inclusion of property in a bequest that was actually in the possession of the heir. Nevertheless, the concern about intervivos gifts is a genuine one, and it is worthwhile to control for that factor by looking at what testators with all minor children did. Table 2.5 compares their treatment of sons and daughters. The differences, though less extreme than those for the sample as a whole (see Tables 2.2 and 2.3), still indicate daughters were at a clear disadvantage vis-à-vis their brothers and that the majority of fathers used wills to give girls less than intestacy provided.

TABLE 2.4 **MOTHERS' TREATMENT OF SONS AND DAUGHTERS IN WILLS COMPARED TO SHARES ALLOWED UNDER INTESTACY LAW, BUCKS COUNTY, 1685–1756**

Treatment in comparison to intestacy	Percentage of sons (N = 35)	Percentage of daughters (N = 35)
More	2.9	11.4
Same	40.0	31.5
Less	34.3	31.4
Some more/less	22.9	25.8

Note: Because of their small numbers, the categories life estates for more, same, less or some more/less than intestacy are combined with those categories where the bequest was forever.

Among those with all minor children, 29.8 percent of testators gave their sons less than intestacy, while 56.6 percent did so with daughters. Moreover, the percentage of testators giving sons less was greater than in Table 2.2, not because some daughters were doing better but because mothers with all minor children were frequently left the entire estate for a term of years to bring up the family. This meant the children would not immediately get the income from their inheritance, and thus they are counted in the less-than-intestacy category.

TABLE 2.5 **TREATMENT OF SONS AND DAUGHTERS IN WILLS COMPARED TO INTESTACY LAW BY TESTATORS WHO HAD ALL MINOR CHILDREN, BUCKS COUNTY, 1685–1756**

Treatment in comparison to intestacy	Percentage of sons ($N = 87$)	Percentage of daughters ($N = 76$)
More	26.4	19.7
Same	24.1	22.4
Less	29.8	56.6
Some more/less	19.5	1.3

Note: Because of their small numbers, the categories life estates for more, same, less or some more/less than intestacy are combined with those categories where the bequest was forever.

Dynastic Ambitions

Our analysis up to this point indicates that testators used wills to increase equality among sons and to decrease the shares of daughters to below what they might expect from intestacy. Giving daughters cash legacies worth somewhat less than a full child's share of the estate reduced some of the strain on the family firm. If most fathers acted similarly, daughters would be competitive in the marriage market despite their smaller share. The effect of the lesser share on their relative power in the marriage, of course, is unclear; most likely it reinforced the notion of female inferiority. The more egalitarian treatment of sons, however, complicated any strategy for continuing the family firm over the generations because it presupposed several family firms rather than one. Nor did dynastic ambitions take the form of trying to insure that specific properties would remain in the patrilineage after passing to the next generation. Fewer than 4 percent of Bucks County testators relied upon entails, life estates, conditional fees, and trusts to prevent sons and daughters from alienating property; and the affluent used them no more frequently than those with more modest estates.[5] When they do appear in wills, they usually served to stop wives from being able to liquidate property.

The dynastic strategies embraced by the Bucks County testators took another form. For one thing, most made sure no wealth was dissipated through the making of bequests to nonnuclear family members. Table 2.6 indicates that among those with children, only 3.7 percent made charitable contributions, and no more than 7.2 percent left legacies beyond some token remembrance, such as funeral gloves, to nonkin. The percentage who gave to kin other than children—grandchildren and wives—was somewhat larger, 17.5 percent, but still extremely small considering that it means over four out of five testators who were parents chose *not* to remember parents, siblings, or in-laws in any meaningful way.[6]

There was also a clear disinclination to allow the liquidation of the estate despite the fact that almost half of the testators in this sample still had minor children when they wrote their wills and that many had heavy debts to be paid before either children or wife could inherit. Of male testators, 57 percent said nothing about liquidation at all. Only 6.4 percent directed that their whole estate be sold; the rest specified only a portion that could be alienated. When it came to the family firm (in almost all instances a farm or farms), only 12.6 percent agreed in their wills to liquidation.

Based on whether testators directed that their entire estate be sold, that some of it be sold, or that executors do some disposing of the es-

TABLE 2.6 **PERCENTAGE OF TESTATORS MAKING BEQUESTS TO KIN, NONKIN, AND CHARITY, BUCKS COUNTY, 1685–1756**

Recipient of bequest	All testators (*N* 387)	Testators with child(ren) (*N* 291)
Kin[a]	26.9	17.5
Nonkin	12.2	7.2
Charity	5.0	3.7

[a]Those other than spouse, children, and grandchildren.

TABLE 2.7 **TESTATORS' WILLINGNESS TO LIQUIDATE THEIR ESTATES, BUCKS COUNTY, 1685–1756**

Independent variables	b	Significance level (f test)
Number of minor sons	.164	.048
Number of adult sons	−.033	.360
Number of minor daughters	−.043	.523
Number of adult daughters	.014	.824
Gross personal wealth (Ls)	−.000	.250
Percentage of wealth in intangible assets	.385	.212
Post–1730 will[a]	−.257	.161
Farmer[a]	.073	.676
Able to sign will[a]	.293	.074
Married[a]	−.214	.258
Female[a]	−.433	.155
Constant	.873	.001

Note: OLS regression: $N = 223$; $R^2 = .067$. Willingness to liquidate, the dependent variable, is measured on a scale from 0 (no mention of liquidation in will), through 1 (executor given authority if necessary to liquidate), and 2 (some of estate liquidated by order of testator or executor), to 3 (all of estate ordered liquidated).
[a]Dummy variables, 1, 0 codes.

tate if necessary, we concocted a measure of "willingness to liquidate." We then ran a regression to see what variables—aside from indebtedness, which we could not measure—best accounted for such a willingness. Table 2.7 shows the results, which are largely negative. Most of the variables seem not to have affected the decision to dispose of an estate. When other factors are held constant, neither wealth nor being a farmer had an impact on willingness to liquidate. Liquidation did not become more popular later in the colonial period. In fact, the influence of time (will written after 1730) was negative, although the coefficient was not significant at an acceptable level ($p = .161$). Being married and being a female testator also discouraged liquidation, but again neither result was statistically significant. Even already having a high percentage of one's estate in intangibles (financial assets) did not attain significance. Although being able to sign one's will (a proxy for educational level) was positively related to a receptivity toward liquidation, and although this variable had a better significance level ($p = .074$) than all of the others save one, it is unclear exactly why. Possibly illiterates had more fears about the costs of converting an estate from tangibles to money. Of the variables tested, the one most influential in promoting liquidation (and the only one statistically significant at the .05 level), however, was the number of minor sons the testator had. This was of more importance than having adult sons or minor daughters or adult daughters, none of which was significant.

Obviously Bucks County testators in the colonial period were wary about liquidating large portions of their estates. They preferred, unless debts intervened, to pass on the bulk of their property in kind, particularly their business or farm. Of all testators, 82 percent (of male testators, 90 percent) disposed of a business in their will and seldom chose liquidation. Table 2.8 compares the method of disposition for testators in different circumstances. Aside from liquidation, they could allow one son to buy out the other heirs; pass on the business entirely to one son or some other heir; transfer it whole to joint owners; divide it into parcels for several heirs; give it to spouse; or allow her to hold it during life, widowhood, or the minority of the children. Testators who had more than one adult son and were affluent preferred to spread the business among heirs, either providing for joint ownership or dividing it into parcels; 71 percent made one of these two choices in Bucks County. The recipients of these shares were invariably the two or three eldest sons not, in a big family, all of the children, as intestacy rules dictated. Parcels were meant to be viable units.

TABLE 2.8 **TESTATORS' DISPOSITION OF FAMILY FARM OR BUSINESS, BUCKS COUNTY, 1685–1756**

	Percentage of				
Method of disposition	All (N = 317)	Those with more than 1 child (N = 224)	Those with more than 1 son (N = 167)	Those with more than 1 adult son (N = 115)	Affluent and with more than 1 adult son (N = 38)
Liquidation	12.6	12.5	9.6	5.2	5.3
One son buys	6.6	7.1	7.8	7.8	7.9
All to one son	20.5	22.8	19.2	19.1	15.8
All to another	4.7	1.8	1.2	1.7	0.0
Joint ownership	18.3	21.4	23.4	27.4	31.6
Parcels	21.1	23.7	26.3	29.6	39.5
All to spouse	5.7	2.2	1.2	1.7	0.0
All to spouse for set term[a]	10.4	8.5	11.4	7.0	0.0

[a]For life, widowhood, or minority of child or children.

It is also important to note that the choices in the disposition of their business made by a hefty minority of testators insured that some siblings would be economically bound to one another long after the death of the parent. Among those with two or more children, those testators who had one son buying out other heirs,[7] put the business under joint ownership, or gave it to the spouse constituted about 40 percent. Nor did the percentage change much when testators had some money and adult sons. Wives were no longer caretakers, but the percentage of joint owners jumped up to compensate for it. Entails and life estates may not have been popular, but forcing sibling cooperation clearly was. The hope must have been that recombinations of resources within the family and additional wealth brought in through marriage would make for several viable household firms where only one had existed before. Apparently the high costs of alienation made the dividing of physical assets, rather than liquidation, seem the most efficient way to achieve this goal.

The Situation of the Widow

So far we have not discussed how the widow fit into the arrangements her husband made for the transferring of family wealth. The law obligated men to make provision for their spouses, for, at marriage, women lost control of property and husbands took over. Although a Pennsylvania widow had once been able to obtain the same portion as intestacy provided (a third of personalty forever and a third of realty for life) if her husband disinherited her or if she found the portion willed her unsatisfactory, she lost the claim on personalty at the beginning of the eighteenth century. Because dower lands in Pennsylvania could be used to pay the debts of the deceased husband, she could not count them for her old age either. A wife's protection against an arbitrary or wastrel husband, therefore, was not great, and she could only hope that should he decide to write a will, he would give her not less than she might receive under intestacy.

Table 2.9 makes this comparison. Almost half of the married male testators gave their wives a larger share than they could have expected under intestacy. The catch was that they usually affixed to their legacies a time limit beyond the one-third of realty for life provided by the intestacy statute. Most widows who got more than intestacy were re-

TABLE 2.9 **MALE TESTATORS' TREATMENT OF SPOUSE, BUCKS COUNTY, 1685–1756**

Treatment compared to intestacy	Percentage of married men		
	All (N = 250)	Affluent only (N = 81)	Pre-1730 (N = 72)
More	17.6	12.3	27.8
Same	10.8	11.1	4.2
Less	16.8	18.5	15.3
More, for widowhood/minority of child	21.6	21.0	30.6
More, for life only	8.4	6.2	8.3
Same, for widowhood/minority of child/life	3.6	2.5	2.8
Less, for widowhood/minority of child	12.0	17.3	2.8
Less, for life only	9.2	11.1	8.3

quired to give up the extra amount or sometimes their entire portion upon remarriage or when a child reached majority or at some other designated time. Those whose rights were for life only could neither sell nor will the property.

The major way, then, that husbands controlled the claims widows made on their estates was to limit their rights to a specified period. At least some part of the widow's legacy was restricted in this way in 70 percent of wills. Many testators went beyond the one-third realty for life clause in intestacy law and penalized the widow for remarrying or made it difficult for her to do so. Time restrictions were also attached to personalty, a sharp departure from traditional custom. With slaves and other personalty growing in importance, testators apparently were reluctant to bequeath such property unconditionally to their wives. These limitations favored the lineage over the spouse and protected family property from the depredations of an avaricious stepfather. To the extent that remarriage might have provided a more stable economic situation, however, they may in the end have been less beneficial to the children than a more generous settlement. Cutting off a widow when she took a new husband may have been pennywise but pound foolish.

It is also noteworthy that although nearly half of testators gave wives more than intestate law provided, almost 40 percent gave less, and sometimes that "less" was not even a legacy wives could liquidate because of the "for widowhood," "minority of child," or "life only" clauses. One of the cheapest ways to dispose of the claims of a widow was to have her portion consist mainly or solely of specified amounts of room space, food, and firewood, and 23 percent of married male testators used such provisions. Most wives who received less than intestacy for widowhood or life received bequests of this type.

Affluent testators tended to be less generous with their wives than the nonaffluent, perhaps because the amount required to maintain a widow was a smaller proportion of their estate. Table 2.9 reveals that nearly half gave their wives less than intestacy. They were also more likely to bequeath food and lodging instead of control over capital. The widows' position also deteriorated over time. In the pre-1730 period, a much higher percentage of women (27.8 percent) got more than intestacy than received it later.

In comparison with the way testators treated female lineal heirs, fewer testators gave wives less than intestacy, and fewer excluded them from having some rights over realty. About 40 percent of testators chose to substitute tangible and intangible personalty for the widow's share of dower land, but this was on a lesser scale than daughters' exclusion from inheriting land. The attempt to get rid of the claims of the widow through a cash payment, so obvious in the case of female heirs, was not prevalent either; only 7 percent of husbands gave their spouses legacies in this form. Rather, wives' shares were deeply embedded in the general estate, particularly that part ultimately destined for male heirs. The use of widowhood, minority of child, and life only clauses in wills and the substitution of food and lodging for capital greatly reduced the power and independence of the widow if not her actual standard of living.

The main beneficiaries of the economies practiced on widows were male heirs. Table 2.10 compares the treatment accorded sons and daughters by those testators who gave their wives less than the portion allowed them under the intestacy statutes. Of husbands who bequeathed their wives less than intestacy, 58.7 percent awarded their sons more, and an additional 33.7 percent gave at least one son more although others may have received less. With daughters, however, 61.9 percent of them, like their mothers, received less than intestacy permitted. Clearly in this colonial community, at least, the patrilineal impulse triumphed over all others.

Wills also enabled husbands to stop their widows from administering their estates and from obtaining custody of minor children. In this Bucks County sample, men did not do the latter very frequently. Only

TABLE 2.10 **TREATMENT OF SONS AND DAUGHTERS
BY PERCENTAGE OF TESTATORS WHO GAVE
THEIR WIVES LESS THAN INTESTACY,
BUCKS COUNTY, 1685–1756**

Treatment[a] compared to intestacy	Sons (N = 92)	Daughters (N = 84)
More	58.7	21.4
Same	5.4	7.1
Less	2.1	61.9
Some more/less	33.7	9.5

Note: Less than intestacy for wives includes the categories less property given forever, less for widowhood, less for minority of child, and less for life only.

[a]Because of their small numbers, the categories life estates for more, same, less, or some more/less than intestacy are combined with those categories where the bequest was forever.

8.6 percent of those with minor children left them entirely in the care of others; another 4.3 percent named the mother and someone else jointly. As Table 2.11 indicates, excluding the spouse from executrix- ship was more common: 37.7 percent of all married male testators and 44.0 percent of those falling into the affluent category named some- one other than their wives. The proportion who excluded their wives, moreover, grew over time. Before 1730 less than 20 percent did so, whereas after 1730 the percentage was 45. Among those who did name their wives, the most popular option was to name other persons also as either executors or overseers. These were about evenly divided among sons, other kin, and nonkin. Daughters were almost never named either as sole executrix or to help their mothers.

TABLE 2.11 **PERCENTAGE OF HUSBANDS NAMING WIFE
EXECUTRIX, BUCKS COUNTY, 1685–1756**

	Married testators	
Those appointed	All (N = 257)	Affluent only (N = 82)
Wife only	17.5	14.6
Wife and other[a]	44.7	41.4
Wife excluded	37.7	44.0

[a]Co-executors and overseers.

The appointment of someone other than the spouse might have been viewed as an aid to the unworldly widow, but it still diminished her power and her wealth. Executors could claim a certain amount for their services. In addition the common law provided that in the absence of express legacies to executors and provisions for the disposition of the residue of an estate left after all bequests had been awarded, executors could claim whatever remained.[8] Appointing overseers to assist a widow might have been preferable, but it was a custom that was slowly dying out. In Bucks County before 1730, 44 percent of husbands who named their wives as sole executrixes also appointed overseers. After 1730 only 23 percent did so.[9]

So, in sum, we find male testators in Bucks County equalized portions among male heirs, made daughters portions smaller than intestacy provided, and reduced the power their widows could exercise over capital. They still passed on their physical estates, shunning liquidation, but they did not attempt to limit their children's ability to alienate property from succeeding generations. Life estates or legacies for a term of years were only common in bequests to wives. How does this behavior compare with that in other regions of colonial America?

TESTAMENTARY BEHAVIOR THROUGHOUT THE COLONIES

Though it is difficult to compare our research and other colonial inheritance studies on all points of interest, there is enough common ground to allow generalization on most of the critical issues. For example, we know that elsewhere wills were also heavily used to distribute land to other children, primarily to other sons. Two-thirds to 90 percent of landholding testators might do this. Daughters tended more often to get land as part of portions earlier in the colonial period. By mid eighteenth century seldom did more than a third of testators award such legacies. The failure to get land would not necessarily have to mean that daughters got smaller total amounts of assets; holdings of slaves, money, and livestock were often sufficient to make up for being given no land. But it seems from what evidence has been collected that daughters' portions were smaller than sons' on the average and, as in Bucks County, probably smaller than what intestacy provided.[10]

Younger sons, providing there were not too many of them, generally did better than under intestacy. Many researchers working on southern communities see them coming out nearly as well as their eldest brothers. Those who have investigated the situation in the northern colonies more often stress the upward mobility advantage of the eldest while noting that certainly more than one son received substantial resources.[11] When fathers had the means, they set up several sons.[12] The emphasis in study after study is the viability of the portion. Liquidation was low, judging by the high proportion of testators who devised land to sons and slaves, livestock, and household goods to daughters. Marriage clearly was intended to help in making portions viable. Thus family firms could be reconstituted and then continued. Fathers seemed very concerned about having property go to the next generation. They did not, on the whole, attempt to tie up estates for the patrilineage over many generations. The use of entails, trusts, life estates, and conditional fees (such as inheritance contingent on the birth of an issue) were relatively rare: fewer than 5 or 10 percent of testators included such clauses.

There were, however, several important exceptions to these generalizations. In the plantation South during the eighteenth century, the devices for perpetuating property within the lineage became more popular. In parts of Maryland a majority of fathers put such limitations on their land bequests, and over one-third attached them to legacies of slaves. In the South Carolina low country, trusts and conditional fees cropped up in the wills of nearly half the testators devising land and in over one-third of those making gifts of slaves. Entails alone, in Virginia, ran as high as 20 percent in some tidewater counties.[13]

What explains this southern departure from common practice in rural communities of New England and the Middle Colonies? Great wealth in the South tended to be heavily in land and slaves, while in the North so much wealth tended to be held in intangible or more transitory tangible personalty: notes, bills, shares of ships, and stock-in-trade.[14] Affluent northerners may have wanted to keep their sons in "business," but grandiose schemes for perpetuating estates intact over many generations were beyond their powers given the state of equity law and the ephemeral nature of mercantile fortunes. Entails traditionally had applied to realty and had been stretched in some colonies to apply also to slaves. It was difficult to use the existing instruments—trusts, life estates, and conditional fees—for tying up or safeguarding personalty for long-term dynastic purposes. True dynastic strategies for this type of wealth required a more fully developed law on trusts, a larger professional class to serve as trustees, and corporate institutions to accept investments.

Trusts, life estates, and conditional fees in the colonial period, then, were usually employed for short-term purposes and found disproportionately in bequests to daughters, and they sometimes accompanied a trend toward daughters getting more equal portions with their male siblings. In the Charleston district of South Carolina, this seemed to be the case, as in other towns and cities where personalty was the predominant form of property and fathers perhaps worried that their daughters' portions might disappear into the coffers of their sons-in-law without benefiting anyone in the testators' lineage.[15] Generally daughters received better sized portions when estates consisted primarily of personalty or were liquidated. Historians have argued that in New York City, Petersburg, Virginia, and Germantown, Pennsylvania there was little discrimination between sons and daughters in allocating shares of the estate.[16] At the same time, these researchers report frequent use of life estates for daughters. This practice seems associated with the late colonial and early national period. Thus some of the increased use of restrictions on children's ownership of property was to insure that wealth would not be dissipated by nonlineage members. The one advantage of giving women land was that their husbands could not, under the common law, sell the property. No such restraints existed on personalty. These devices, then, interfered with husbands' moving around all types of property. What seems to have occurred through most of the colonial period was a practice of giving daughters less with no strings attached; but when daughters' legacies became closer to equal to those of their brothers, the strings began to appear.

If restrictions on the length of time children might hold property and to whom they might give it were not widely used in most of America, the same cannot be said about bequests to wives. The colonial Bucks County testamentary patterns were repeated throughout the other colonies. Both the size of a widow's share and the restrictions placed upon it depended largely on the number of children she had, their ages, and the wealth of her husband. In the early settlement period, particularly in the South, mortality tended to be high, and husbands frequently died with no lineal heirs or all minor children, and the portions awarded widows could be quite generous. The widow's share shrank and the restrictions grew, however, as the population lived longer and as wealth accumulated. Land held for widowhood only and personalty for life became commonplace. Two studies of different counties in Maryland have found a situation comparable to what we discovered in Bucks County. By the post-1750 period, two-thirds of these testators were giving their spouses either a smaller share or a more restricted tenure over it than intestacy provided.[17]

The type of bequest that rendered a widow most dependent was the portion that specified a set number of rooms and provisions that heirs, usually sons, were to allow for her maintenance until she died or re-married. Generally, when husbands made this type of arrangement for wives, they gave them very little else in the way of property. While such women were old enough to have an adult child, they were not nec-essarily geriatric cases. Used frequently in Bucks County wills and in those of New England, this type of bequest less often surfaced in testa-ments of the tidewater South.[18] Part of the explanation for this differ-ence may be that the higher mortality in the South resulted in fewer testators with adult children clamoring to take over the productive capi-tal. Greater wealth among the southern white population may also have reduced the number of such bequests. Although in Bucks County, affluence slightly increased the likelihood of these maintenance clauses appearing in wills, very few of these farmers had as much wealth as those in the top third of most probate samples from the tidewater South. Rich planters often gave their widows less than intestacy, but confining their portions to food and roomspace would not have been appropriate.[19] The presence of slaves in the South may be an additional factor of importance. The labor that a widow's bound servants could perform on her son's plantation or someone else's could insure her maintenance without the need to specify what provisions were neces-sary for her to live.

Besides the size of the portions awarded wives and the stipulations placed upon their use of the property they were willed, there is also the issue of how much control husbands granted them over the administra-tion of the estate and the guardianship of their children. Unfortunately, guardianship has not been extensively treated by historians, so it is difficult to say much about trends in naming. Perhaps the most interest-ing fact about guardianship in Bucks County and apparently in some areas of the Chesapeake was how infrequently testators with minor children named *anyone*. This might prove that fathers assumed their widows would be guardians, were it not that widowers and widows often omitted appointment of a guardian as well. Courts, of course, had the last word in deciding guardianship, and it seems as if most testators were willing to grant them the first word as well. This policy, of course, never affected fathers because married mothers had no right to draft wills or name guardians. Widows were the ones who had to worry about losing out to a stranger.[20]

What has been studied for most parts of colonial America is the incidence of naming or excluding widows as executrixes. During the colonial period, husbands who excluded their wives from sole or joint executorships were in the minority (see Table 2.12). There is a clear trend over time, however. In the seventeenth and early eighteenth centuries, the proportion of those who excluded wives generally stayed below 20 percent, but in the second third of the eighteenth century, it began to rise and in many communities reached 30–45 percent or more. Several explanations have been offered. The lack of adult sons and collateral kin in the early settlement period is the primary cause cited. Indeed, in

TABLE 2.12 **HUSBANDS' EXCLUSION OF WIVES AS EXECUTRIXES IN COLONIAL AMERICA**

Place	Date	Percentage excluded
New England:		
Essex Co., Mass.	1638–1681	19.5
Hartford, Conn.	1638–1681	36.9
New Hampshire	1650–1700	20.0
	1730s	30.0
Hingham, Mass.	— –1720	58.0
	1721–1760	64.0
	1761–1800	85.0
Middle Colonies:		
New York City, N.Y.	1664–1695	15.0
	1696–1750	14.0
	1750–1775	26.0
Bucks County, Pa.	1685–1730	18.9
	1731–1756	45.1
South:		
St. Mary's and Charles Co., Md.	1640–1710	11.0
	1711–1750	10.0
	1751–1777	12.0

TABLE 2.12 (*continued*)

Place	Date	Percentage excluded
Somerset Co., Md.	1640–1710	12.0
	1711–1750	15.0
	1751–1777	32.0
Baltimore Co., Md.	1660–1709	14.4
	1710–1749	14.0
	1750–1759	18.4
Frederick Co., Md.	1720–1790	51.7
Tidewater, Va.	1660–1676	11.0
	1720s	16.0
York Co., Va.	1700–1729	2.0
	1740–1749	15.5
Albemarle Co., Va.	1750–1759	29.8
	1760–1769	42.9
	1770–1779	52.5
Amelia Co., Va.	1735–1745	35.0
	1746–1755	38.0
	1756–1765	43.0
	1766–1775	57.0
Charleston Co., S.C.	1670–1740	25.0
	1760s and 1790s	36.0

Sources: Kim Lacy Rogers, "Relicts of the New World: Conditions of Widowhood in Seventeenth Century New England," in *Woman's Being, Woman's Place: Female Identity and Vocation in American History,* ed. Mary Kelley (Boston: Hall, 1979), 32–33; Laurel Thatcher Ulrich, "Good Wives: A Study in Role Definition in Northern New England 1650–1750 (Ph.D. diss., University of New Hampshire, 1980), 111—since revised and published as a book by Knopf in 1982 under the title *Good Wives: Image and Reality in the Lives of Women in Northern New England, 1650–1750;* Daniel Scott Smith, "Inheritance and the Position and Orientation of Colonial Women" (Paper presented at the Second Berkshire Conference on the History of Women, Cambridge, Mass., 1974); David Evan Narrett, Patterns of Inheritance in Colonial New York City 1664–1775: A Study in the History of the Family (Ph.D. diss., Cornell University, 1981), 172; Lois Green Carr and Lorena S. Walsh, "Woman's Role in the Eighteenth Century Chesapeake" (Paper delivered at the Conference on Women in Early America, Williamsburg, Va., November 5–7, 1981); Gail S. Terry, "Women, Property, and Authority in Colonial Baltimore County, Maryland: Evidence from the Probate Records, 1660–1759," and Elizabeth A. Kessel, "The German Family in Frederick County, Maryland 1720–1790" (Papers presented at a conference, The Colonial Experience: The Eighteenth-Century Chesapeake, Peabody Library, Baltimore, September 1984); Carole Shammas, "Women and Inheritance in the Age of Family Capitalism" (Paper delivered at the 1980 American Historical Association meeting in Washington, Daniel Blake Smith, *Inside the Great House: Planter Family Life in Eighteenth-Century Chesapeake Society* (Ithaca, N.Y.: Cornell University Press, 1980), 239; Linda E. Speth, "More than Her 'Thirds': Wives and Widows in Colonial Virginia," in *Women, Family, and Community in Colonial America: Two Perspectives* (New York: Haworth, 1983), 16; John E. Crowley, "Family Relations and Inheritance in Early South Carolina," *Histoire sociale/Social History* 17 (1984): 46.

Bucks County the percentage of sons and kin acting as executors did rise over time, but the use of nonkin (some of them functioning in a professional capacity) also went up, suggesting perhaps that other causes, including increased wealth and the establishment of a legal profession, may have been operating as well.

The evidence on widows' portions and on executrixship indicate that wives were often left less than their intestacy share and that over the colonial period their control over their portions and over the estates of their husbands may have declined. One school of thought holds that this treatment of women was necessary in order to provide for the lineage; that widows were taken care of by their families, even though they might not themselves have much property or control over assets; and that their concern for the welfare and prosperity of their children made them accept the system. Just how cheerfully is difficult to ascertain. Widows in colonial society were a notoriously impoverished group.[21] Apparently, the household economy safety net had some serious holes in it. In most colonies, widows who wished to overturn their husbands' wills could not claim their intestacy thirds. Instead all they could elect was one-third of the realty for life, and, in a colony such as Pennsylvania, that third was also at risk to be taken by creditors. In the one colony, Maryland, where a widow could claim the full third of personalty and realty, widows in fact did not meekly stand by and suffer their fate. A majority of those in pre-Revolutionary Somerset County who were given less than their intestacy share went to court and demanded their rights. In other Maryland counties, the percentage was lower, but it still averaged about one-third, a not insignificant proportion. Widows of wealthier testators and those who had no children were the most likely to renounce their bequests in favor of dower.[22]

It is worthwhile noting that, in regard to economic power, the life-cycle experience of women differed noticeably from that of men. As men matured they could generally count on having increased control over capital. That was not true of women. Single women, though they might receive smaller portions than their brothers, did have legal rights over their own property, but when they married, they lost those rights. The young widow with minor children was more likely to get control over property than was an older widow. Judging by testamentary patterns, the increased authority and power that some societies awarded the elderly matriarch was little in evidence in Anglo-America.

THE MINI-DYNASTIES OF EARLY AMERICA

The family capitalism that prevailed in colonial America produced an inheritance system designed to keep the family firm going for at least a generation. Two-thirds of those testators who had "firms," usually farms, to pass on kept them intact although doing so demanded much family cooperation. Out of the remaining third, most testators divided the productive capital into parcels that could be viable units. These testators were most often wealthier men with two or more sons. Liquidation was the choice of only one in eight testators. Intestacy procedures in nonprimogeniture colonies often served to keep the firm intact as well.

The price of not liquidating was that the lives of siblings and widows were tied together for a long time. An eldest son had responsibilities for buying out his brothers and sisters. Or brothers received property jointly and had to work out some arrangement over time. Young widows were to manage, but not sell, property that they would have to relinquish when their sons came of age. Older widows had to content themselves with room space and food allotments in a household they had once run, or live off the income of property they could not alienate. Even some of the cash gifts they received were for life or widowhood only. Daughters were usually freest, in the sense that they more often received cash portions; but there was a price involved there as well: They routinely received less than their intestacy share.

Inheritance in the colonial period, therefore, did involve a high degree of economic planning and saving. On the other hand, only a distinct minority of testators tried to perpetuate property in the family indefinitely. Entailing, trusts, and even life estates enjoyed popularity only among the planter class of the tidewater South. As we suggested earlier, colonists belonged to abbreviated lineages that did not extend very far either horizontally or vertically.

Tension in the System:
Changes and Attempted
Changes in Postrevolutionary
Inheritance Law

By the end of the eighteenth century, most of the states had formalized their rules on inheritance, and, in the process, some changes were made. They abandoned primogeniture and drafted laws on the division of land among children. Legal definitions of dower and escheat appeared in the statutes, and states made explicit what a widow would receive if she renounced her husband's will. A few states went even further and included provisions such as those of Massachusetts, New Hampshire, and Rhode Island making it necessary for a father to show intent in his will to disinherit a child.[1] Maryland, Virginia, and South Carolina discussed the rights of illegitimate children in their postrevolutionary statutes on inheritance.[2] The tendency was to codify common law provisions and, on some issues such as the rights of illegitimate children, to go beyond the common law to create entirely new regulations.

The movement toward codification was speeded by colonial separation from the mother country. Lawmakers in the new United States felt a strong need to create statutes that could substitute for common law axioms. They did not generally change English rules; in fact, they adhered to many traditional regulations in order to guarantee security in land titles. Instead, they acted to show where American law differed from English law and to delineate those areas in which standard English customs would continue.[3]

Early national statutes on inheritance were not equally comprehensive. Pennsylvania and Maryland refrained from defining dower, and Georgia neglected to explain what a widow would receive if she renounced her husband's will. Most states did not define the rights of ille-

TABLE 3.1 **U.S. INHERITANCE LAWS CIRCA 1790**

		When there is no will:			
	Date of Law[a]	Division among children		Widow's share if children	
State	(1)	Real. (2)	Pers. (3)	Real. (4)	Pers. (5)
Connecticut	1784	Eld. share double	Eld. share double	⅓ life	⅓
Delaware	1794	Equal	Equal	⅓ life	⅓
Georgia	1789	Equal	Equal	⅓ life or child's share	Child's share
Maryland	1798	Equal	Equal	⅓ life	⅓
Massachusetts	1789	Equal	Equal	⅓ life	⅓
New Hampshire	1789	Equal	Equal	⅓ life	⅓
New Jersey	1795	Sons double	Equal	⅓ life	⅓
New York	1787	Equal	Equal	⅓ life	⅓
North Carolina	1784	Sons equal	Equal	⅓ life	[d]
Pennsylvania	1794	Equal	Equal	⅓ life	⅓
Rhode Island	1798	Equal	Equal	⅓ life	⅓
South Carolina	1791	Equal	Equal	⅓	⅓
Virginia	1792	Equal	Equal	⅓ life	[e]

Sources: John D. Cushing, comp., *The First Laws of the State of Connecticut* (Wilmington, Del.: Glazier, 1982); idem., comp., *The First Laws of the State of Delaware*, 2 vols. (Wilmington, Del.: Glazier, 1981); Delaware, *Session Laws,* January 1794; John D. Cushing, comp., *The First Laws of the State of Georgia*, 2 pts. (Wilmington, Del.: Glazier, 1981); Virgil Maxy, comp., *The Laws of Maryland* (Baltimore, 1811), vol. 2; John D. Cushing, comp., *The First Laws of the Commonwealth of Massachusetts* (Wilmington, Del.: Glazier, 1981); New Hampshire, *Session Laws,* February 1789; William Paterson, ed., *Laws of the State of New Jersey* (New Brunswick, N.J., 1800); John D. Cushing, comp., *The First Laws of the State of North Carolina*, 2 vols. (Wilmington, Del.: Glazier, 1984); North Carolina, *Session Laws,* April, October 1784; James T. Mitchell and Henry Flanders, comps., *The Statutes at Large of Pennsylvania from 1682 to 1801* (Philadelphia, 1896–1911), vol. 12; John D. Cushing, comp., *The First Laws of the State of Rhode Island,* 2 vols. (Wilmington, Del.: Glazier, 1983); New York, *Session Laws,* February 1786, January, February 1787; Thomas Cooper, ed., *The Statutes at Large of South Carolina* (Columbia, S.C.,

gitimate children or establish rules for disinheriting children. Few states defined the rights of widowers in the estates of their wives.[4] Compared with earlier efforts, however, the postrevolutionary statutes were both inclusive and well written.

EQUALITY IN CHILDREN'S INHERITANCES

Table 3.1 displays U.S. inheritance laws circa 1790. Probably the most significant postrevolutionary development in American inheritance law was the end of primogeniture everywhere. Although some

TABLE 3.1 (*continued*)

		When there is no will:			When there is a will:	
Widow's share if no children		When widow gets all	Escheat when no		Widow's share if she disregards will	
Real. (6)	Pers. (7)	(8)	Real. (9)	Pers. (10)	Real. (11)	Pers. (12)
⅓ life	½	Never	Next of kin	Next of kin	⅓ life	None
½ life	½	No kin	Next of kin	Next of kin	Intestate share	Intestate share
½	½	Never	Parents or descending kin, whole blood	Parents or descending kin, whole blood	Dowerᵇ	None
⅓ life	½	Real—no kin; pers—children of sibs.	Kin of spouse	Kin to 5th degree	Dowerᵇ	⅓
⅓ life	½	Never	Next of kin	Next of kin	⅓ life	None
⅓ life	½	Never	Next of kin	Next of kin	⅓ life	None
⅓ life	½	Never	Descending kin, half blood	Next of kin	⅓ life	None
⅓ life	½	Never	ᶜ	Next of kin	⅓ life	None
⅓ life	⅓	Never	Kin	Kin	⅓ life	ᶜ
½ life	½	Never	Kin	Kin	Dowerᵇ	None
⅓ life	½	Never	ᶜ	ᶜ	⅓ life	None
½	½	Never	Kin	Kin	⅓ life	None
⅓ life	ᵉ	No kin	Kin of spouse	Kin of spouse	⅓ life	ᵈ

1836–1839), vols. 2–5; William Waller Hening, comp., *The Statutes at Large: Being a Collection of All the Laws of Virginia from the First Session of the Legislature, to the Year 1819* (Richmond, Va., 1809–1823; reprint, Charlottesville, Va., 1969), vol. 12.

ᵃEarliest date in which all provisions in the table were in effect.

ᵇNo statutory provision; common law in effect, ⅓ realty for life.

ᶜLand acquired by purchase: next of kin. Land acquired by gift, descent, or devise: Kin of the blood of the original owner.

ᵈWidow's share if children: ⅓ if two or fewer children, child's share if more than two children. Widow's share if she disregards will: same as if children, except slaves for life only.

ᵉWidow's share if children: ⅓, except slaves for life only. Widow's share if no children: ½, except slaves for life only. Widow's share if she disregards will: ⅓ slaves for life.

colonies had taken this step in the seventeenth century, others needed a push from revolutionary events to make the break with English tradition. Stanley N. Katz believes revolutionary-era statesmen focused on revising inheritance law "in order to promote egalitarian ideals and to establish the foundation of a republican polity."[5] Because the English custom of primogeniture had functioned primarily to perpetuate an aristocratic social structure and political system, it could be abandoned in a republic. In the new United States, lawmakers acted to encourage wide ownership of property and, thus, widespread participation in government. As Jefferson argued, "The consequences of this enormous inequality producing so much misery to the bulk of mankind, legislators cannot invent too many devices for subdividing property, only taking care to let their subdivisions go hand in hand with the natural affections of the human mind."[6] Jefferson himself promoted the revision of inheritance law in Virginia.

Preferential treatment of eldest sons and male heirs continued in Connecticut, New Jersey, and North Carolina, demonstrating that inheritance laws did not become totally egalitarian immediately after the Revolution.[7] Therefore, although republican sentiment may have contributed to the abolition of primogeniture in some states, it is more likely that American independence simply provided jurists with a convenient excuse for moving in a desired direction. After all, the adjustments had begun in the seventeenth century when settlers' wealth in land and poverty in goods prompted colonies to pass partible inheritance statutes. As noted in the last chapter, colonial testators also tended to divide their lands into several viable parcels when they had more than one son.

When several children inherited a single tract of land, one of the heirs usually bought the others out.[8] At the end of the eighteenth century, new forms of financial assets made land sales and liquidation easier, probably freeing some siblings from the kind of long-term family obligation that buy-outs had occasioned in the past.[9] In Bucks County it also appears that eldest sons less often exercised their option to purchase the family holding. Between 1752 and 1765, court-appointed appraisers evaluated twenty-seven estates. In 81 percent of the instances the appraisers decided that farms could not be divided without hurting their value. They recommended partitions in only three cases. (The other two cases involved liquidation of estates, probably by the agreement of all the heirs, although that is not specified.) In sixteen of the twenty-two buy-outs (73 percent), the eldest son took the farm. But out of the sixty-one buy-outs among the seventy-nine actions to settle estates during the period 1787–1801, the eldest son was the purchaser in only thirty-four or 56 percent, of the cases.[10] Of course, whether this was the pattern for the much larger number of cases that were probably handled privately, we have no way of knowing.

States that waited until after the Revolution to change the law on primogeniture (South Carolina, Virginia, Maryland, and New York) adopted rules on the division of estates similar to that of Pennsylvania.[11] In South Carolina, for example, the statute of 1791 abolishing primogeniture contained provisions that gave courts of equity or common pleas the right to order partitions and sales. Legislators ordered that partitions should be made only when they would not cause "manifest injury" to any party. "But," the assembly ordered, "if it should appear to the court that it would be more for the interest of the parties that the same should be sold, then they shall direct a sale to be made, on such a credit and on such terms as to them shall seem right; and the property so sold shall stand pledged for the payment of the purchase money." [12] Early colonial innovations in the manner of distributing estates were thus accepted in the more traditional jurisdictions. Republican sentiment finally forced the change, but the system adopted had existed in New England and Pennsylvania since the seventeenth century, and it worked because of New World economic conditions: an abundance of land and ready purchasers.

By 1800 in most states, sons and daughters received equal shares in real and personal property; there was no longer any meaningful distinction for purposes of children's inheritances. For daughters who were married, increased rights to realty could bring a significant advantage. When a married women inherited personalty, her husband assumed ownership of her estate, but an inheritance of realty remained hers both during marriage and after her husband's death. He could not permanently alienate it without her consent, although he was entitled to the rents and profits during his life. [13] The rarity of partitions between heirs in Bucks County may indicate that few women gained any advantage, however, from the legal change. When daughters' inheritances of land were converted into cash settlements, laws governing personalty took over. Once again husbands had the right to claim wives' inheritances, a point to which we return in the next chapter.

THE WIDOW'S SHARE

The end of primogeniture brought changes in widows' rights as well. A traditional dower share was by metes and bounds. That is, the widow was entitled to a one-third share for life of each separate tract. This system worked best when a family estate remained intact. Once administrators began to divide an estate among all the children, however, dower proved extremely cumbersome. Therefore widows increasingly received cash sums in lieu of dower by metes and bounds. When an estate could not be divided without reducing its value, the widow had no right to dower in the land itself. The other heirs could demand a sale, and she would receive her share of the proceeds along with everyone else. Of the seventy-nine actions to settle estates in Bucks County between 1787 and 1801, for example, forty-seven mentioned a widow's share. In only one instance out of the forty-seven did the widow receive dower in land. In all other cases her dower was computed according to the annual interest that could be expected on one-third the valuation of the land.[14]

Although widows of intestates were receiving cash sums in lieu of traditional dower, Pennsylvania law continued to insist that they be paid in annual payments rather than lump sums. According to a Pennsylvania statute of 1764, the child who purchased the estate was responsible for paying the widow what amounted to an annual rent of her dower share. If the child fell behind in making payments, the mother could recover "by distress or otherwise, as rents in this province are usually recovered."[15] In partitions, each child became responsible for a proportionate share of the total dower payment. In eighteenth-century Pennsylvania, lawmakers assumed that the best provision for a mother was a guarantee of a child's role in caring for her.

Many widows probably agreed, but it is doubtful they appreciated another aspect of the law on partitions. When no child took the property and it was sold, the widow still could not claim her dower share as a cash payment. Instead the purchaser became responsible for paying her the annual interest on her share of the purchase price.[16] Even when family property came under the control of a nonfamily member, a woman did not gain control over her inheritance. If not dependent on her children, she became dependent on a stranger. *Beeson* v. *M'Nabb* (1833) demonstrates the plight of one widow forced to sue a purchaser for payment of the very first annual installment.[17] And Justice Hutson, in *Gheen, Executor of Osborn* v. *Osborn* (1828) spoke well, if unconsciously, on the situation of widows when he explained why the payment was an annual one: "In case of intestacy and valuation, or partition of the lands, her share is left in the lands, and charged on them by law, and the interest to be paid annually. . . . It is always intended as a provision for life: it is such in its nature, though generally made payable at a stated period; yet this is done to prevent the trouble and irritation which would arise from a weekly or daily demand."[18] By the late eighteenth and early nineteenth centuries, widows' dower rights were perceived more and more as an "irritation." They interfered with the transfer of property, operating, as Morton Horwitz noted, as a "clog" to economic development.

Shortly after the Revolution, South Carolinians took an approach more favorable to women. In the revision of 1791 they gave widows control over cash sums raised when lands were sold as a result of partitions or creditors' demands. The move was in line with the southern state's greater willingness to make husbands and wives equals for purposes of inheritance, for in 1791 South Carolina also had acted to give widows and widowers the same fee simple (absolute ownership) rights to family property.[19] This dramatic innovation in eighteenth-century law was imitated only in Georgia, which offered widows a choice between a fee simple estate in a child's share or a life estate in one-third.[20] For the most part, however, widows continued to receive their dower shares as life estates, as did widowers their curtesy; and except in South Carolina, the shares of men and women remained vastly different.

For widows, unlike for children, inheritance laws in most states continued to distinguish between real and personal property. When a Pennsylvania widow renounced her husband's will, she could claim only dower, that is, a share of the family's realty, plus her paraphernalia.[21] The law failed to recognize that increasingly, family wealth was made up of personal property as much as land. By neglecting to provide a remedy for the widows of intestate men who owned the bulk of their estates in personalty (a merchant's stock in trade or shipping interests, for example), lawmakers were ignoring economic change. But in the late eighteenth century when legislators rewrote their laws on inheritance, they were interested more in codifying and clarifying the law than changing it on such points as dower. In most states, widows' rights to personal property would be addressed only in the mid nineteenth century.

SOUTHERN RULES

Just as they had in the colonial period, a few jurisdictions—Maryland, Virginia, and North Carolina—guaranteed widows who renounced their husbands' wills shares of personalty as well as realty.[22]

The value of slave property combined with the difficulty of operating plantations without slaves had caused southerners to deal with the issue of personalty earlier than northerners.[23] The particular value of slaves probably also led to a unique provision in the inheritance laws of North Carolina. There, the widows of intestates received only a child's share of personalty if there were more than two surviving children.[24] Generally widows received a full third (or half if there were only one child) of intestates' personalty, but in North Carolina the legislators believed all members of a deceased man's family should inherit his slaves equally. The new North Carolina statute on intestacy continued to guarantee widows a full third of intestate husbands' realty, indicating that the move was not an attempt to reduce the value of dower generally but only with regard to personal property.[25] The fact that the statute guaranteed widows who renounced their husbands' wills shares of personal property, including slaves, mitigates the hardship of this new provision on personalty, for most states guaranteed no share of personalty to a woman who renounced her husband's will. Instead of restricting widows' rights, North Carolina lawmakers had expanded them beyond what was allowed under the common law.

Southern states were not consistently willing to grant women more property rights than they had known under English law, as demonstrated by the North Carolina provisions favoring sons over daughters for inheritances of land. In Georgia, women suffered an even greater hardship. Although a woman inherited land with her brothers under the state's intestacy statutes, she lost that land to her husband upon marriage,[26] for her new spouse gained absolute rights to her realty as well as her personalty. Men could sell or mortgage their wives' lands as readily as their own. Georgia women did have one advantage already noted, however. In cases of intestacy they could choose between a child's share of realty to hold in fee simple or a traditional life estate in a third.[27] The right to own land in fee gave Georgia widows, along with the women of South Carolina, a privilege others would not gain until the mid to late nineteenth century.[28] In Georgia, however, the fee simple right was still a poor replacement for the loss of all realty upon marriage. Women in other states retained title to their own realty after the deaths of their husbands and in addition received dower.

The changing rules of Georgia and South Carolina on widows' rights were in line with a general southern trend favoring what has been called modernization in the law. Virginia, for example, was the first state to allow widows and widowers fee simple rights to the estates of their deceased spouses when there was no "kin" to inherit.[29] Maryland applied the rule to widows only.[30] Lawmakers were acknowledging that those related by marriage had a claim on an inheritance paramount to that of the state. No longer would the land escheat for want of a lineage. Similarly, these two states also were the first to include the wife's or husband's kin in the line of succession.[31] Many other states still had not adopted such a rule by the end of the nineteenth century. Virginia, and Maryland to a lesser extent, were also aggressive in defining the rights of illegitimate children. Common law rules giving illegitimates no inheritance rights at all continued in most states after the Revolution. According to Tapping Reeve, who wrote the first American treatise on domestic relations, published in 1816, an illegitimate child was "*filius nullius* . . . having no inheritable blood." As a matter of policy, "to discourage illicit commerce betwixt the sexes," a child born out of wedlock could inherit from neither father nor mother unless they included a provision for the child in their wills. For the same reason, an illegitimate child could transmit to no one but spouse and children, "for all other kindred but his children must be traced through a common ancestor to him and the relations. But he has no ancestor: He, therefore, can have no relations in the ascending, or collateral line; and if he should die intestate, without any issue, no person could lay claim to his estate."[32] Reeve admitted that this reasoning could not apply to a child's mother but noted that in Connecticut, his own state, the Supreme Court supported the rule. Pennsylvania also upheld it until 1855.[33] A Virginia inheritance statute enacted in 1785, however, gave illegitimates the power to inherit from and transmit to their mothers as though they were legitimate.[34] Along with Maryland, Virginia lawmakers also gave men the power to legitimize children by marrying their mothers and acknowledging paternity.[35] Other than South Carolina, which acted only to limit the inheritances of illegitimates to no more than one hundred pounds, other states made no provisions for children born out of wedlock.[36]

Illegitimate children benefited under the Virginia statute in several ways. As noted, they became assured of inheriting intestate mothers' property and of transmitting their own estates to their mothers if they died intestate. This aspect of the law obviated the necessity of making testamentary dispositions. But another aspect of the statutory change was even more beneficial. By giving illegitimate children the rights of legal heirs, Virginia lawmakers allowed them to succeed to property *through* their mothers as well as from their mothers. They became the heirs of those who gave property to women and their legal "issue" or women and their "heirs." After 1785 in Virginia illegitimate children occupied a recognized place in the line of succession, alongside the legitimate children of their mothers and ahead of mothers' ascendant and collateral relatives. While children always had been able to inherit under specific testamentary bequests, they had never before been recognized as heirs in the general line of succession.

CONTINUITY AND CHANGE IN PENNSYLVANIA INHERITANCE LAW

Like most other middle and northern states, Pennsylvania remained true to its colonial tradition, which increases its usefulness as a case study. Rules on the treatment of illegitimate children as well as those defining widows' shares and creditors' rights all remained unchanged in 1800. That rules enacted in the late seventeenth and early eighteenth centuries remained in force through the first decades of the nineteenth century indicates Pennsylvania's reticence to institute reforms even in light of shifting economic conditions. Over the course of the eighteenth century, Pennsylvania lawmakers had moved away from the spirit of innovation displayed by their predecessors. Now they clung to the standards created for earlier times.

Increasing egalitarianism in the treatment of sons and daughters, for example, did not influence Pennsylvania lawmakers to place wives and husbands on a more equal footing. Husbands kept their curtesy rights, still undefined by statute, while widows' smaller dower shares continued to be subject to creditors' demands, as they always had been in Pennsylvania. In other states, widows received dower before creditors could claim estates, and they retained it until their deaths.[37] Pennsylvania widows had never enjoyed this common law privilege, and therefore unless they owned realty in their own names, an unlikely event given fathers' preferential devises of lands to sons and the custom on partitions, women could not be guaranteed support during widowhood. Despite a challenge to the practice in 1791—counsel for the widow pointed to English law and the practice of neighboring New

Jersey—the Pennsylvania Supreme Court upheld the unique custom on creditors' rights.[38] Widows, like other heirs, could claim inheritances only when an estate was clear of debt. As Justice Shippen explained the rule, "Our ancestors in Pennsylvania seem very early to have entered into the true spirit of commerce by rejecting every feudal principle that opposed the alienation and partibility of lands. While, in almost every province around us, the men of wealth or influence were possessing themselves of large manors, and tracts of land, and procuring laws to transmit them to their eldest sons, the people of Pennsylvania gave their conduct and laws a more republican cast, by dividing the lands, as well as personal estate, among all the children of intestates, and by subjecting them, in the fullest manner, to the payment of their debts."[39] Increasing economic instability at the end of the eighteenth and beginning of the nineteenth centuries did not prompt revision of this rule. It was not until late in the nineteenth century that women gained the right to keep all property separate from their husbands.[40]

Pennsylvania's reticence to revise established practices worked to the benefit of widows with regard to waste. As demonstrated by Morton Horwitz, the New England states of Massachusetts and Connecticut reduced widows' dower rights in the postrevolutionary period by denying them dower shares in uncultivated lands. Jurists argued that dower in wilderness lands purchased for speculative purposes had no value to widows. It produced no income they could use for their present support (the purpose of dower), and clearing and planting the lands to produce an income would result in a lawsuit by the future heir.[41] Under the common law, widows could not clear timber—commit "waste"—on lands they held under life estates.

Other jurisdictions, including Pennsylvania, continued to support colonial policy on the issue of waste.[42] Without risking a suit for waste, widows could clear timberlands if doing so gave them the income they needed to live. Moreover, as a Pennsylvanian observed in *Hastings* v. *Crunkleton* (1801), "Lands in general with us are enhanced by being cleared, provided a proper proportion of woodland is preserved for the maintenance of the place."[43] The Pennsylvania Supreme Court obviously held a different opinion from that of the high courts of New England on the value of uncleared lands. Horwitz probably is correct in his analysis that the New England rule was meant more to restrict dower generally than to prevent development of timberlands. If so,

Pennsylvania's decision not to limit dower by adopting the old English rule on waste was beneficial to women. Their options remained open. They could still clear and farm the timberlands they received as dower.

In another area of the law, Pennsylvania partially reformed one long-standing colonial policy. Beginning in 1770 Pennsylvania wives gained the right to veto land conveyances arranged by their husbands. By accepting the right of wives to private examinations, Pennsylvania law came into line with English law as well as that of the other American colonies.[44] New York, which like Pennsylvania did not enforce the procedure in the colonial period, also accepted the procedure at the end of the eighteenth century.[45] Through this right to join—or not join—in conveyances of family property, women were able to protect their dower shares. Men who sold property without the consent of their wives left purchasers liable to future dower claims, to avoid which, purchasers needed women's signatures as well as those of their husbands. Through private examinations, court officials guaranteed themselves that women were signing voluntarily and not out of "compulsion, dread or fear" of their husbands.[46]

Colonial Pennsylvania did not guarantee widows' dower in lands sold by their husbands during marriage; women, like children, could claim shares only in the property their husbands owned at death. Probably for this reason colonial officials had remained unconcerned about administering private examinations. The assembly did not require the procedure, although some purchasers demanded it to strengthen their land titles. In 1770 the Pennsylvania assembly enacted a statute reforming practice on private examinations;[47] they would be required thereafter for any conveyance of a woman's right to realty. Because women had no dower right in husbands' lands sold during marriage, the procedure applied only to lands women inherited or purchased before marriage. The protection was an important one despite its limitation. The fact that Pennsylvania and neighboring New York had long ignored the need for private examinations indicates the willingness of American jurisdictions to deviate from English law. Their move to require the procedure is evidence of what John Murrin called anglicization, the increasing desire of the colonists to adopt English practices.[48] Even here, however, Pennsylvanians did not move completely away from colonial tradition. While accepting the need for private examinations in theory, they continued to enforce them haphazardly,[49] leaving

Pennsylvania women with less protection than women had elsewhere. They still were ahead of Massachusetts matrons, however; that colony and state never did require the examination procedure.[50]

THE ALTERNATIVE TO DOWER; JOINTURES AND SEPARATE ESTATES

Through formal contracts, usually executed as trust estates, women or their relatives and friends could arrange for separate property during marriage and specific support during widowhood. Marriage settlements creating separate estates for femes coverts could be designed so that a woman had the right to both manage and devise her property. Often, however, husbands and wives together, or even husbands alone, managed the estates. Most separate estates were exempt from claims by husbands and their creditors, executors, or administrators. Unless a wife voluntarily used her estate as collateral, it could not be taken to pay her husband's debts. Women with separate estates therefore enjoyed a security not known to those without them. This was particularly true in Pennsylvania, where creditors could seize all of a man's estate, leaving only a few essentials (her clothes, some cooking utensils) for his widow. Many couples created separate estates to provide their families with just this sort of financial security.

The interposition of trustees in separate estates was designed to protect women from coercion, when husbands pressured wives to give up settlement property against their wishes.[51] Eventually, however, settlements executed without trustees—called simple marriage settlements—became valid. Pennsylvania accepted the English precedent in 1793.[52] Support for direct contracts between husbands and wives demonstrates a new official commitment to women's autonomy. Courts now regarded women as capable of protecting themselves against coercion from husbands or husbands' creditors. Undoubtedly the numerous instances of corrupt and thieving, or simply incompetent, trustees helped jurists realize that third parties could be more trouble than they were worth. Most creators of separate estates gave powers of control to women or their husbands rather than to trustees anyway. Trustees has become, in most instances, a mere formality, expensive and without purpose.[53] In addition, changing family relationships in the eighteenth century, particularly the rise of the companionate marriage, weakened the belief in the power of husbands to coerce.[54] The law no longer maintained that men possessed secret means of controlling their wives. As Reeve pointed out, wives could use the same procedures available to all who found themselves subject to coercion;[55] the law's general remedy provided enough protection. Simple marriage settlements pointed the way to even greater independence for women in the future, when mid-nineteenth-century jurists would recognize the right of women to hold and devise their own property, even without the benefit of such a settlement. Settlements without trustees marked an intermediate step on the way to complete independence for female property holders through the married women's property acts.

Whether made through trustees or as direct contracts, separate estates were favored particularly by widows, who needed to protect their dower property upon remarriage. Earlier marital experience or life as a widow had taught them the value of independent property rights. In addition, widows often had children from earlier marriages to consider. Settlement terms therefore indicate their desire to manage separate property and devise it at death. Fathers were the other primary creators of separate estates. Worried about turning daughters' marriage portions and inheritances over to sons-in-law, they used trusts to protect the property. Although the daughter, her husband, or the two of them together managed the estate, clauses generally restricted the claims of husbands' creditors and might prevent use of the principal or alienation. Settlements created by fathers usually arranged for automatic descent to the children of the marriage, thereby assuring a man that his estate would not be wasted before his grandchildren came of age.[56]

One kind of marriage settlement, the jointure, guaranteed women certain property in the event they outlived their husbands. Prenuptial jointures had the advantage of spelling out exactly what women could expect during widowhood but the disadvantage of barring dower. (Postnuptial jointures did not bar dower. The widow could take her choice of the jointure estate or her dower share.) In addition, prenuptial jointures did not allow wives to benefit from an increase in their husbands' estates during marriage and prevented couples from conveying the property covered in the contracts. In America, where conveyances were more common than in England, reliance on dower provisions or testamentary dispositions was the norm. Jointures may have been avoided because they interfered with the ready transfer of property.[57]

Marriage settlements designed to provide wives with separate estates could contain clauses giving women testamentary rights. Such a power gave mothers the privilege to bestow or withhold inheritances in the same manner as fathers. Children—or a husband—could be controlled through the promise of future gifts. In Pennsylvania some women took advantage of the powers they held under marriage settlements to make unequal dispositions. In *Administrators of Elizabeth Stone* v. *Charles Massey* (1798), a feme covert decided to turn her separate estate over to her husband rather than leave it to descend automatically to her infant daughter.[58] Elizabeth Stone's trustees gave the estate to the husband "at the repeated instance and reqest of the said Elizabeth in her life time."[59] When the daughter died shortly after her mother, Elizabeth's siblings stood to lose family property. They refused to release the estate of their sister, but the state supreme court found against them. Women with powers of disposal over their separate estates could give it to whomever they pleased.

In certain special cases, when courts of chancery had to interpose to assist a married woman in acquiring property (as in a will dispute, for example) they ordered the creation of a separate estate. When chancellors made such orders they usually gave the husband lifetime managerial rights and provided for the automatic and equal distribution of property among all the children at the death of the survivor of the marriage. Femes covert in such instances did not, then, have the right to make wills or deny husbands' curtesy rights. In a South Carolina case, *Postell and wife and Smith and wife* v. *Executors of James Skirving* (1789), the chancellor ordered O. B. Smith "to make the usual settlement" on his wife.[60] It consisted of a life estate for the survivor of the marriage with equal distribution among their children. A Maryland chancellor noted in *Helms* v. *Franciscus* (1818) that in his court, the creation of a marriage settlement "in general" resulted in a provision for a wife and her children after the death of the male family head.[61]

Court-ordered settlements were not designed to give a woman any present benefit. Her husband had the use of the interest or profits during his lifetime. Only if she outlived him could she gain access to her settlement property, and even then she could not control the principal, which remained in trust for her children. Unusual circumstances occasionally prompted chancellors to deviate from this pattern. When a husband became indebted, and in particular when he proved insolvent, courts would order that the wife receive payments directly.[62] This rule was consistent with the most common reason for employing separate estates, protection of some family property from husbands' creditors. In general, however, settlement property was kept in reserve, a fund for the support of a woman and her children during widowhood. A settlement of this sort did not bar a woman from claiming dower in her husband's estate. It was meant as additional, not supplementary, support.

Despite the advantages of separate estates for married women and their children, few couples had them. In a study of marriage settlements in South Carolina, only 1–2 percent of couples who married between 1785 and 1810 bothered to create a separate estate.[63] Apparently most people were satisfied with common law rules governing married women's property rights. Men, in addition, may have been unwilling to give up their extensive common law rights. Unless a fiancé or husband agreed, a woman could not make a legally binding separate estate. Fathers or others could, however, do so even against the husband's wishes. Still, most did not, even in South Carolina where the legal system lent them full support.

Elsewhere the law was not as sophisticated and supportive. In such states as Pennsylvania, Massachusetts, and Connecticut, settlements were even more rare. The absence of separate courts of chancery on the English model in these jurisdictions meant that English precedents and rules for governing marriage settlements were often poorly understood, rejected, or simply not known. States such as New York and Maryland, which did have independent chanceries, were more accepting of separate estates and developed sophisticated bodies of law concerning them, just like South Carolina.[64] The issue goes deeper than this, however. While the structure of a legal system was significant for determining acceptance of separate estates, ideological concerns were also important. Some colonies and states placed more emphasis on female dependence than others. The law of separate estates thus varied significantly from state to state, creating further confusion in an already complicated area of the law.

THE LIMITS OF REVOLUTION

Only one development significantly affected the economic relationship of family members in the postrevolutionary decades, the abolition of primogeniture. Rules were clarified in the new statutes on inheritance, but they entailed few breaks from the past. Except for occasional reforms that pointed the way to the future—South Carolina's equation of widows' and widowers' inheritance rights or the Virginia inclusion of illegitimate children in the line of succession, and the rise of simple marriage settlements—states continued their colonial traditions. As a result, the rules on inheritance became more and more out of step with economic reality, particularly with regard to the increasing value of personalty and women's property rights.

PART TWO

Family, Property, and the Rise of Corporate Capitalism

At the start of the nineteenth century, both would-be dynasts and lovers of domestic tranquility faced formidable problems in devising satisfactory inheritance plans. Fertility in America was high, seven being the average number of children born to women living through their childbearing years. Given the new postrevolutionary intestacy laws, to pass on the family "firm" intact to one offspring now required a will in all states.

The proliferation of new financial instruments, which facilitated liquidation and cash portions, made the perpetuation of wealth in the family line more difficult. The mechanisms for preserving financial assets were more poorly developed than those available for keeping realty in the family. Still, skimping on a daughter's or widow's portion because a future husband would find it easier than ever to dissipate the legacy ran counter to the postrevolutionary trend in intestacy laws and the supposedly enhanced status of motherhood.

In Chapter Four, we examine how these dilemmas resulted in a major change in property law, and therefore inheritance, during the nineteenth century. We consider, in Chapter Five, the impact of the new legislation, along with changes in capital and fertility, on nineteenth-century testamentary behavior.

4

Inheritance Law and the Rights of Women and Children in the Nineteenth Century

If the biggest change in inheritance law during the eighteenth century was the abolition of favored treatment for eldest sons and a new equality among children as heirs, then in the nineteenth century it was surely the transformation of the married woman's position as heir and testator. From about 1850 on, most states passed legislation allowing married women, rather than their husbands, the ownership and control over all personal and real property they had inherited or been given. These acts automatically endowed women of the capitalist class with rights only obtainable previously through the complicated marriage settlement process. Married women's inheritances became separate property that they could will to whom they chose and daughters could finally benefit from the intestacy laws that gave them a share equal to that of the eldest brother. The nineteenth-century reforms substantially increased the number of testators who were women and the amount of wealth they bequeathed. The virtual universality of married women's property acts did not mean, however, that uniformity reigned in America when it came to either women's rights or inheritance law generally. States devised different ways to allow married women to hold property. Some territories chose to enter the union as community property states, which meant that they not only recognized separate property of husbands and wives but also something known as conjugal or community property that had its own set of inheritance laws attached to it. States also differed on their treatment of illegitimacy and in other areas affecting inheritances of children.

THE LAWS IN THE FIFTY STATES AND TERRITORIES IN 1890

Appendix B lists the inheritance laws of the United States in the year 1890. Eight jurisdictions—Arizona, California, Idaho, Louisiana, Nevada, New Mexico, Texas, and Washington—had adopted the community property system, and the rest stayed with the common law. Wives in community property states automatically inherited one-half of community property, that property which had been acquired during the marriage and which neither spouse had received as part of an inheritance or gift. The common law only recognized separate property. As a result, property acquired during a marriage, because it was usually purchased or contracted for by the husband, became his separate property. At death, the spouse was entitled to an intestacy share of it; in the case of a will, the spouse could ignore the legacy bequeathed and claim dower (if a widow) or curtesy (if a widower). Some states also enlarged these powers of election against a will by allowing a share of personalty in addition to the dower or curtesy share of realty. But the major change wrought by the new acts in most common law states was that now wives could will separate real and personal property, and husbands had to be content with only a portion of a wife's personalty at her death rather than all of it upon the exchange of marriage vows. Because for most couples the bulk of an estate was property acquired after marriage and not part of an inheritance, the community property system generally benefited widows more than did the common law rules. Women, however, were still not on an equal footing with their husbands in the community property states. The most obvious inequality was the inability of a wife to will her half of community property. In four of the eight community property states, if she died first, all community property went to her husband. If he died first, she could only claim half.[1] He could will his half to whomever he pleased. Both legal systems considered the husband the head of the family, and that role carried with it a variety of privileges in different states.

Appendix B shows that the variation in inheritance laws between the two legal systems was much less marked among most of those nineteen common law and community property territories that entered the union from 1850 on. This group (hereafter called the post-1850s group) consists of a little over one-third of the states and excludes all jurisdictions east of the Mississippi and a few west of it. (The older states are here-after referred to as the pre-1850s group.)[2] Naturally the division does not work perfectly. Oregon joined the union in 1859 but conforms to-tally to the inheritance law pattern of the older states. Neither do the two far-flung states, Hawaii and Alaska, fit the pattern of the post-1850 jurisdictions very well.[3] On the other hand, the community property state of Texas does fit, even though its admittance date was 1845. The cutoff point of 1850, then, is somewhat arbitrary but ultimately useful in revealing the new direction legislation took. The post-1850s states were receiving American settlers, codifying laws, and forming consti-tutions during those decades in which lobbying on the "woman ques-tion" was most intense.[4]

Table 4.1 contrasts the inheritance laws of the post-1850 and pre-1850 jurisdictions. First, among the post-1850s group there was a trend toward making equal the intestacy shares given to husband and wife. In some community property states and a few common law jurisdictions, equality was achieved by increasing widows' shares to one-half; in others, by reducing the widowers' percentage to a third. Whatever the proportion, all post-1850 jurisdictions passed intestacy provisions that treated husbands and wives equally except Oregon, Alaska, and the four community property states that gave widowers' all the communal assets.

Second, the post-1850 group replaced widow and widowers' life-time tenure in realty with fee simple tenure (tenure forever). By the

TABLE 4.1 **DIFFERENCES IN INHERITANCE LAWS BETWEEN THE PRE–1850 AND THE POST–1850 JURISDICTIONS**

	Percentage of jurisdictions having such a provision in 1890	
Provision	Pre–1850 (*N* = 31)	Post–1850 (*N* = 19)
Spousal equality in intestacy shares	51.6	68.4
No "for life only" intestacy shares	16.1	73.7
Dower and curtesy both abolished[a]	25.8	68.4
Substantial homestead exemption[b]	41.9	84.2
Illegitimate child inherits from father who acknowledges	25.8	63.2

Source: Appendix B and Isidor Loeb, *The Legal Property Relations of Married Parties* (New York: Columbia University Press, 1900), 137–141, on dower and curtesy.

1890s, over 80 percent of the post-1850 jurisdictions had abolished curtesy, and over two-thirds had abolished dower. In one sense, this was advantageous to women, for it did away with an inequality. Dower gave widows only one-third of the husband's realty for life, while widowers got all for life. Yet, the advantage of these old devices was that in most states they included all realty that the decedent had been seized of during life, while the new intestacy and election laws usually gave a one-third share of the land the decedent owned at his or her death only.

In place of dower, the post-1850 jurisdictions firmly embraced homestead provisions. The exemption of the homestead from creditors and other claimants in order to prevent widows and children from destitution was initiated by Texas in 1839 and copied in one form or another in every post-1850 state except Oregon.[5] In contrast, the pre-1850 jurisdictions proved reluctant to remove dower and curtesy and institute protective homestead legislation.

Finally, the post-1850s' legislatures were more inclined to countenance illegitimate children inheriting from fathers who acknowledged paternity. Almost all states had altered the common law, which forbade any intestate transmission, by permitting illegitimate children to take an intestate share of their mother's estate. Only a minority, however, allowed these children to receive their portion from their father's estate even though he had recognized them as his offspring, and that minority tended to be in the post-1850s group of states.

There was, then, in the 1890s, a general acceptance in all areas of the country—common law or community property, East or West, original thirteen states or Mexican cession—that married women should have the power to devise and bequeath property they inherited. What was also happening in a significant minority of jurisdictions—most of the new states entering the union—was a move to enlarge the claim women had on "conjugal" property, whether formally designated community assets or not. There was a trend, also, to make personalty and realty more alike by doing away with intestacy shares, dower, curtesy, and election rights that provided for lifetime use rather than absolute ownership. Lifetime restrictions applied only to the dwelling house or homestead of the family. Then there was the effort to extend to illegitimate children an equal share of their parents' estate.

Why were married women granted inheritance rights, and what forces were promoting these other changes in inheritance statutes as new territories and states formed their constitutions and laws? The extensive literature on the married women's property acts has focused on the role of three separate movements that, as Norma Basch has put it, formed a "confluence of interests" promoting legal change.[6] There was the movement to protect debtors' families from destitution; the push for codification of laws, which stressed "modern" statute law over relics of "feudal" custom; and the crusade for women's rights.[7] The women's movement was formally organized, while the other two movements actually consisted more of a body of opinion shared among certain legal and business groups. Legislators and jurists gave their arguments increased coherence in debates and decisions.

There were of course countervailing forces that represented the other side of each of the three positions. Opposed to the debtor protection movement was the creditor, or more accurately, the financial interest, those individuals and institutions that championed the growth of corporate forms and opposed legal barriers to business transactions. Their views frequently coincided with those expressed by the codifiers but clashed with the arguments of the common law advocates, who in turn often allied themselves with the traditional family proponents. Both wished to retain marital unity in the person of the husband.[8] All of these interests exerted an influence on the inheritance law that evolved at the end of the nineteenth century.

Behind the debates, of course, were differing reactions to developments occurring in the economy and the family. The growth in financial institutions and financial assets had introduced a volatility into business activity that worked to the advantage of some but devastated others. The new world of paper wealth was at the center of the economic crises that wracked the country and the legislative battles fought out in the state capitols. Statutes on banking, railroads, canals, trust investment, general incorporation, bankruptcy, and imprisonment for debt preoccupied nineteenth-century lawmakers as they tried to formulate state policy toward corporate capitalism.[9] Inheritance law got caught up in this process. It also became part of the debate on the rules that should govern the relations of family members, husband and wife, parent and child. Age and gender had already been dismissed as criteria in discriminating among children as heirs with the abolition of primogeniture. The feme covert status of married women seemed as riddled with contradictions as the position of the chattel slave, yet a family with two heads seemed unthinkable.

Considering the situation, it is not surprising that, on the one hand, the arguments of the codifiers and financial interests proved victorious, and dower and curtesy were abolished. "It was inevitable," and "natural," wrote one legal scholar in 1900, that after "the development of real estate transactions," there would be a "modification of the rules governing the wife's interest in the husband's lands." Dower was so "inconvenient" and resulted in "hardship" and "injustice." [10] On the other hand, those concerned with the plight of debtor families successfully pressed for homestead exemptions that tied up the dwelling house for a number of years. Nor is it surprising that legislators adopted community property law so wives could have both separate estates and half of the property accumulated during the marriage but at the same time refused to give the wife the right to will that one-half if she should predecease her husband.

To give a sense of the interests involved and the confusion that prevailed, let us trace the development of inheritance law in our case study state of Pennsylvania during the last two-thirds of the nineteenth century. The state, though a leader in commercial and industrial activity, was not in the vanguard when it came to changing the rules on property distribution. Like almost all of the pre-1850 states, Pennsylvania tended toward conservatism in reactions to innovations in inheritance law. Allowing wives to will their separate property as well as be heirs of their children, and granting illegitimate and adopted children some inheritance rights, represented an enormous break with patriarchal and dynastic traditions. There was constant pressure in the legislature and from the courts to hold the line against both the feminists and the modernizers and to salvage somehow the battered notion of marital unity in the husband and the customary rights associated with the common law.

THE EVOLUTION OF NINETEENTH-CENTURY INHERITANCE LAW IN PENNSYLVANIA

In the 1830s, Pennsylvania legislators began to rework the state's outdated code of laws on inheritance. Over the next sixty years they slowly revised the rules, by piecemeal legislation that made the process of change long and confusing. Revised statutes conflicted with others still upholding eighteenth-century values, and judicial decisions occasionally became blatantly contradictory.

The earliest reforms in women's property rights all concerned inheritance. In 1848 the legislature enacted its first comprehensive married women's property statute granting wives the right to own separate property and exercise full powers of control over it.[11] This statute focused centrally on the issue of women's control over property they inherited or received as gifts, and it therefore can be seen as a continuation of the earlier reforms. A desire to protect the inheritances of married women eventually grew into a wish to protect their earnings as well, but the Pennsylvania General Assembly did not take that step until 1872.[12]

What is particularly interesting about the relationship between inheritance law and the married women's property acts is not that new rules on inheritance followed from the expansion of women's right to own property—that seems obvious—but rather, that changing attitudes toward inheritance allowed lawmakers to overcome their misgivings about a separation of property within marriage. The forces for change behind the revisions in married women's property rights, moreover, also produced a different perspective on the rights of husbands and children. The broad basis of reform can be seen in revised rules on entailed estates, the power to appoint guardians, and the inheritance rights of illegitimate and adopted children. Thus while the most startling changes concerned relations between husbands and wives, they were but part of the entire process of both legal change and continuity.

In revising the rules of inheritance, nineteenth-century Pennsylvania lawmakers were responding to forces ranging from the demands of modern economic policies to changes in the popular conception of motherhood. The history of Pennsylvania inheritance law is not one of reform only, however. Powerful conservative forces prevented change in some aspects of the law governing family property. Jurists upheld the principle of marital unity on some questions at the same time they destroyed it on the issue of separate property. The idea of women as family dependents, for example, persisted throughout the century. Provisions for widows remained minimal, and devises in restraint of marriage as well as life estates continued to find support among lawmakers. Illegitimate children only gained inheritance rights from their mother. As a result of legislative and judicial reluctance to change basic family relations, nineteenth-century rules on inheritance were marked by continuity as well as change.

Pennsylvania's Reform Movement

In Pennsylvania the first statute granting separate property rights to married women passed the legislature in 1832. It is appropriate that this reform involved the issue of personalty because it was the growth in this form of property, particularly the financial asset portion, that prompted legislators to push for changes in many parts of the inheritance law. As personalty grew in importance, husbands had a ready defense against reform available. They could write wills and restrict wives' ownership of personal property to life or widowhood (see Chapters Two and Five). Wives and their fathers were in a more difficult position since a woman who did not like what her husband left her in a will could only claim her dower right, one-third of realty for life. If most of his estate was in personalty, she was out of luck. In the Anglo-American inheritance system, fathers had been accustomed to having personalty pass to sons-in-law with no guarantees on how it would be handled. Since the abolition of a double share, all Pensylvania daughters with brothers received more personalty than before, and the estates of heiresses—those without brothers—were more likely to be in personalty than had been the case earlier. Enhanced credit opportunities open to husbands also heightened chances that families might be engulfed in debt. Undoubtedly, these factors helped further the popularity of trusts in the nineteenth century. There were drawbacks to these legal devices, however. The state legislature and the courts were constantly changing the rules governing trusts and the investments that could be made with their assets.[13] It was also sometimes difficult to appoint a competent trustee for one's daughter, and a groom had to agree to the type of settlement where the woman herself essentially managed the trust. Then there was always the possibility that creditors would challenge such an agreement.

The 1832 statute that one Pennsylvania judge termed "the first act securing the rights of married women in Pennsylvania" and another declared "a partial anticipation of the Act of 1848" concerned yet another disability suffered by women, owing to the switch in the balance of wealth away from realty toward personalty.[14] The law provided that any wealth women inherited as a result of the partitioning of realty be considered their separate estate even if the parcel had been converted to cash in the process of division among heirs. Although intestacy laws directed that realty be equally divided among children, daughters often ended up with money payments rather than land because sons, starting with the eldest, had first choice among the parcels in a partition, and statutes specified that money could replace land as long as those who took possession paid a sum equal to the value of the share of realty.[15]

Money was personalty, so the daughter's husband could claim it. Had it remained realty, neither a husband nor his creditors could take it.

Earlier in a decision on *Yohe* v. *Barnet* (1808),[16] the Pennsylvania court had rejected the argument that payments from partitioned land could be treated as realty and remain a wife's separate estate. The case concerned the distribution of an intestate father's estate among his children. One daughter received a cash payment as compensation for her share of the realty. Her portion, therefore, vested immediately in her husband, Jacob Yohe, who owed the estate money that he had borrowed from the deceased. The administrators, two of the woman's brothers, claimed their sister's share for the payment of her husband's debt, and her inheritance was thereby lost. Yohe had hoped to retain the money by arguing that his wife's profits from the partition should be treated like realty and thus be beyond the grasp of his creditors. Though the court professed dissatisfaction with the law as it stood, leaving a wife's real inheritance subject to confiscation by her husband's creditors once it had been converted to personalty as part of a division, they also could find no precedent for doing as Yohe requested.[17] In subsequent decisions, justices attempted to obviate the worst effects of the rule on a wife's inheritance from partitioning, but the truncated equity jurisdiction of the state courts would not allow them to go as far as they wanted.[18]

It was at this point that the General Assembly unveiled its own remedy. The new law provided that in all instances where a daughter inherited money in lieu of real estate, her husband was required to post security "to the satisfaction of the court" that after his death the sum would be returned in full to his wife, or in the event of her death before his, that it would be distributed among her heirs "as if the same were real estate." If a husband refused or was unable to give security, he was asked to relinquish the money to trustees, who managed the principal during his life, while paying into his hands the annual interest.[19]

As might be expected in this first statutory effort at granting women separate property, the provisions of the law blended old and new attitudes toward marital relations. The intent of the legislature in designating certain property as separate was radical. Loss of inheritance by women through the partitioning process had been going on in Pennsylvania since at least the early eighteenth century.[20] The assembly's decision to act, therefore, was a departure. Probably payments in place of land were occurring more frequently by the 1830s because of a brisker realty market and reduced availability of land. Indebtedness of husbands may also have been on the rise. These circumstances may partially account for the legislation. But it also seems that in the nineteenth century there was a new sense of impropriety about a husband having that kind of power over his wife's property. It came out in the regretful tone assumed by the court in their 1808 decision on Yohe and in later court judgments requiring a husband to settle all or a part of his wife's inheritance on her as a condition for assisting him in gaining access to the property. Under the statute of 1832, this limited option was expanded and generalized to make it more effective. All property inherited by married women under partitions was defined as separate property, not just what the court decided was adequate on a case-by-case basis.

The lawmakers managed, however, to formulate the statute in a manner that expressed this righting of a gender inequity in a traditional way. The statute aimed at preserving women's estates for their blood relations. Like much state legislation around this time that tried to protect a wife's property from her husband's creditors, it was the product of legislators' dislike for seeing one lineage have to pay for the mistakes of another.[21] But the law stopped short of giving a wife actual control of the property, and it provided her with a mechanism for relinquishing her rights to her husband if she so desired.[22] The legislation was also traditional in that the remedy added restraints and conditions onto personalty, making it as cumbersome to transfer as realty and thus clashing with the aims of the modernizers who were trying to remove the so-called feudal devices—dower, curtesy, and estates for a fixed term—that interfered with business transactions. It was just this kind of conflict that eventually made it necessary to grant women separate property rights.

The influence of those modernizers who wanted to codify common law custom can be seen in another piece of legislation passed in the same session. This law recognized the legitimacy of a married woman's will written with the consent of her husband and, therefore, merely codified existing law.[23] Rather than indicating support for an expansion of women's limited testamentary capacity, the act probably resulted from the growing legislative distrust of rules affecting transmission of wealth that were not governed by statute. As such, it anticipated the numerous revisions of inheritance law to follow.

A very different sort of motivation, however, was probably behind the next Pennsylvania act concerning inheritance. In 1833 legislators voted to allow mothers inheritance rights in their children's estates even when fathers were living, whereas previously, fathers had inherited children's estates to the total exclusion of mothers.[24] Under the new law mothers became equal inheritors of personalty absolutely and of realty as tenants of the entirety. If they outlived their husbands, they gained absolute ownership of all the real estate by right of survivorship. Husbands could not deny them access to the property, and creditors had no permanent claims on the realty or half of the personalty. This marked a dramatic improvement over the dower share in land wives could claim when fathers only inherited children's estates, as under the old statute of distribution dating from 1794.

So once again the Pennsylvania General Assembly had given women the right to own personal property after marriage without the benefit of a marriage settlement.[25] Unlike the statute on partitions, the appearance of this statute cannot be attributed to changing attitudes toward debtor–creditor relations. Nor was the statute a codification of an old equitable or common law rule. More than any previous law expanding the property rights of women in nineteenth-century Pennsylvania, this one exemplified the legislature's desire to improve the status of women, and thus it stands as testimony to what many have seen as the rising power of women within the family as the cult of domesticity took firm hold on the imaginations and sentiments of the nation toward midcentury.

By granting mothers separate property rights within marriage, Pennsylvania lawmakers moved closer to acknowledging all women's rights to own property independently of their husbands. This exception to the general rule together with that protecting women's inheritances of personalty under partitions demonstrate the gradual evolution of a policy supporting separate property. The first exceptions necessarily were specific, designed to benefit women in particular situations, but they indicate a slowly changing attitude toward the principle of marital unity. A decade and a half later, the assembly was ready to move a step further and enact the first comprehensive married women's property act in the state.

The Married Women's Property Act of 1848 specified that everything the wife owned before marriage or acquired afterward "by will, descent, deed of conveyance or otherwise,"[26] whether real or personal, was subject to her disposition. It automatically gave women the separate estates that previously had only been possible through complicated trusts and marriage settlements, and moreover, it allowed them the complete testamentary capacity of femes sole (unmarried women).

The terms of the statute of 1848 aimed primarily at improving women's property rights in personalty. Before the act took effect, women already exercised some control over the disposition of their real estate. (Men could not convey their wives' estates without permission, and at their deaths, the property stayed in the possession of their wives.) The provisions on realty remained unchanged by the women's property act; the clause of the statute governing conveyances repeated the traditional rule: "Nor shall such property be sold, conveyed, mortgaged, transferred or in any manner encumbered by her husband, without her written consent first had been obtained, and duly acknowledged before one of the judges of the court of common pleas of this commonwealth, that such consent was not the result of coercion on the part of her said husband, but that the same was voluntarily given and of her own freewill." [27] The statute gave women no new right to convey realty separately from their husbands but, as this clause demonstrates, assumed that men still would be making decisions about conveyances, while women simply gave consent. [28]

With regard to personalty, however, the statute brought women considerable relief. Even after marriage, they could manage their personal property, including the rents and profits of their real estate, with or without the permission of their husbands. For this reason, contemporaries regarded the statute not as a conferral of all property rights on married women but as a support of their rights to personalty. In his decision on a case tried in 1889, Justice Penrose of the Pennsylvania Supreme Court defined the statute as "preserving the ownership of personal property to women notwithstanding marriage." [29]

Certainly concern about husbands' creditors and modernizers' dissatisfaction with the complicated devices required to safeguard married women's property both played a big role in the passage of the 1848 act but could hardly account for all its sweeping provisions. There was no necessity to give women complete testamentary power over their separate estates when descent and distribution laws could operate instead. Furthermore, the new law gave widows who elected against taking the legacy left them by their husbands an absolute share in personalty in addition to their dower third in land. They could inherit one-third if there were children and one-half if none, the same portion they could claim if their husbands died intestate. The right to a share of personalty under dower, which had been lost in colonial times in Pennsylvania, was now being restored to widows. The new testamentary authority and the enhanced right of election indicate a clear desire to improve women's status in the family. The ability to write a will gave mothers new influence over heirs. The revised election rights made it impossible for a husband to convert all his wealth to personalty and escape a widow's claim on his estate.

Less well studied than the diminution of patriarchal power brought about by the married women's property acts are the alterations occasioned by statutes concerning the intergenerational transmission of wealth. Devices that had in earlier times been tools to further the fortunes of the patrilineage seemed in the later nineteenth century to be impediments to the proper functioning of the economy and the family.

In 1855 the Pennsylvania legislature finally abolished entails, ordering that "whenever hereafter by any gift, conveyance, or devise, an estate in fee tail would be created according to the existing laws of this state, it shall be taken and construed to be an estate in fee simple, and as such be inheritable and freely alienable."[30] This law undoubtedly was part of the legal housecleaning sponsored by the codifiers and probably had little practical effect. Our will samples from Bucks County in the colonial period and the 1790s show that, even then, fathers almost never entailed the land they devised to their children.

The other two developments were of more moment and concerned not only paternal authority but also maternal power. One of the greatest patriarchal prerogatives enjoyed by fathers was the testamentary right to appoint the guardian of their children. Although they retained this privilege throughout the nineteenth century, the Pennsylvania General Assembly, in the same year that they abolished entails, passed a statute limiting the control of unfit fathers over their children.[31] Among the provisions of this act was the stipulation that when a father "for one year or upwards previous to his death" neglected to provide for his children, he lost the right to appoint a testamentary guardian to his will. It was 1881, however, before mothers had a legal right to appoint testamentary guardians, and at no time in the nineteenth century could they overturn an appointment made by a "responsible" father.[32]

Also in 1855, the assembly began dealing with the issue of illegitimacy. In comparison with the post-1850s states, Pennsylvania took a conservative position. Not fathers, but only mothers and the children they bore outside of wedlock, could inherit from one another. Still, this marked an improvement over no intestacy rights for illegitimate sons and daughters. They now occupied an official place in the line of succession, alongside the legitimate children of their mothers, and ahead of mothers' ascending and collateral relatives.[33] Like entailing, the legitimate–illegitimate distinction was an important traditional tool in dynastic management. Unlike entailing, it was still in use, so this law had greater significance.

Finally, adopted children also gained inheritance rights in 1855. Under the new rule that appeared several weeks after the one on illegitimate children, they obtained the status of legal heirs. In addition they gained a right withheld from illegitimates, the right to inherit from and transmit to the other children of their parents.[34] The common law had made no provision for adoption, for it had developed other methods for dealing with lineage failures. But as dynastic strategies declined in importance, a new egalitarianism in the domestic circle was allowed.

Drawing the Line on Reform

While many lawmakers sought to protect women's property during economic fluctuations and to acknowledge the importance of women in the family, a few also advocated a goal that was more radical and therefore more controversial: an increase in women's financial autonomy for its own sake. The forces of change behind nineteenth-century reforms went beyond the economic and social ones with which Americans felt most comfortable. From the 1830s on, feminists began to demand equal property rights for women. Enough influential politicians and jurists supported them to make the movement for reform dangerous to the status quo.[35]

In the eyes of many, the legislation of 1848 went too far. Financial interests, though usually on the side of modernization, were no friend to women's separate property rights, which they considered an obstruction to commerce. Consequently, they worked to narrow the property wives could claim as their separate estate, and for some time the state courts and the legislature cooperated with their objectives. In 1853 a supreme court decision held that even though the statute of 1848 specified that "all such property of whatever name or kind, which shall accrue to any married woman during coverture by will, descent, deed of conveyance or otherwise, shall be owned, used and enjoyed by such married woman as her own separate property,"[36] earnings received after marriage were not covered.

Feminist reformers decried the supreme court's ruling as a narrow interpretation of the law, but the legislature upheld the court's verdict in 1855. This action was consistent with the view that the primary goal of separate property was to protect wives' assets from husbands' creditors, not to give women independence.[37] Women still had an obligation to help support their families if husbands proved unable to do so alone. The assembly, to protect the interests of local tradespeople and landlords, required wives to use their separate property to cover debts for family necessities.[38] The exclusion of women's earnings remained until 1872, when the assembly finally reversed itself. Concern for creditor interests surfaced, however, in those clauses that placed the burden on the wife to "show title and ownership" in her separate property to prevent its confiscation and required wives to petition and register in the local court their intention to claim separate earnings.[39]

Other critics of the 1848 law were less concerned about the impact the legislation had on commercial relations and more disturbed about its effect on the traditional family. The statute gave women the right to dispose of all their property, real and personal, to the exclusion of their immediate families. Curtesy was swept aside, as was the automatic right of children to inherit their mothers' realty. The law gave wives a powerful option husbands did not possess, the right to cut off a spouse without a penny. A husband had no right to elect against his wife's will.

How did this happen? There are a couple of possible explanations. First, in Pennsylvania as in most other jurisdictions, one purpose of the married women's property acts was to codify existing equity law rules. There were no election rights for husbands in those rules because under the equity arrangements a husband or a third party giving a wife property had to approve her making of a will. Second, election rights for widows were an extension of the male head's responsibility to support his wife. Because women had no traditional obligation to maintain their husbands, the legislature initially may have overlooked the fact that wives could disinherit their spouses.

Whatever the case, the assembly in 1855 corrected its decision to grant women absolute testamentary powers. The public might be ready to expand the rights of women but not to give them privileges unknown to men. With the passage of the act, men gained the same election rights as women had or, alternately, could claim curtesy in all of a wife's lands.[40]

At the end of the nineteenth century, State Supreme Court Justice Mitchell looked back on the 1848 provision on married women's testamentary power and declared that it had created an inequitable situation in which women had gained an unfair advantage over men. As he explained it, "The pendulum had swung too far. From the entire absorption of her personal property by the husband at common law, the wife was now not only freed during marriage, but vested with a testamentary control, to his exclusion, far greater than his control of his own or against her." Mitchell believed that the act of 1855 was passed "to remedy this last condition." Its "plain intent" was to produce equality.[41]

That Mitchell claimed that the 1855 law produced equality is curious considering that men could elect curtesy in all the lands of their spouse, something wives had no power to do. Nor did he mention that in intestacy cases husbands received all a wife's realty for life while wives received only a lifetime third of a husband's land. Often the land was partitioned among the heirs, and the widow's share took the form of an annual rent. If, over the years, the children or the buyers of the land failed to keep up the payments, she had to go to court to enforce her rights.[42] It was a cumbersome system. Husbands never faced partitioning because they inherited all the parcel.[43]

The courts and the legislature also refused to outlaw clauses in husbands' wills making a wife's possession of realty contingent upon her remaining unmarried, even though, since the married women's property acts, there was no danger that the second husband could take control of it from her without her collaboration. Some of the opinions justifying the restraint on remarriage indicated a fear that women might sacrifice their children's interest for that of a new husband. Other decisions argued that a man should not have to suffer the indignity of having his widow, her new husband, and their children enjoying his property. As one chief justice bluntly put it, "It would be extremely difficult to say, why a husband should not be at liberty to leave a homestead to his wife, without being compelled to let her share it with a successor to his bed, and to use it as a nest to hatch a brood of strangers to his blood."[44] Perhaps it was this kind of reasoning that prevented the passage of a homestead exemption in Pennsylvania.

These acts and decisions regarding election rights, intestacy shares, and restraints on remarriage continued to uphold a double standard. As head of the family, widowers got larger portions of their wives' estates than widows did of their husbands'. Women could expect no more of lawmakers than support for their right to be maintained. If the husband had devised a way to keep his widow unmarried and dependent, the courts would not intervene. Jurists reiterated time and again their stand that the married women's property acts had not aimed at changing the basic economic relationship of marriage. Legislators wanted to protect women's property by giving them control over it, but they did not want to destroy the idea of marital unity, for doing so, they feared, would also destroy the family.

Marital unity was the notion that upon marriage a man and a woman became legally one. The famous Blackstone dictum "and that one is the husband" suggests the problem with this concept after the married women's property acts were passed. What particularly needed to be clarified was whether property jointly given to a married couple or purchased by them still made them tenants of the entirety, as it had when husbands controlled all, or whether the spouses became tenants in common, each with a 50 percent interest that each was free to sell or will. With tenancies of the entirety, neither partner could dispose of the property alone; and upon the death of one spouse, the survivor claimed all the property. Although the courts in 1870 finally decided that a woman's interest in tenancies of the entirety was her separate property, they also ruled that all the rights and obligations of that tenancy were to be observed.[45] It is not clear who benefited by this ruling. Judges argued they were protecting women, and indeed the decision probably worked to wives' benefit because their claims on husbands' separate property were much less than husbands' claims on theirs. Also men were more likely than women to try and sell their shares without a spouse's knowledge. We are less interested here in the question of who gained the advantage, however, because our research has shown that, at least in Bucks County, very few nineteenth-century couples held land jointly (see Chapter Eight). What is significant about the issue, from our standpoint, is that the debate occasioned an outpouring of support from the bench for the sanctity of marital unity. Husbands and wives could not bring actions against each other in the courts, so they could not hold as tenants in common where such suits were possible. In passing the 1848 act, "the design of the legislature was single," wrote

Justice Strong in 1867. "It was not to destroy the oneness of husband and wife" but to protect her property.[46] This oneness made possible survivorship in the entirety, but it also justified female dependency.

During the nineteenth century, Pennsylvania inheritance law, though it had its peculiarities, was in the mainstream. The law supported married women's right to bequeath their separate property and choose their heirs instead of having their husbands and fathers do it for them. In making reforms, lawmakers were influenced by arguments for the bettering of women's status in the family. Of course such arguments would have been of little effect without the growth of financial institutions and intangible assets and the change in debtor–creditor relations it engendered. Yet the forces that might be associated with some of the modernizing tendencies in the law wanted only limited reform; commercial and financial interests had no desire to see married women's claims to property expanded. Assets accumulated by the labor of both spouses generally became the husband's separate property unless the wife was paid directly in wages and registered that fact with the local courts. The wife had no testamentary power over this conjugal wealth, and her intestacy share was what it had been in the colonial period. Husbands had greater claims on their wives' separate property than their wives had on theirs, and the courts refused to intervene when a husband in his will punished his wife for remarrying.

THE NEW SYSTEM

The patrilineage dissolved in the nineteenth century. Entails went the way of primogeniture; mothers could inherit from their children; illegitimate and adopted children barged into the line of succession; and most significant, wives shook loose their inherited property from their husbands. The question is, what took its place? Inheritance law did not really become conjugally oriented. Children, not spouses, inherited the bulk of each parent's wealth in most states. In fact, it became more difficult to disinherit a child in America as the number of states passing laws requiring parents to state in their wills their specific intention to leave out a son or daughter jumped from three to twenty.[47] Nor was there any big move to give spouses the entire estate if no children or grandchildren survived.[48]

There seemed to be a nod toward a more bilateral descent system as a way to give women greater status in the household yet keep them subordinate to the head of the family, the husband. A mini-matrilineage emerged as married women could bequeath to and inherit from their children both legitimate and illegitimate. Women from affluent families gained a great deal, but in most states—ones like Pennsylvania—the average woman, who had no separate property and whose assets primarily consisted of those derived from the labor she had put into her marriage, would have noticed little change in her situation. Her husband controlled and willed that wealth, and typically, she could claim no more than a third of it.

In the inheritance law of a minority of states, however—those entering thc union in 1850 or after when the "woman question" was being hotly debated—there was a sign of the direction in which things would move. Some of the post-1850s territories entered as community property states. Others did not go that far but moved to improve the intestacy share widows received of their husband's separate property, which was where most of the "conjugal" assets ended up in common law states. All provisions specifying lifetime only tenure in realty were abolished in most of the post-1850 jurisdictions. At the same time, homestead exemptions were introduced to make sure widows and minor children were not thrown out of the family domicile. But of course what happened in the statute books is only half the story; testamentary behavior is the other half.

5

Testamentary Behavior in the 1790s and 1890s

Two changes, one legal and the other economic, had the potential for transforming testamentary behavior in nineteenth-century America. The first was the passage of the married women's property acts, which permitted wives to retain control over assets and write wills. The second was the proliferation of corporate forms and the concomitant increase in intangible property. Corporations made it possible to separate the ownership from the management of business, taking the succession problem out of family hands. Just as important, this change provided an alternative form of property to distribute among family members in lieu of physical wealth. Family firms could be liquidated, and the money from the sale could be converted into the stocks and bonds of other companies or put into trusts that in turn would make such investments.[1] The growth in personalty, mainly intangible personalty, had much to do with the enactment of the period's married women's property statutes.

The property holdings of Bucks County residents whose estates were probated provide some indication of the pace of this development. In the colonial period, about 10.5 percent of probated wealth was in cash and financial assets, and that percentage grew to 28.7 by the end of the eighteenth century. The biggest jump, however, came during the nineteenth century, when intangible assets ultimately comprised over two-thirds of total wealth.[2] In colonial times, most intangible wealth took the form of book accounts (debts owed by buyers of goods), mortgages, personal bonds, and notes. These types of financial assets retained their importance, but the real growth was in stocks and bonds issued by banks; municipalities; mining, water, energy, and transport industries; and authorities such as those for railroads, canals, turnpikes, and bridges. Insurance policies were also important, as were groups such as the Dairying Association peculiar to rural areas. In probate files of the 1890s (those for Los Angeles County as well as Bucks), paper assets are ubiquitious.

These alterations in law and property, moreover, occurred as the demographic structure of families was being transformed. Fertility declined 50 percent between 1800 and 1900. In the two Bucks County samples from the 1790s and the 1890s, the average number of children mentioned in wills dropped from 4.2 to 1.8. Undoubtedly, these numbers are underestimates because some testators omitted bequests to one or more children. Still, there is no indication that these omissions followed a systematic pattern or were greater in one period than the other. Both the proportion of testators who had no children and of those who had fewer children increased over time. In the 1790s, out of those testators with children, 19 percent had one or two, while over half had five or more. Those proportions were just about reversed in the 1890s.

There is a question, of course, about the nature of the association between inheritance and fertility. In which direction does the causal arrow point? The land availability thesis of Richard Easterlin suggests inheritance strategies resulted in a fertility decline, that concern about providing farm land to sons kept family size down in more settled regions of the country. It is also possible, however, to posit the reverse: that fertility is the explanatory variable, and testation patterns are the phenomenon to be explained. How did the number of children affect inheritance behavior? To what extent did the portions allotted to lineal descendants and spouse depend on the number of children in the family?[3]

DYNASTIC AMBITIONS

There is some continuity in the dynastic behavior of Bucks County wealthholders. Testators with children in both the 1790s and the 1890s were no more likely than their colonial counterparts to bequeath property to kin outside the nuclear family, to nonkin, or to charitable institutions (Table 5.1). In fact, in the case of kin, colonials with lineal heirs were twice as likely (17.4 percent to 8.6 percent) as those in the late-nineteenth-century sample to give to relatives possibly because the former were more inclined to make their sons-in-law legatees. At the opening and the close of the nineteenth century, 90 percent or more of testators with children confined their bequests to wives, sons, daugh-

TABLE 5.1 **PERCENTAGE OF TESTATORS MAKING BEQUESTS OUTSIDE THE IMMEDIATE FAMILY, BUCKS COUNTY**

Bequests to	1685–1756	1791–1801	1891–1893
	All testators		
N	387	352	351
Kin[a]	26.9	23.0	31.3
Nonkin	12.2	11.6	11.1
Charity	5.0	6.5	7.1
	Testators with children		
N	327	274	222
Kin[a]	17.4	10.9	8.6
Nonkin	6.7	5.1	4.5
Charity	3.7	4.1	2.3

[a]Excludes spouse, children, and grandchildren.

ters, and grandchildren.[4] Any increased amount of property going to nonnuclear family members resulted from the larger number of childless testators.

In most other ways, however, the 1890s testators sharply departed from earlier patterns. The percentage of testators who transferred a family firm to an heir, whether farm (the main industry in Bucks County) or other business, plummeted. Table 5.2 indicates that this was not only because fewer testators owned a business at the time they wrote a will, a situation that could be due to an earlier transfer of property to family members, but also because testator- and court-ordered liquidations grew. Thus, of testators with a farm or other business in the colonial period, 87 percent passed it on to heirs. The proportion declined somewhat in the 1790s, with 71 percent in that category. But by the 1890s, only a little more than one-third made that choice. The findings are nearly the same if we consider only male testators. There was of course no guarantee that the heirs of that one-third would actually keep the business. A study of Iowa farmers in the late nineteenth and first half of the twentieth century found that a little over half of the tracts transferred in this manner stayed in family hands for two generations or more.[5]

TABLE 5.2 **PERCENTAGE OF TESTATORS TRANSFERRING FARMS AND BUSINESSES IN WILLS, BUCKS COUNTY**

Period	All	Male only	All with farm/business	Male only with farm/business
1685–1756	71.6	77.5	87.4	87.1
	(387)	(341)	(317)	(303)
1791–1801	53.9	61.0	70.9	71.5
	(352)	(292)	(268)	(249)
1891–1893	10.8	17.6	36.2	36.9
	(351)	(216)	(105)	(103)

Note: Included under transfer of a farm or business to heirs are those cases in which an heir bought the firm from the estate and also those cases in which the firm was a closely held corporation and a majority interest in the stock was bequeathed, the latter situation being extremely rare. Also counted as transfers are all businesses willed to wives forever. Number of observations appear in parentheses below percentage.

The tendency of 1890s testators either not to have a business or to liquidate rather than pass on to the next generation was of course not an overnight development.[6] Even in the 1790s, a greater proportion of testators (29.1 percent) opted to liquidate their farms or businesses than had been the case in the colonial period (12.6 percent), and among those who did pass the family firm on to heirs, fewer specified joint ownership, a method of disposition that bound together adult family members for long periods (see Table 5.3).

The decline in the proportion of testators who transferred a business

TABLE 5.3 **TESTATORS' DISPOSITION OF FAMILY FARM OR BUSINESS, BUCKS COUNTY**

	Percentage of testators	
Method of disposition	1685–1756 (N = 317)	1791–1801 (N = 268)
Liquidation	12.6	29.1
Eldest son buys	6.6	7.8
All to eldest son	20.5	11.9
All to another heir	4.7	6.7
Joint ownership	18.3	12.7
Parcels	21.1	19.4
All to spouse	5.7	2.2
All to spouse, time limit	10.4	10.1

to heirs did not mean that everyone had lost the desire to conserve family wealth. The development of trusts and their use by the affluent in Bucks County indicates that in certain circles there was a continuing interest in estate planning. Trusts differed from entails and life estates in that testators nominated a person or institution as trustee. This trustee was formally in charge of the bequest and usually had the power to move around the assets for the benefit of the trust's recipient. Trusts were a more appropriate means of handling and safeguarding property composed mainly of intangible personalty. Table 5.4 shows the increase in the use of trusts by testators over the course of the nineteenth century. It rose from 11 to 29 percent among all testators, with most of the increase being in trusts set up for wives. Among affluent testators, however, there was also a dramatic jump in the employment of trusts for male and female heirs. Some of these trusts were for the

TABLE 5.4 **TRUSTS, 1790s AND 1890s, BUCKS COUNTY**

Type of trust	Percentage of [a]	
	All testators	Affluent testators [b]
1791–1801		
N	351	103
None	88.6	82.5
For spouse	5.7	6.8
For some/all male heirs	2.9	5.9
For some/all female heirs	3.5	3.9
Other: charitable, etc.	1.1	3.9
1891–1893		
N	351	75
None	70.7	54.7
For spouse	16.2	24.0
For some/all male heirs	5.7	12.0
For some/all female heirs	8.3	20.0
Other: charitable, etc.	3.7	6.7

[a] Percentages in columns exceed 100 because some testators had more than one type of trust.

[b] Those with personal estates of £500 in the 1790s and $7,000 in total estate in the 1890s. For more information on cutoff points, see Appendix A.

guardianship of wealth bequeathed to minors, but that type was by no means the only kind drawn up. In the 1890s, 20 percent of affluent Bucks County testators left trusts for some or all of their female heirs, a fivefold increase, while trusts for male heirs doubled, going from 6 to 12 percent. The fact that female heirs were more frequently the recipients of these trusts indicates that testators had more confidence in men's than women's ability to handle wealth and pass it on to lineal heirs. In fact, the kinds of trust arrangements found in the 1890s are seldom the comprehensive type drafted in the twentieth century to include all principal heirs. Rather, trusts were set up for specific legatees—those who, for one reason or another, the testator felt needed supervision.

INEQUALITY IN BEQUESTS TO SONS AND DAUGHTERS

If the passing on of a business intact to the next generation had become less of a necessity in the nineteenth century, one might expect that it became easier to equalize portions among children. The abolition of primogeniture and double shares in state intestacy statutes at the end of the eighteenth century would also have contributed to a climate hostile to discrimination among siblings. Yet, in the 1790s, after the passage of the new intestacy laws in Pennsylvania, Bucks County testators continued to discriminate against daughters in about the same proportions as they had in the colonial period, although it seems that the degree of inequality between sons' and daughters' portions had diminished.[7] By the 1890s, however, the situation had changed markedly. In Table 5.5 the two periods are compared, showing the testamentary choices made by all testators and by the affluent. The treatment of sons and daughters by the entire sample of testators at the end of the nineteenth century is nearly identical. Only among the affluent did some discrimination against daughters remain. Affluent testators gave sons more than intestacy more frequently, and they more often placed time restrictions on bequests to daughters.

Wealth, then, continued to produce some inequality in bequests, but what about the role of fertility? How much of the change in treatment of children can be explained by a drop in the number of offspring for which a testator had to provide? Perhaps it was not a change in senti-

TABLE 5.5 **TREATMENT OF SONS AND DAUGHTERS, 1790s AND 1890s,
BUCKS COUNTY**

Treatment compared with intestacy	Percentage of			
	All testators		Affluent testators[a]	
	Sons	Daughters	Sons	Daughters
1791–1801				
N	260	262	83	80
More	37.3	14.9	49.4	17.5
Same	14.6	16.0	14.5	20.0
Less	21.2	50.4	9.6	48.8
More but life[b]	1.5	1.1	—	2.5
Same but life	0.8	2.3	1.2	1.3
Less and life	0.8	6.9	2.4	6.3
Some more/less[c]	23.1	7.3	22.9	3.8
Some more/less and life	0.8	1.1	—	—
1891–1893				
N	136	133	35	32
More	12.5	12.8	20.0	9.4
Same	18.4	20.3	37.1	31.3
Less	47.8	48.1	22.9	31.3
More but life[b]	1.5	0.8	—	3.1
Same but life	2.9	3.8	5.7	9.4
Less and life	2.2	3.0	—	—
Some more/less[c]	11.0	7.5	5.9	6.3
Some more/less and life	3.7	3.8	8.6	9.4

[a] For the description of "affluent," see Table 5.4.
[b] Some or all legacies contain a clause limiting ownership of property to the life of the legatee.
[c] Some sons/daughters got more than intestacy and others less.

ment at all but a reduced pressure on resources that enabled testators
to abandon unequal shares. The fact that wealth caused testators to be
less egalitarian, however, casts doubt on attributing bias in legacies to
simple population pressure. Still, the influence of this demographic
shift should be measured.

The effect of family size on bequests differs by sex. Discrimination among siblings could be of two types. One was the favoring of
one or more sons over other sons. Table 5.5 shows that nearly one-
quarter of testators in the 1790s gave some sons more than intestacy
and others less, but by the 1890s that percentage had dropped to about

15 percent. It turns out that the declining number of sons had something to do with that. Table 5.6 breaks down the treatment of sons by
number of sons. At the start of the nineteenth century, testators clearly
tried to avoid discriminating much among male offspring. It took three
sons before many fathers gave less to some sons so that one or two
could have more than intestacy, and it was not until there were four
sons that a greater proportion of testators (44.8 percent) discriminated
against some sons than gave all sons more than intestacy (41.4 percent). In the 1890s there was some change in sentiment. More testators
with several sons gave them all the same or all less than intestacy, but
many parents continued to discriminate. For instance, among those
with two sons, only 12.9 percent discriminated between them; but
among those with three sons, 45.8 percent did so. What partially
brings down the percentage in the sample that discriminated is the fact
that the proportion of testators with three or more children fell. Thus
the drop in discrimination among sons can to some extent be attributed
to the decrease in fertility.

Table 5.7 displays the impact number of sons made on the treatment

TABLE 5.6 **TREATMENT OF SONS IN TESTATORS' WILLS BY NUMBER OF SONS,
BUCKS COUNTY**

Treatment compared with intestacy	Percentage of testators by number of sons					
	1	2	3	4	5+	All
1791–1801						
N	64	67	44	29	39	243
More	40.6	44.8	45.5	41.4	28.2	40.7
Same	20.3	20.9	11.4	6.9	7.7	15.0
Less	39.0	19.4	9.1	6.9	17.9	21.0
Some more/less	—	14.9	34.1	44.8	46.1	23.0
1891–1893						
N	60	31	24	11	8	134
More	20.0	9.7	12.5	9.1	12.5	14.9
Same	30.0	19.4	20.8	45.5	12.5	26.1
Less	50.0	58.1	20.8	18.2	37.5	43.3
Some more/less	—	12.9	45.8	27.3	37.5	15.7

Note: For life and forever categories of bequests are combined because there were small numbers of observations in the life estate categories.

TABLE 5.7 **TREATMENT OF DAUGHTERS IN TESTATORS' WILLS BY NUMBER OF SONS, BUCKS COUNTY**

Treatment compared with intestacy	Percentage of testators by number of sons						
	0	1	2	3	4	5+	All
1791–1801							
N	26	60	60	42	28	33	249
More	7.7	21.1	13.3	11.9	21.6	21.2	16.5
Same	38.5	18.3	20.0	14.3	7.1	9.1	17.7
Less	50.0	48.3	61.7	71.4	64.3	45.5	57.0
Some more/less	3.8	11.7	5.0	2.4	7.1	24.2	8.8
1891–1893							
N	34	45	22	19	7	4	131
More	—	20.0	22.7	10.5	14.3	25.0	13.7
Same	35.3	26.7	18.2	26.3	42.9	25.0	28.2
Less	52.9	51.1	36.4	47.4	14.3	50.0	46.6
Some more/less	11.8	2.2	22.7	15.8	28.6	—	11.5

Note: For life and forever bequests are combined because there were small numbers of observations in the life estate categories.

of daughters in wills. Here, the effect is different. In the 1790s, as number of sons increased, the percentage of testators who left less than intestacy grew as well—up to a point. Some of those with five or more male children chose to give some daughters more and some less rather than just uniformly bequeath all less. In the 1890s sample, the total proportion of those who gave less than intestacy dropped, from 57 percent to 46.6 percent, but that was due to an across-the-board improvement in daughters' bequests unrelated to the number of sons testators may have had. Daughters received less than intestacy as often from a parent who had 0–2 sons as they did from one with more. Many daughters continued to inherit less than intestacy because of the proportion of the estate given to widows for lifetime use.

The remaining questions have to do with the effects of changes in capital and in property law. Discrimination as to type of property bequeathed to males and females, still apparent in the 1790s, had ended by the 1890s. Because liquidation was so prevalent, realty was not devised all that frequently to either males or females.[8] Most heirs received intangible personalty as their legacy. It seems that the trend toward substituting cash and financial assets for tangible personalty and realty in intergenerational transfers coincided with a decline in favoritism toward sons among all but the richer testators. These testators also were more likely to use trusts to tie up intangible property the way entails and life estates had functioned for physical wealth earlier. Still, if we add the intestacy cases, in the vast majority of estates going through probate at the close of the nineteenth century, siblings were treated fairly equally. No doubt the married women's property acts aided in this development. After their passage, fathers could be more certain that the personal property their daughters inherited would not be dissipated by sons-in-law. Apparently such legislation was needed before wealthholders were willing to give out equal portions to daughters. Certainly the sample for the 1790s indicates that the egalitarian spirit that had inspired the abolition of primogeniture and double shares for eldest sons had not affected appreciable numbers of testators and that legislation safeguarding married women's inherited personalty was required to aid in the retirement of sex discrimination as a dynastic strategy.

TREATMENT OF THE WIDOW

We found in the colonial period that a majority of Bucks County married male testators, like their counterparts elsewhere in America, restricted the ownership of personalty and realty beyond the limitations imposed by the intestacy laws and that over a third also reduced the actual share they gave. As Table 5.8 indicates, the situation got worse before it got better: About two-thirds of testators in the 1790s gave their widows less than intestacy provided. Over 80 percent restricted the time some of the property could be held beyond the limitations imposed by the intestacy statutes.

One of the reasons widows received so little control over economic resources in the 1790s is that a practice used by a minority (23 percent) of testators in the colonial period became standard procedure in the 1790s. Nearly two-thirds (63 percent) of 1790s testators made the major part or all of the wife's legacy roomspace and provisions for life or, more often, for widowhood. It has been suggested that more widows in later periods received less because, as colonies matured,

TABLE 5.8 **TREATMENT OF SPOUSE BY MALE TESTATORS, BUCKS COUNTY**

Treatment compared with intestacy	1685–1756	1791–1801	1891–1893
Percentage of all married male testators			
N	250	200	125
More	17.6	4.5	28.8
Same	10.8	6.0	7.2
Less	16.8	8.0	4.0
More but life/wid/min[a]	30.0	25.0	46.4
Same but life/wid/min[a]	3.6	5.5	8.0
Less and life/wid/min[a]	21.2	51.0	5.6
Percentage of married male testators with all adult children			
N	97	105	74
More	15.5	2.9	13.5
Same	5.2	1.0	8.1
Less	21.6	8.6	5.4
More but life/wid/min[a]	25.7	20.0	54.1
Same but life/wid/min[a]	3.1	3.8	9.5
Less and life/wid/min[a]	28.9	63.8	9.5

[a]Life/wid/min refers to legacies given either for the life time of the widow, during her widowhood, or during the minority of children. To fall into one of the life/wid/min categories, the time restrictions had to be more stringent than what was provided by the intestacy statutes.

more families had all adult children when the head of household died. When we control for the age of children, however, by considering only testators with all adult offspring, there is still deterioration in the widow's position between the colonial period and the 1790s. By the 1890s the situation had improved as legacies of lodging and food practically disappeared and a majority of husbands left their wives a share greater than that provided by intestacy. Time limitations, however, continued to be very popular, with 60 percent of married male testators employing them.

A similar trend surfaced with executrixship. Over the course of the eighteenth century, male testators increasingly excluded their spouse from handling probate. In Bucks County, this exclusion reached a high point in the 1790s with over three-fourths of male testators barring their wives from being executrixes and even a greater percentage of affluent testators doing so (Table 5.9). The proportion dropped back down in the 1890s, although it still remained higher than it had been in the colonial period.

TABLE 5.9 **HUSBANDS' EXCLUSION OF WIVES AS EXECUTRIXES, BUCKS COUNTY**

	Percentage of	
Period	All testators	Affluent testators
1685–1756	37.7	43.9
	(257)	(82)
1791–1801	77.0	82.8
	(200)	(70)
1891–1893	58.5	66.8[a]
	(135)	(36)

Note: Number of observations appear in parentheses below percentage.

[a] Adjusted figure; see Appendix A.

Unless one wants to argue that husbands just got meaner as the eighteenth century progressed, explaining these developments is no simple matter. Of the theories that might be advanced, most involve changes in the economic structure—increase in improved land, the growth in financial assets and institutions, establishment of corporations, the rise of the professions—and are best measured on the macro or aggregate level. Our testamentary data, however, contain microlevel variables; they tell us about individual choices and individual characteristics. The data sets—covering, as they do, three disparate periods—alert us to the fact that some aggregate changes were going on but cannot specifically identify what they were. The best we can do is look at the effect of the same individual characteristics on the colonial, 1790s, and 1890s will samples. While these characteristics are related to certain societal changes and may act as proxies for them, they are imperfectly related, and also, not every aggregate variable has a microlevel stand-in.

Husbandly generosity or stinginess to a spouse in a will can be explained in several ways. It can be seen as a response to a demographic situation. In the early colonial period, the presence of many immigrants, which tended to delay nuptiality and, in some areas, cause higher mortality meant that fewer male testators had adult children and that those who did had smaller numbers of them. Wives received larger portions than normal when they had children to raise, while fathers with older children, especially boys, had to use the patrimony to set them up for life.[9] In fact, in Bucks County, the number of adult sons and adult daughters per married male testator in the 1790s sample was double the figure in the colonial testaments and then declined again in the 1890s.

Another theory has it that as America matured during the eighteenth century, many long-settled communities found that land availability for legacies to children was becoming a problem.[10] Thus there would be pressure on the small farmer to reduce his widow's rights to profits from realty or to the patrimony in general. The choices of farmers are of particular interest. We have argued that the growth in personalty made husbands increasingly reluctant to give widows their full third of it forever, especially when the instruments to safeguard and manage financial assets and cash were in such a rudimentary form.

The results of the regressions run to test these propositions appear in Table 5.10. Having an adult son or sons (the number did not matter) did certainly decrease spousal generosity toward wives.[11] It had its greatest effect in the 1790s but was important in all periods. The number of adult daughters also bore an inverse relationship to the gener-

TABLE 5.10 **GENEROSITY OF MALE TESTATORS TOWARD WIVES, BUCKS COUNTY**

Independent variables	1685–1756	1791–1801	1891–1893
Presence of adults son(s)[a]	−.800	−1.057	−.679
	(.005)	(.001)	(.040)
Number of adult daughters	−.009	− .174	−.114
	(.926)	(.024)	(.341)
Farmer[a]	−.482	− .403	.480
	(.107)	(.123)	(.116)
Personal wealth (ln)[b]	−.220	− .374	−.242
	(.023)	(.001)	(.019)
Constant	4.471	5.119	4.138
	(.000)	(.000)	(.000)
Adj. R2	.068	.215	.112
N	224	180	95

Note: OLS regression. Generosity to wife was measured on a scale of 5–0. Those who gave spouse more than intestacy were coded 5; those who gave more but had time restrictions on legacy received a 4; those giving the same as intestacy were coded 3; the same but with time restrictions were given 2; less than intestacy earned a 1; and less than intestacy and time restrictions received a 0. Numbers in parentheses are significance levels of F test.

[a]Dummy variables, 1, 0 codes.

[b]The natural log of personal wealth (personalty). In the colonial period and the 1790s wealth was measured in Pennsylvania pounds current and in the 1890s in hundreds of dollars. The respective means in natural log form are 5.123, 5.968, 3.187.

osity of husbands toward wives, but that effect was only statistically significant in the 1790s. Being a farmer had a negative effect in the two earlier periods, but became a positive force in the 1890s. In no period, however, were the coefficients statistically significant at the .05 level. In all the samples, the natural log of personal wealth had a negative and statistically significant effect. Taking the three coefficients at their respective means, wealth had a larger effect than any of the other variables on the predicted value of spousal generosity in all periods, although it exerted the most influence in the 1790s.[12]

What conclusions can we draw? It seems the more wealth husbands had, the less generosity they showed to their wives. Having an adult son further reduced the widow's portion. The life-cycle factor, then, appears important, but only where sons were involved. Having an adult daughter did not reduce a widow's portion from what intestacy would provide. Only in the 1790s did daughters clearly cut into the widow's share, and it was not the presence of an adult daughter but the number of adult daughters that led to the effect. In other words, if a husband had many adult daughters, he might have to reduce his wife's portion or the length of time under which she held it. This, along with the discrimination practiced by those in the 1790s with many sons, are the only signs that high fertility might be taking its toll on this cohort. When all sons and daughters (minor and adult) are put in the regression, the results are the same. It is presence of a son or sons in all periods and number of daughters in the 1790s that are statistically significant factors in lowering the widow's share.

The Malthusian argument that wives got less because land scarcity was gradually impoverishing farmers in settled regions of the Northeast has to be rejected because it was those with greater personal wealth who were most likely to be least generous and also because being a farmer was not statistically significant in any period. Because a prime factor in deciding the generosity of a husband was his personal wealth, it is tempting to say that these regressions prove that the growth of personalty led to a reduction in widows' shares. The problem is, we cannot really discern whether a husband gave less because he was rich or because he was rich in personalty. Putting realty into the equation for those years in which we have enough observations for the variable would not solve the problem because in most of the cases where realty values are known it is because the testator had ordered that the land be sold and converted into personalty. Again, it may have been structural changes in the economy that were operating here, and trying to measure them with microlevel proxies is awkward.

Thus we can only infer that the growth of personalty and the rise in liquidations swelled the size of the portions widows would potentially inherit and led husbands in the 1790s to be less liberal than their colonial counterparts had been, particularly when there was an adult son to take over the farm and supply the widow with provisions. Both the coefficients for personal wealth and the presence of adult sons are smaller in the colonial period, and number of adult daughters is totally insignificant. It is probable that the exceptional period was not the 1790s, but the earlier era when there was much wealth invested in unimproved land. Considering the small amount of variation in the dependent variable that we have predicted, there is still much left to explain.

Until the very recent past, most widowed spouses resided with their adult children. The question, then, is, why in the colonial period were a number of widows given outright ownership of larger personalty shares and devised lifetime use of realty that allowed them to strike their own bargains with their sons or move out entirely, whereas widows later were stuck with roomspace and annual provisions? The relatively privileged status given to women in newly settled areas has already been noted (and comes up again in Chapter Nine, in the discussion of the inheritance practices of another area dominated by migrants, Los Angeles County, in the 1890s). The flexibility given widows in the colonial sample may be partially related to the undeveloped nature of the Bucks County economy in the earlier eighteenth century. Historical studies of migration have revealed that the first generation of immigrants tend to move around a bit and experience more relocations than subsequent generations.[13] Many colonial testators, even though they had an adult son, may not have had a well enough established farm to encumber it with the support of both a son's family and the widow. Colonial widows, then, were given more freedom and economic power, but there may have also been more risks involved.

We may also assume that the married women's property acts had something to do with the reduced impact of adult sons and personal wealth on husband's generosity in the 1890s sample. As Table 5.8 shows, more male testators gave shares greater than provided by the intestacy statutes, although they continued to tie the legacies up with time restrictions. The development of trusts facilitated this inclination.

TABLE 5.11 **PERSONS CHOSEN AS EXECUTOR OR CO-EXECUTOR BY MALE TESTATORS, BUCKS COUNTY**

Relationship of executor(s) to testator	1685–1756	1791–1801	1891–1893
	Percentage of all married male testators		
N	257	200	135
Wife	62.3	23.0	41.5
Son(s)	27.0	53.0	30.3
Daughter(s)	2.8	2.0	5.2
Other kin	24.5	25.5	14.8
Nonkin	26.5	32.0	33.3
Professional	2.0	1.0	0.7
	Percentage of married male testators with adult son(s)		
N	134	141	63
Wife	53.8	2.1	22.2
Son(s)	60.1	71.7	62.3
Daughter(s)	2.2	0.7	4.8
Other kin	10.4	30.4	15.8
Nonkin	19.4	24.0	30.2
Professional	2.2	1.4	1.6

Note: Percentages in columns exceed 100 because many testators named more than one person as executor.

Liquidations were so common that being a farmer actually increased the generosity of husbands.

The trend in widows being named as executrixes in their husbands' wills paralleled that for their shares: a 1790s trough and a partial recovery in the 1890s. Apparently, to husbands of the period, a legacy of roomspace and provisions went along with exclusion from executrix-ship. Whom then did they appoint? Table 5.11 shows the persons chosen by all married male testators and then by married males who had an adult son or sons. Among those testators in the 1790s who had adult sons, only in 2.1 percent of the cases was a wife named executor or co-executor, a drop from 53.8 percent in the colonial period. Adult sons increased their percentage from 60 percent to nearly 72 percent; but increases were greater for kin (10.4–30.4 percent), and even non-kin registered a proportional rise similar to that experienced by sons (19.4–24.0 percent). When a husband wanted someone to assist his son in the handling of an estate, he chose male kin or nonkin rather than his wife. While wives regained some of their authority by the end of the nineteenth century, the probating of wills remained largely a male preserve. This was true even though husbands no longer were leaving their wives legacies that made them lodgers in their son's homes. Again we wonder if the growth in financial assets and the frequency of liquidations resulted in complexities that women were believed incapable of handling. It is noteworthy that among male testators as a whole, daughters are even less in evidence as executrixes than widows. They of course had always been excluded in favor of their brothers, even in the colonial period, and the passage of the married women's property acts did little to change that practice.

WOMEN AS TESTATORS

If the married women's property acts did not make women the full equals of men in the eyes of male testators, they did radically alter the participation of women in testation. With a greater proportion of the patrimony going to women, greater numbers of single and widowed women as well as wives drew up testaments. The percentage of testators who were women grew from 17 percent in the 1790s to 38.5 percent a hundred years later (see Table 5.12), and the percentage of total personal testate wealth they owned rose from 7.3 percent to 35.8 percent, nearly the same proportion as their share of the testates.[14]

What did female testators do with their new found power? Most married women did not award their entire estate to their husbands, nor did they usually give him his intestacy share. Nearly three-fourths of the wives either willed their husbands less than intestacy or placed

TABLE 5.12 **WOMEN AS TESTATORS, BUCKS COUNTY**

Period	N	Percentage of testators who were women	Percentage of total personal testate wealth owned by women
1685–1756	387	11.9	5.8
1791–1801	352	17.0	7.3
1891–1893	351	38.5	35.8

time restrictions on the shares they bequeathed. Women named their spouse as executor a bit more often than men named their wives. The big difference between men and women, however, was mothers' greater willingness to appoint their daughters. Only about 8 percent of widowers nominated their daughters as an executrix or co-executrix, whereas almost a quarter of widows did so. The other major difference was that each sex favored a child of their own gender when they treated their offspring unequally. That is, fathers were more likely to give more than intestacy to one or two sons and less to the rest of the boys and all of the girls, while mothers would do the opposite: some of the girls, along with all of the boys, would get less, but one or two daughters would get more. Whether these preferences were demonstrations of greater affective ties between parents and children of the same sex is unclear.

LIQUID PORTIONS AND FEMALE WILLS

The evidence in Bucks County wills suggests that by the end of the nineteenth century testamentary behavior had changed substantially from what it had been in the colonial period. The majority of testators in the 1890s no longer used wills to transfer a business to the next generation. Fewer testators had a farm or business at the time they drew up a will, and of those who did, the majority ordered sale or liquidation of the enterprise. The kind of mutual obligations of parent and children and among siblings that were, earlier, made inevitable by the need to pass a firm on yet also insure a portion for everyone were no longer necessary. Dynastic ambitions were not dead, but they took different forms and mainly persisted among the top stratum of wealthholders. Affluent testators used trusts to conserve rentier assets, setting them up for male and female heirs as well as for spouses. They also continued to discriminate against daughters in their bequests. Most of the testators, part of the emerging middle class,[15] had less need for these strategies, and consequently their treatment of daughters became nearly indistinguishable from that of sons both in the size and type of the portions.

Compared to the colonial period, fewer historians have researched nineteenth century testamentary behavior, and therefore it is more difficult to know if Bucks County trends hold true in other parts of America. The timing of the changes is also a question mark because we only have information about the situation at the beginning and the end of the century. Studies of communities in upstate New York and Ohio suggest that growing sexual equality in portions was well underway by the 1840s, and another investigation of several Connecticut towns detected a trend toward equality by the 1820s. At that point, wealthholders began distributing property in separate, discrete bundles according to share-and-share-alike principles. They did not so much set up children with a direct inheritance of productive property, the author found, as give them a potential cash fund. Testators in urban areas and communities with substantial mercantile activity (and thus considerable wealth in financial assets) more frequently exhibited this kind of behavior. While it seems testamentary behavior followed rather than led intestacy legislation, both were moving in the same direction. Intervivos transfers most often resulted in retention of farms by families, but even in a late-nineteenth- and early-twentieth century area of Iowa with a substantial ethnic population, fewer than one in five farms were transferred in this way.[16]

Our conclusion that the 1790s marked a nadir in the fortunes of testators' wives seems reconfirmed by findings in other studies where gradual improvement in portions was at least post-1820.[17] The first solution of fathers to a lack of liquidity, high fertility, and the new egalitarianism toward daughters was to shrink further the portions of their widows. Sons rather than daughters had traditionally benefited the most from smaller-than-intestacy shares. Only in the 1790s did having many daughters result in a reduction of the widow's portion. When, later in the nineteenth century, the proportion of an estate going to widows grew, the bequest was in the form of a life estate or trust rather than given absolutely. The percentage of wives named executrixes in husbands' wills does not seem to have returned to early colonial levels anytime in the nineteenth century.[18] Figures on female testation for comparison with our data are not generally available.

We have argued that corporate capitalism came to dominate the economy of nineteenth-century America. The growth of financial assets and financial institutions permitted liquidation and cash portions that could be reinvested in stocks and bonds from enterprises managed by others. This liberated many family members from the "firm" and was particularly advantageous for younger male siblings and daughters. The married women's property acts reassured fathers that the generous portion to a daughter would be less likely squandered by a wastrel son-in-law. The acts apparently did less for wives, although the share they inherited for life did rebound from the turn of the century low point. Most important for women, they surface as testators in the nineteenth century. Whether it was wealth from fathers, husbands, or their own labor, for the first time in the history of the common law system, significant numbers of women from the propertied class had the opportunity to distribute sizeable amounts of property to the next generation. This right could only have enhanced their position in the family.

PART THREE

State Capitalism and Inheritance Today

If the emergence of corporate forms characterized the capitalism of the nineteenth century, what has been its distinctive feature in this century? In our view, it has been the role of the state, and each of the chapters in this section analyzes the impact of specific governmental actions on the transmission of wealth in America. Chapter Six traces the history of one of the most controversial taxes ever levied in America, the estate tax, from its inception as a Progressive reform in the early twentieth century to its partial dismantling under the Reagan administration. Our focus is on how well it functioned in its assigned tasks as a revenue source and an instrument for the redistribution of inherited wealth. Given the growth of trusts and foundations during the twentieth century, there is a real question as to whether it hampered or aided the implementation of dynastic strategies.

The seventh chapter deals with another major revolution in government, the establishment of social insurance—social security and Medicare—and their companion, the old age pension. Income derived from these sources has transformed old age and made the elderly more financially independent than their counterparts in previous centuries. The growth in retirement communities, old age homes, and nursing homes testify to the change that has occurred. The elderly are also living longer and thus are more at risk to consume their own estates. Chapter Seven reviews these changes and

123

explores the impact they have had on family relationships and inter-generational support mechanisms.

"Inheritance Law and the Unfinished Revolution" is the title of Chapter Eight. It picks up where we left off in Chapter Four and examines the role of legislatures and courts in women's fight for equal rights to family property in the twentieth century. While earlier the property at issue was what a woman had inherited from her own kin or from a previous husband, more recently it has been the disposition of conjugal property accumulated during a marriage. This chapter evaluates the changes that have occurred in intestacy laws in response to the call for equal rights.

Finally, Chapter Nine considers the impact all these changes wrought by the state have had on contemporary testamentary behavior. How have male and female testators, both the affluent and with more modest estates, reacted to the taxing of inheritance, the presence of social insurance, and increased sexual equality under the law? Their decisions in wills measure the extent to which dynastic sentiments and a lineal orientation have been replaced by concern for spouse, other kin, friends, the community, or simply self.

6

The Federal Estate Tax and Inheritance

Since 1916 the federal government has been a principal heir to the fortune of every affluent American decedent. Whatever people may think about the desirability of estate and gift taxes for the society as a whole, it seems probable that, on an individual level, wealthholders would prefer to minimize the take of this statutory legatee. The question is, just how much has government taxation affected the process of inheritance? Have loopholes and estate planning nullified the progressive nature of the tax, made it a revenue source barely worth collecting, and left relatively untouched intergenerational wealth transmission? Or, to express another popular view, has the tax been so burdensome that many have lost the incentive to save?

Opinions on this issue have always been colored by feelings about the justice of progressive taxation, the necessity for additional government expenditure, and the vitality of capitalism. Historically, reformers who believed in reducing inequality in American society have promoted estate and inheritance taxes, but they seldom succeeded without the help of a national emergency, most often a war. Congress enacted the first death duty in 1797 in the midst of an international crisis. When the crisis ended, so did the tax. Although the secretary of the treasury suggested another such levy during the War of 1812, no further taxing of inheritance took place on the national level until the Civil War.[1] Meanwhile states began to assert their prerogative to tax inheritance and opposed federal competition for this revenue source. The Civil War tax was lifted in 1872 and despite the efforts of Progressive reformers, did not resurface until the Spanish American War. Clearly, preparations for World War I made possible the passing of the 1916 estate tax.[2]

In the first third of the twentieth century, neither the rates of taxation adopted by the states nor by the federal government were of a magnitude to threaten the breakup of vast fortunes. Most states exempted spouse and children from inheritance tax altogether and kept taxation of collaterals to a flat rate below 10 percent. Federal taxes, although they contained a graduated scale and fewer exemptions, also featured modest rates. It took the Depression of the 1930s to establish the steeper percentages that more or less remained in effect until the Reagan administration's Economic Recovery Act of 1981. The acceptance of stiff progressive taxation was a watershed in the development of the state in America and in defining its role in the economy. It affirmed the right of the government to redistribute wealth for the public good at a time when the state was assuming responsibilities that formerly had been identified as the obligation of the family.

The period from the mid-1930s to 1980 might well be called the golden age of the estate tax. What actually happened during those years, though, has been the subject of debate. Conservatives have argued that the taxation of wealth transfers diminished the incentive to accumulate capital and therefore lowered the productive capacity of the nation. In the 1970s their criticism of the estate tax intensified as inflation accelerated and pushed estates into higher brackets that were taxed at proportionately higher rates. In a 1977 book published by the American Enterprise Institute, Richard Wagner complained that while the estate tax had remained relatively unchanged during the period 1942–1976, consumer prices had jumped 275 percent.[3] A taxable estate of 1 million dollars in 1941, he noted, would have amounted to about 674,300 dollars after taxes. The same estate in 1976 would be worth 3 million in current dollars, but taxes and conversion to 1941 dollars would have reduced the heirs' share to 578,800 dollars, almost 100,000 dollars less than the 1941 value. Bracket creep prevented the accumulation of capital and the intergenerational transfer of small businesses.

In 1981 the Reagan administration and Congress responded to these critiques by lowering tax rates in top brackets, so that the maximum rate was reduced from 70 to 50 percent, increasing the amount of an estate exempted from tax to 600,000 dollars, allowing lineal descendants of each child of a decedent a tax-free inheritance of 240,000 dollars, and eliminating all taxes on spousal transfers.[4] This legislation marked the end of an era for the estate tax.

Not all, however, have portrayed the golden age of the estate tax as a period when government captured increasing amounts of capital from the affluent. Beginning in the 1950s, tax law experts and economists interested in the federal budget started drawing attention to the small and continually declining percentage of national revenue contributed by estate and gift taxes.[5] These levies brought in much less than had been envisioned when the New Deal rates were enacted. Part of the problem, it seems, rested with special exemptions allowed in the 1940s and early 1950s, most notably the marital deduction permitting one-half of the estate to pass to a spouse tax free. Another source of lost revenue was the generation-skipping trust. A life estate given in trust to one or two or even more generations escaped estate taxation. While the law against perpetuities stopped donors or, as they are technically known, "settlors" of trusts from creating an infinite series of life estates, trusts could exist for perhaps as long as one hundred years and only be subject to tax twice, when the settlor died and when the final heir expired. All the generations that only had a life interest in the trust escaped estate taxation at death. The Treasury Department and the Brookings Institution produced detailed studies on the status of the estate tax and trusts at midcentury and indicated the amount of revenue lost by allowing this loophole to continue.[6] Congress in 1976 finally made life estates in trusts subject to death duties; but the 1981 legislation, which raised the exemptions and drastically reduced the rate schedule, also postponed implementation of the 1976 tax on generation skipping.

More recently, critics have concentrated on the long-term inadequacy of the estate tax as a tool for reducing inequality. At the same time that American Enterprise Institute economists such as Wagner railed against the insidious effects of bracket creep on the industrious of America, Lester Thurow was struck by the ineffectiveness of the progressive taxation system in changing the economic order. "For all practical purposes," he maintained in *Generating Inequality,* "gift and inheritance taxes do not exist in the United States. They do not stop wealth from being transferred from generation to generation."[7]

So some have alleged that great fortunes have been decimated and the government shamelessly enriched because of the tax rates and the impact of inflation. Others claim, however, that exemptions and loopholes make the estate tax unsatisfactory as a source of revenue and a leveler of society. To sort out the actual trends, we turned to a body of material that, despite its accessibility, has not been examined systematically by other investigators: the published reports of the Internal

Revenue Service. From the inception of taxes on estates, gifts, and trusts, the agency annually issued a summary of these returns. Unfortunately, in the mid-1950s, however, the reports began appearing less frequently, the last bulletin on any of these taxes being for 1977. In addition to the irregularity of their issuance, there are the problems of variations in category definitions and in bracketing that sometimes make comparability over time difficult. On several occasions, the Treasury Department commissioned special cross-sectional samples, which have been extensively analyzed elsewhere; but these, as they include only the years 1945, 1957, and 1959, are of limited use in any historical study.[8] For our purposes, the published IRS reports, though far from ideal, are the best source available.

THE ESTATE TAX OVER TIME

To begin, it is useful to know if the percentage of the population that pays federal estate tax has changed over time and if the amount paid has also changed. Table 6.1 shows the percentage of decedents

TABLE 6.1 **FEDERAL ESTATE TAXPAYERS AND TAXES, 1922–1977**

Year	Percentage of decedents over 25 paying federal estate taxes	Tax per estate in constant (1958) dollars[a]
1922	1.2	24,573
1923	1.1	17,988
1924	1.1	14,945
1925	1.2	17,468
1926	1.1	25,804
1927	0.8	28,884
1928	0.6	43,455
1929	0.6	48,374
1930	0.7	43,982
1931	0.6	63,906
1932	0.5	40,943
1933	0.6	34,532
1934	0.7	38,328
1935	0.8	53,601

TABLE 6.1 (*continued*)

Year	Percentage of decedents over 25 paying federal estate taxes	Tax per estate in constant (1958) dollars[a]
1936	0.8	61,391
1937	1.0	68,115
1938	1.2	64,522
1939	1.1	60,020
1940	1.1	52,187
1941	1.1	54,871
1942	1.1	49,496
1943	1.0	55,079
1944	1.0	63,747
1945	1.1	71,930
1947[b]	1.4	50,865
1948	1.6	50,745
1949	1.4	45,828
1950	1.4	38,132
1951	1.4	39,592
1954	1.9	38,592
1955	1.9	37,829
1957	2.2	42,246
1959	2.6	33,658
1961	3.0	38,168
1963	3.4	34,615
1966	3.9	35,100
1970	5.3	26,385
1973	6.6	24,910
1977	7.8	21,242

Sources: Public Health Service, *Vital Statistics of the United States,* 1949–1977, (Washington: Government Printing Office, 1950–1979); Robert D. Grove and Alice M. Hetzel, *Vital Statistics Rates in the United States 1940–1960* (New York: Arno, 1960); Bureau of the Census, *Historical Statistics of the United States, Colonial Times to 1970* (Washington: Government Printing Office, 1976), 224, 1113; IRS, *Statistics of Income, Estate Tax Returns,* 1958, 1972, 1976 (Washington: Government Printing Office, 1961—1979).

[a] The estate tax is the amount paid to the federal government plus the credit for state taxes paid. GNP deflators with 1958 as the base year were used to determine constant dollars.

[b] IRS, *Statistics of Income, 1945* (Washington: Government Printing Office, 1947), 1, reports that "no information for [1946] estate tax returns is included in this report; the . . . returns not having been processed." After 1951, estate tax return information was published irregularly.

over the age of 25 whose estates were subject to the tax from 1922 to 1977, the first and last dates for which data are available. Clearly the estate tax has always affected a very small percentage of the population. For the first thirty-odd years or so of the tax, less than 2 percent of decedents had estates taxable under the law. There were increases during the New Deal period when the legislation became more strongly progressive. Improvements in the economy after World War II also made more decedents eligible, although the marital deduction passed in 1948 exempted many estates that would otherwise have had to pay. (The marital deduction allowed decedents to bequeath half of their estates to their spouses, thereby eliminating estates up to double what was then the standard exemption of 60,000 dollars.) From the mid-1950s onward, the proportion of decedents paying estate taxes went up, and by 1977 nearly 8 percent paid some estate tax. Undoubtedly the biggest cause for increasing percentages of decedents being subject

TABLE 6.2 **PERCENTAGE OF TAXABLE RETURNS WITH A GROSS ESTATE OVER ONE MILLION DOLLARS**

Year	Returns
1938	2.1
1939	2.4
1940	2.4
1941	2.2
1942	2.2
1943	2.4
1944	2.5
1945	2.7
1947	2.4
1948	2.4
1950	2.5
1954	2.8
1955	2.8
1957	3.4
1959	2.8
1961	3.2
1963	3.5
1966	3.6
1970	3.3
1973	3.3
1977	3.2

Source: IRS, *Statistics of Income, Estate Tax Returns,* 1937–1976 (Washington: Government Printing Office, 1940–1979).

to these taxes was the inflation that existed throughout the postwar period but which grew most rapidly from the late 1960s on. These new recruits, plus the added revenues provided through bracket creep, meant more dollars for the government. For example, between 1957 and 1977 the amount collected increased 220 percent in real dollars.

Table 6.1 also indicates that, while more estates were being drawn in and pushed up the tax schedule, the average amount paid per estate actually declined after 1945. In real dollars, the amount was about the same in the 1970s as it had been in 1926–1927. Is this anomaly due to a *proportional* decline in the number of large estates taxed? Apparently not. Table 6.2 lists the percentage of estates having a gross estate value of over one million dollars from 1938, the first year when such information is available, to 1977. This group is an important one because it usually pays half or more of the estate tax bill. As the table demonstrates, the percentage of one-million-plus estates increased slightly, from about 2.5 to 3.5 percent, not decreased. Why the average real amount paid in taxes per estate, therefore, has gone down is still a mystery. Is it that estates in all the brackets paid less than they had earlier or just in some of the brackets? Moreover, does this reduction under- or overcompensate for the greater amounts levied because inflation pushed estates into higher tax brackets? To answer these questions requires us to control for inflation and bracket creep over time.

THE EFFECTS OF INFLATION AND BRACKET CREEP

What we need to determine is whether estates with the same real gross estate value paid more or less in taxes during periods of high inflation. Because the IRS reports gross estates in groups, it is not always easy, going from one year to the next, to find comparable categories. For example, the one million to two million dollar category in 1966 differed from the same category in 1970 because of about a 20 percent increase in prices. But the inflation was insufficient to make the category comparable with the next bracket, the two to five million dollar group.

As prices approximately doubled between 1938 and 1955 and doubled again between 1955 and 1977, and as these are years for which the IRS published comparable data, it is possible to link several different estate categories at those three points.[9] There were changes in the tax law during this period, of course. Rates were raised somewhat further in the early 1940s, and in 1948 the marital deduction was instituted. In 1976 the estate tax underwent a major overhaul; but the 1976 changes do not affect the figures we use here because they only applied to decedents dying after 1976, and those observations we removed from the 1977 calculations.

Table 6.3 indicates what happened to three groups—what we call the poor rich, the middling rich, and the rich rich—over the thirty-nine-year period. In 1938 the poor rich were those with estates worth between 30,000 and 40,000 dollars. In 1955 they were those with gross estates between 60,000 and 80,000 dollars, while in 1977 those in the 120,000- to 160,000-dollar range were the poor rich. The brackets for the other two estate categories also exactly doubled between the years: 250,000–500,000, 500,000–1 million, and 1–2 million dollar estates were the middling rich in 1938, 1955, and 1977 respectively. The rich rich had over 2.5 million in 1938, over 5 million in 1955, and over 10 million in 1977.

Each of the estate groups had somewhat different experiences over time. Between 1938 and 1977, the poor rich went from paying nothing to paying an average of 5,399 dollars, a rise of about 1,000 real dollars, or 4.4 percent of their gross estate. This sum was before credits, so it included much of what was owed to states for inheritance tax as well. The biggest increase occurred in the 1955–1977 period. The situation of the middling rich is more puzzling. There, the big leap occurred from 1938 to 1955, and the increase in the second period came nowhere near to equaling it. The middling rich went from paying on the average nearly 10 percent to paying almost 20 percent of their gross estate in taxes. Most perplexing are the figures for the rich rich estate category. There the amount of tax paid in real dollars actually declined, going from a mean of 1,912,518 dollars in 1938 to 1,346,847 dollars in 1977. The proportion of an estate going to taxes, after staying at 28 percent for nearly twenty years, dropped to 18 percent in 1977, a proportion lower than that paid by the middling rich out of their gross estates. To find out what happened, it is necessary to look at the deductions and exemptions used to transform the gross estate into a taxable estate.

TABLE 6.3 **ESTATE TAXES 1938, 1955, AND 1977 BY GROSS ESTATE GROUP, CONTROLLING FOR INFLATION**

Year	Dollar value of estates included	Number of estates taxable and nontaxable	Mean tax in dollars	Mean tax in constant (1938) dollars	Tax as percentage of gross estate
		Poor rich			
1938	30,000–40,000	—	—	—	—
1955	60,000–80,000	8,553	160	77	0.2
1977	120,000–160,000 ^a	29,393	5,399	1,264	4.4
		Middling rich			
1938	250,000–500,000 ^b	1,208	34,054	34,054	9.1
1955	500,000–1,000,000	1,392	115,482	55,788	17.1
1977	1,000,000–2,000,000	2,629	266,132	62,326	19.1
		Rich rich			
1938	2.5 million and up ^c	92	1,912,518	1,912,518	28.4
1955	5 million and up	48	3,090,583	1,493,035	28.6
1977	10 million and up	79	5,751,038	1,346,847	18.6

Source: IRS, *Statistics of Income, Estate Returns,* 1937, 1954, 1976 (Washington: Government Printing Office, 1940–1979).

Note: 1977 figures are only for those whose estates were filed in 1977 but who died before 1977 and thus were not affected by the 1976 tax reforms. GNP deflators are used with 1938 as the base year.

[a] Bracket in published IRS report ends at $200,000, not $160,000. Estimate obtained by assuming that, for both taxable and nontaxable returns, 25 percent of the returns and 20 percent of the tax and aggregate gross estate in the $150,000–200,000 bracket fell into the $150,000–$160,000 range.

[b] Bracket begins at $200,000. Estimate obtained by assuming that (1) for taxable estates, 30 percent of returns and 50 percent of tax and gross estate in the $200,000–$300,000 bracket fell into the $250,000–$300,000 range; (2) for nontaxable estates, 20 percent of the returns in the $200,000–$300,000 bracket were in the $250,000–$300,000 range and 50 percent of the aggregate gross estate.

[c] Bracket begins at $2,000,000. Estimate obtained by assuming that for taxable estates in the $2,000,000–$3,000,000 bracket, 20 percent of the returns and 33 percent of the tax and gross estate fell in the $2,500,000–$3,000,000 range. There were no nontaxable estates in that range.

ESTATE PLANNING AND THE CASE OF THE
DWINDLING TAXABLE ESTATE

Table 6.4 goes a long way toward explaining what happened to the various estate categories over time. Testators and professional estate planners (lawyers, accountants, and bank officers) had a number of exemptions and deductions at their disposal with which to reduce the size of the taxable estate. Among the poor rich in 1955 the standard, or specific, exemption of 60,000 dollars allowed to all estates wiped out most of the tax liability, and the marital deduction (permitting half of the estate to pass tax free to the spouse) did the rest. In 1977, with inflation pushing what had previously been 60,000-dollar estates into the 120,000-dollar category, the specific exemption only covered 30 percent of gross estate value. In contrast, the exemptions and deductions of the middling rich, though changing in nature, remained, throughout the forty-year period, at approximately 40 percent. Deductions do not really explain much about changes in the taxable estate for this category. Inflation made the specific exemption of less value in 1955 and 1977, but the marital deduction made up for most of this loss. As far as the rich rich are concerned, it appears the growth in charitable giving and the introduction of the marital deduction in 1948 account for the decline in the taxable estate. If there is one change that the estate tax has made, it is in the area of charitable bequests (100 percent deductible) by the extremely wealthy. Although the rich rich are a small group, the effect of their behavior on taxes and the general economy is far from trivial. In 1977 the amount given to charity by those with gross estates exceeding 10 million dollars was equivalent to 28 percent of the total estate tax going to the federal government from all estates. The tax paid equaled nearly 5 billion dollars, and charitable bequests from the rich rich totaled 1.4 billion.

While it may be that the rich rich simply have bigger hearts than the rest of us, it seems more likely that their eleemosynary gestures, which have often constituted one-half or more of their wealth, are the result of high rates in the top brackets and of estate-planning strategies. For most of the period under consideration, the rich rich were taxed at over 70 percent on wealth above ten million dollars. By making charitable contributions, it was possible to influence where all of that money went and also to secure a monument of one sort or another to one's memory.

TABLE 6.4 **DEDUCTIONS AND EXEMPTIONS AS A PERCENTAGE OF GROSS ESTATE (TAXABLE AND NONTAXABLE), 1938, 1955, AND 1977**

Year	N	Aggregate gross estate (in millions of dollars)	All exemptions and deductions (%)	Specific exemptions (%)	Debts and other exemptions (%)	Marital deduction[a] (%)	Charity deduction (%)
			Poor rich[b]				
1938	—	—	—	—	—	—	—
1955	8,553	599.3	111.6	85.6	9.5	15.3	1.7
1977	22,835	4,619.0	51.8	30.0	5.6	14.7	0.8
			Middling rich[b]				
1938	2,046	592.7	39.3	13.9	18.8	2.5	4.1
1955	1,392	941.6	41.3	8.9	9.6	17.6	4.9
1977	2,629	3,660.0	41.2	4.3	11.3	18.4	7.3
			Rich rich[b]				
1938	134	703.5	31.1	0.8	14.7	0.9	14.7
1955	48	519.1	49.8	0.6	8.4	16.4	24.4
1977	79	2,448.0	70.2	0.2	11.7	10.4	48.0

Source: IRS, *Statistics of Income, Estate Returns,* 1937, 1954, 1977 (Washington, D.C.: Government Printing Office, 1940–1979).

[a] In 1938 there was no marital deduction, but property that had been taxed within the previous five years did receive special treatment.

[b] Wealth categories are the same as in Table 6.3 except that there are no corrections made in those instances where a bracket did not exactly double the bracket from the previous year. Thus the poor rich in 1977 were those estates with gross values between $120,000 and $150,000; the middling rich in 1938 were those between $200,000 and $500,000; and the rich rich in 1938 were those in the $2 million or over bracket. Making corrections on the amounts of all the exemptions and deductions could have introduced more error than it rectified. Furthermore, the percentages for the deductions and the exemptions were not much affected by the slight bracket inconsistencies.

Through a device known as a charitable front-end annuity trust, it is possible to do even more. The lion's share of an estate can be deducted and heirs can *still* ultimately inherit fully. Under this arrangement, the charitable bequest is used to pay a fixed sum annually to charity for a specified period, at the expiration of which full ownership of the assets reverts to the heirs.[10] We do not know what proportion of charitable bequests fall into this category, but it is believed that this type of trust is not widely used outside of New York City, America's financial capital.

Proposals to impose a limit, similar to the one that exists for income taxes, on the portion of a charitable contribution that estates can write off have met with strong opposition.[11] The unrestricted deduction, it is argued, has brought much-needed dollars into the coffers of charitable organizations, and these contributions have more than made up for the loss in tax revenue. Supposedly, educational and social welfare institutions are particularly popular with testators. If tax policy discouraged this philanthropy, then the government would have to spend more in these areas.

Empirical research on charitable bequests in the post–World War II period, however, casts some doubt on these defenses of the unlimited deduction. Among the rich rich group, the primary philanthropists, statistical analysis indicates that because some bequests would have occurred without the tax incentive, the extra contributions generated by the policy have not fully covered the value of the forfeited revenue.[12] The heirs of the rich rich also get more than they would have with no charitable deduction because the portion of the estate they inherit falls into a lower bracket.

The idea that the charities supported by bequests are fulfilling a function that government would assume in their absence is also open to question, largely owing to the fact that it is difficult to know exactly where bequests go. The American Association of Fund Raising Counsel issues annual reports showing that estates contribute more often to education, social welfare, and the arts and humanities than to religion; but there are problems with assuming that, therefore, government would be supporting those needs if charity did not. First, the fact that money goes to schools or for welfare purposes tells us nothing about who is the ultimate beneficiary and how generally available these gifts are to the public at large. In education, the only category for which the reports make a distinction between private and public institutions, the former received from twice to six times the support given annually to the latter.[13]

The other difficulty with characterizing the recipients of charitable bequests is that the biggest portion of bequest money goes to foundations rather than directly to organizations. In 1973, one of the years in which the American Association of Fund Raising Counsel collected information on this point, it appears that among the big estates, those transferring a million dollars or more to charity, 56 percent of the money went to foundations; 21 percent to the arts and humanities; 14 percent to education; and the remaining 9 percent was shared by health and hospitals, social welfare, religion, and foreign and international agencies. Civic and public affairs received nothing.[14]

Foundations are not particularly easy institutions to study, despite the fact that, since 1969, the IRS requires yearly filing. The Treasury Department has released reports for the years 1962 and 1974–1979 that furnish information about the number of foundations and the value of their assets, receipts, and grants. All types of private foundations are lumped together—corporate and civic as well as those endowed by wealthy individuals. According to these sources, the number of foundations doubled between 1962 and 1979, going from about 14,000 to nearly 28,000. The majority of foundations are small, having assets under one hundred thousand dollars. Those with holdings over ten million dollars only constitute 1–2 percent of the organizatons, but their assets account for nearly two-thirds of total foundation wealth. Foundation wealth is skewed in the same way personal wealth is.

During the 1960s and 1970s, foundation receipts from gifts, bequests, and investments did not keep pace with the growth in the GNP. If the value per estate of total gross estates is compared with the value of foundation assets per foundation, however, it appears that foundations have kept up and even exceeded the growth in the value of estates left at death. In 1962 the market value of assets per foundation were 1,093,979 dollars, while by 1977 they had grown to 1,257,340 dollars, an increase of about 15 percent. This was much less dramatic than the rise in foundation numbers and did not compensate for the effects of inflation, so the average value in real dollars actually declined. Nevertheless foundation assets did outperform the growth in the value of the average gross estate. In 1961 (1962 statistics are not available), the gross estate figure was 226,565 dollars, while in 1977 it was 240,000 dollars, only a 5 percent rise.[15] The increase in the numbers of foundations and the comparison with gross estate numbers suggest that the rich continued to endow foundations at a steady or perhaps even an increased rate but that their resources did not grow as quickly as the economy as a whole. That is, while there is some question whether the resources of wealthy decedents have been increasing (more on this issue below), it does seem that a larger share of the wealth of the affluent may be going into foundations. To the rich, the establishment of foundations has been preferable to outright charitable bequests for several reasons. For those who wish to pass a closely held corporation to heirs, bequeathing a chunk of nonvoting stock to a foundation and devising the voting shares to one's family allows kin to maintain control. In the past, it has also been possible to foist off on foundations the full burden of paying the tax on that portion of the estate inherited by heirs and make other arrangements beneficial to a decedent's family.[16]

Considering that there is a high correlation between wealth on the one hand and conservative political views on the other, we might expect that the charitable giving of the foundations would reflect that predisposition. Unfortunately, it is very difficult to analyze patterns in awarding grants. As of 1979, the IRS counted 490 foundations with assets exceeding ten million dollars. Some of these organizations— Ford, Carnegie, Rockefeller—have large professional staffs and publish detailed annual reports, but most do not. The IRS does not provide much in the way of breakdowns on the recipients of foundation largesse. Only the Foundation Center, an organization funded by the foundations themselves and dependent on voluntary reports of its members, offers data of this type. One would have to do a very careful investigation of the thousands of funded projects listed in their annual directory to come to any firm conclusions about the relative accessibility to and bias of foundation funding. Ironically, the only time foundations ever received substantial criticism from Congress about the ideological nature of their grants was when the Ford Foundation gave money to certain civil rights activists and liberals in the 1960s.[17] Government subsidies can, of course, have biases too, but they are susceptible to correction every two to four years in the voting booth. Whether biases in foundation grants differ from those of the government has yet to be empirically demonstrated, but it is indisputable that the charitable deduction has resulted in an increasing proportion of wealth falling under private, as opposed to public, scrutiny and control.

What we have found in the way of a general trend in the history of the taxable estate is increased erosion of the estate tax during the golden age. The establishment of new deductions and the more frequent use of the charitable deduction, especially by the rich rich, produced this result. With the rich rich, so much wealth was shifted to philanthropy that by 1977 their group actually paid, despite bracket creep, fewer real dollars in estate tax than estates of comparable size had paid forty years earlier. How this increased charitable giving has affected heirs is not completely clear. If the rich rich would have given nothing to charity were it not for the deduction, then clearly heirs have lost. But, because some bequests would certainly have gone to charity even if taxed, heirs have actually done quite well and have probably gotten as much as, or more than, they would have without the deduction. They would, of course, do even better without any estate tax at all. The point is that the estate tax did shift substantial resources from private hands to the public, and the goal of estate planners during the past forty years or so has been to recapture those resources for the private sector. Though thwarted somewhat in the lower brackets by inflation, the estate planners have been remarkably successful in achieving their goals for the rich rich. As a result, the tax brought in less than originally intended and became less progressive. This deterioration had begun long before the Reagan tax legislation of 1981.

The history of the taxable estate and deductions, however, is not the whole story. A remaining issue concerns the tax base itself and whether it grew or shrank during the golden age. Conservatives have argued that there has been a dwindling in the size of prefisc (before taxes) intergenerational transfers among the affluent. Others, of more liberal persuasion, maintain that the rich have not pursued the most rational policies in conserving their wealth and do not always take advantage of the available loopholes.[19] There are actually two questions here: first, whether the wealthy have been good savers for the next generation, and second, whether the estate tax or some other factor explains their savings behavior.

A DWINDLING GROSS ESTATE?

In an interesting study of intergenerational wealth transmission in mid-twentieth-century America, Paul Menchik came up with some surprising results in comparing what a sample of decedents had inherited and what they bequeathed at death.[20] He found that a significant percentage left less than what he called the real present value of their inheritance: the principal and the increase obtained through the investment of that principal during their lifetime. In addition, a smaller number were actually depleters, bequeathing less in real dollars than they had been given. Depending on what rate of return is chosen as the standard, from 40 to over 75 percent of the heirs studied fell into one of these two categories. They not only failed to enlarge the patrimony through their own industry but also consumed much of the profits and, in 20 percent of the cases, some of the principal itself.

The aggregate gross estate figures for the three years discussed ear-

TABLE 6.5 **THE TREND IN GIFT GIVING, 1933–1966**

| Year | Taxable and nontaxable gifts (in millions) | | Gifts as a percentage of disposable income |
	Current dollars	Constant (1958) dollars	
1933	241.0	613.2	0.5
1934	888.7	2,105.9	1.6
1935	2,130.5	5,001.2	3.4
1936	482.8	1,130.6	0.7
1937	431.2	969.0	0.6
1938	399.8	910.7	0.6
1939	371.6	860.2	0.5
1940	570.1	1,298.6	0.7
1941	1,081.5	2,291.3	1.1
1942	480.2	906.0	0.4
1943	412.6	726.4	0.3
1944	499.0	857.4	0.3
1945	535.5	897.0	1.1
1946	755.7	1,133.0	0.4
1947	777.6	1,042.4	0.4
1948	740.9	930.8	0.4
1949	708.4	895.6	0.3
1950	1,064.2	1,326.9	0.5
1951	999.5	1,167.6	0.4
1953	1,012.1	1,146.2	0.3
1956	1,357.5	1,444.1	0.4
1959	1,870.0	1,840.6	0.5
1961	2,316.1	2,214.2	0.6
1963	2,650.0	2,472.0	0.6
1966	3,961.9	3,478.4	0.6

Source: Bureau of the Census, *Historical Statistics of the United States, Colonial Times to 1970* (Washington: Government Printing Office, 1975), 197, 225, 1113.

lier—1938, 1955, and 1977—also suggest a dwindling in the amount left at death. To make the aggregate wealth groups comparable, we included estates over 60,000 dollars in the 1938 mean aggregate estate figure, only those over 120,000 dollars seventeen years later, and those above 240,000 dollars in 1977. Deflators put the amounts in real (1938) dollars. Accordingly, in that base year the mean aggregate gross estate amounted to 242, 452 dollars; in 1955, 165,989 dollars; and in 1977, 160,309 dollars.

One explanation for the absence in growth between 1955 and 1977 and the steep decline between 1938 and 1955 could be an increase in intervivos transfers—gifts made and trusts established during the life of decedents. It is impossible to link specific decedents with gifts and trusts, but national trends in gift giving and trust income can be charted. Table 6.5 shows the dollar amount of gifts from the mid-1930s, when gift taxation began in earnest, to the 1960s, when the last figures are available. Because of population growth and inflation, however, the raw figures mean little, so the gift amounts are compared with disposable income. The ratio between gifts and disposable income seems not to have increased over time. It was at about 0.6 percent in the late 1930s and, after some fluctuations, returned to the same level in the mid-1960s.

The gross income reported by fiduciaries to the IRS probably reflects changes in the amount of capital held in trusts better than any other available time series. Table 6.6 gives total trust income as a percentage of disposable income, 1937 to 1974. The figures reveal a fairly consistent decline in the proportion, going from 1.7 percent, down 40 percent, to 1.0 percent between these years. There also seems to have been a relative decline in the number of trusts in all income

TABLE 6.6 **THE TREND IN TRUST INCOME, 1937–1974**

Year	Per capita trust income in current dollars[a]	Per capita trust income in constant (1958) dollars	Trust income as a percentage of disposable income
1937	9.2	20.6	1.7
1938	7.7	17.5	1.5
1939	8.2	18.9	1.5
1954	19.5	21.8	1.2
1956	23.1	24.6	1.3
1958	22.1	22.1	1.2
1960	22.6	21.9	1.2
1962	25.2	23.8	1.2
1965	34.3	30.9	1.4
1970	36.7	27.1	1.1
1974	48.6	28.6	1.0

Sources: IRS, *Statistics of Income: Fiduciary Income Tax Returns, 1937–1939, 1953–1973* (Washington: Government Printing Office, 1939–1977); Bureau of the Census, *Historical Statistics of the United States, Colonial Times to 1970* (Washington: Government Printing Office, 1975), 197, 225; idem, *Statistical Abstract of the United States* (Washington: Government Printing Office, 1979), 442.

[a] Both taxable and nontaxable total gross income from trusts as recorded in fiduciary returns. From 1937 to 1939, income from trusts and income from unsettled estates was not separated. For these years, we assumed trust income to be 77 percent of the total. Between 1940 and 1953, nontaxable trust income was not reported, so those years are omitted.

groups vis-à-vis the number of individuals filing personal income returns. Table 6.7 shows the proportion for different income levels. Note the comparatively high ratio of million-dollar-plus incomes from trusts to individuals receiving that income. For example, in 1958, fiduciary returns show there were 154 trusts in that bracket, and personal income tax returns reveal 244 individuals in that category. As trusts can have numerous beneficiaries, and some individuals receive income from more than one trust, we cannot say that 154 of those 244 people obtained their money from this source. Still, the implications about the derivation of large incomes are fairly clear.[21]

For the purposes at hand, what is of particular relevance in this table, however, is that it offers no support for the notion that trusts can account for the failure of gross estates to grow between 1955 and 1977. In the late 1950s in the over-one-million-dollar income group the number of trusts was 55–60 percent of the number of personal income returns in that bracket; by the mid-1970s they were little more than one-third. In the 500,000–1,000,000 dollar category, the change was from about half to one-quarter. All other brackets also showed a decline in the ratio. The trust income relates to both intervivos and testamentary trusts, but there is no reason to believe that there was a rise in the former that was masked by a drop in the latter.

The trends in gift giving and trust making exhibited in these tables

TABLE 6.7 **TRUST INCOME AS A PERCENTAGE OF PERSONAL INCOME BY INCOME GROUP, 1954–1974**

Year	$50,000– $100,000	$100,001– $200,000	$200,001– $500,000	$500,001– $1,000,000	Over $1 million
1954	6.9	13.4	24.9	54.9	56.7
1956	7.6	15.3	28.5	56.1	58.1
1958	7.7	12.3	24.9	47.3	63.1
1960	6.9	14.5	25.3	36.9	51.6
1962	6.3	14.3	26.0	37.0	49.3
1965	6.4		15.9[a]		32.6	54.6
1970	4.0	8.4	18.9	29.1	47.7
1974	2.7	5.4	13.0	22.9	35.6

Sources: IRS, *Statistics of Income: Fiduciary Income Tax Returns,* 1937–1939, 1953–1973 (Washington: Government Printing Office, 1939–1977); Bureau of the Census, *Historical Statistics of the United States, Colonial Times to 1970* (Washington: Government Printing Office, 1975), 197, 225; idem, *Statistical Abstract of the United States* (Washington: Government Printing Office, 1979), 442.

[a]In 1965 the categories of $100,001–200,000 and $200,001–500,000 were combined.

coincide with previous research on intervivos transfers.[22] The affluent did not give gifts to any great extent even though, during the period we are considering, the tax rate on these transfers was much lower than the rate according to which estates were taxed. The small amount of information on the prevalence of trusts seems to suggest that, while the raw number of trusts has increased and awareness about these legal devices has grown with the boom in the estate-planning industry,[23] the actual percentage of wealth going into noncharitable trusts has not been growing. Trusts have, of course, been instituted for many reasons other than tax saving: to serve dynastic purposes, to guard against spendthrift heirs, to conserve the wealth of those beneficiaries that settlors believe are unable to manage estates by themselves, and to avoid probate court complexities.[24] Consequently, it could be that while the estate tax and inflation have continually encouraged trust making, other factors—those connected with the dynamics of family life and the structure of capitalism—have worked to depress it. These same forces may also have been shrinking the size of gross estates.

Some suggest that wealthholders are reluctant to make intervivos transfers because of the loss of economic power.[25] In fact, what probably needs to be considered first is why they would part with assets early or save in order to pass on a sizeable estate. Clearly, some have more reason than others to be concerned about intergenerational transfers. For example, it seems those owning a business bequeath a higher proportion of their lifetime earnings than other individuals; ownership of a family firm presumably encourages saving.[26] Any decrease in the prevalence of family businesses would, therefore, affect the size of gross estates left at death. The conjugal emphasis and egalitarian treatment of sons and daughters in wills and the growth in charitable bequests are other indications that traditional dynastic concerns have progressively become less important. Thus, there is less reason to give over economic power early and to save for intergenerational transfers. Heirs, for their part, are sometimes resentful of the restrictions imposed by trusts and increasingly seek to terminate them.[27]

ESTATE TAXES: THE BEGINNING OF THE END?

The estate tax, particularly in the form adopted during the 1930s, strongly affected inheritance by making the federal government a statutory heir who took an ever larger percentage of an estate as the gross value increased. Yet, after 1945, while the proportion of decedents who became subject to the tax rose because of inflation and economic growth, the average tax per estate, paid in real dollars, continually declined. The force and the progressivity of the tax was gradually reduced by the introduction of new exemptions and the increased use of the charitable deduction. More poor rich groups were taxed, and more of the wealth of the rich rich was exempted.

Initially, the estate tax did not give preferential treatment to legacies awarded spouses, largely because a marital deduction interfered with a prime objective of the levy, the breaking up of vast fortunes. With the exemption, the estate, or at least a substantial part of it, would be taxed one less time a generation. The policy of no exemption, however, ran counter to trends within the family encouraging generous settlements to wives. Consequently, in 1948 the first deduction was passed, and in subsequent years further liberalization occurred, to the point that today no spousal transfers are taxed. This exemption greatly reduced the size of taxable estates and to some degree compensated for the bracket creep produced by inflation.

Among the very rich, the estate tax resulted in the growth of private nonfamily sources of capital, specifically, charitable organizations and foundations. Because of the charitable deduction, wealth that would otherwise go to the government could be used for philanthropic endeavors of the testator's choice. Foundations have had the added advantage that they could assist the family in furthering certain dynastic aims while functioning as a charitable institution. The charitable front-end annuity trust allows the best of both worlds, a deduction *and* ultimate ownership by heirs. The charitable deduction became so widely used in the 1960s and 1970s by those with wealth over ten million dollars that, by 1977, their estates paid a lower proportion of their gross in taxes than did estates in the one- to two-million bracket.

In contrast to the use of the marital exemption and the charitable deduction, the affluent seemed to make less use of tax saving through intervivos transfers. When gifts are taken as a percent of disposable income, they seem to have declined over time. A similar trend is found with trust income. The amount of wealth held in trusts is immense. The ratio of trusts to individuals earning above one million dollars a year was over one to three in 1974, the last year figures are available, but this was down from the better than one to two ratio twenty years earlier. Again, changes in the family and the organization of capital may explain the drift away from strict forms of estate planning. There is in fact some evidence that the rich are saving less for future generations than in the past.

The Economic Recovery Act of 1981 gutted at both ends an already weakened New Deal progressive estate tax. Setting the specific exemption at six hundred thousand dollars, it spared the moderately wealthy from any payment and taxed the very rich at a maximum rate of 50 percent. In the last year that 77 percent was the top rate, estates over ten million paid an average of 18 percent of their gross in estate taxes. With the lower rates and much more generous exemptions, we can only speculate on how little will ultimately go to the government. The actual impact cannot be measured because no figures are available nor is it clear when detailed reports will be published or data furnished on tape. Between the 1950s and 1980, the amount of statistics on the wealthy the government compiled and made public dropped dramatically. Only income was well studied, and trying to derive information about wealth from it is confounded by the lumping together of various kinds of nonwage income and by the presence of trusts and foundations. Only recently has the Census Bureau begun asking questions about household wealth in its surveys, and it is unclear how effective such instruments are in measuring assets of the very rich.

In the transference of control over capital from the rich themselves to corporate and professional managers, the importance of keeping track of that wealth somehow came to be regarded as less crucial. It may be, too, that taxing it is considered less necessary. Fears about concentration of wealth in the hands of a few private citizens and the corrupting influence of vast fortunes on the politics and economy of the United States, so often expressed in the first half of the twentieth century, are seldom voiced today. Among politicians, economists, lawyers, and, perhaps, the public at large, support for any form of progressive taxation is at a sixty-year low. The principle is only slightly more popular than five-year plans. Sales taxes and user fees, generally regressive forms of taxation, seem to be the favored types of new revenue.

Under state capitalism, there are clear limits on the ability of the government to regulate wealth. The New Deal reforms resulted not only in the state being a prime heir of the wealthy but in the proliferation of charitable organizations, foundations, and certain kinds of trusts. Some estate-planning strategies, however, came into conflict with trends in family life and the perceived needs of the capitalist system. In the name of free enterprise, savings, venture capital, and conjugal rights, the 1981 tax act was promulgated. Now, in terms of estate taxation and the power of the government to control great personal wealth, we are back to the situation that existed in the 1920s.

Demographic Change, Old-Age Policy, and the Family

Inheritance decisions in the twentieth century are usually made by the elderly. Anything that changes their lives may well have an impact on inheritance. One notable development has been the increased longevity of those over sixty-five. As Table 7.1 demonstrates, the number and proportion of the aged has increased steadily during the past eighty years, going from about 4 percent of the population in 1900 to over 12 percent currently. In the seventeenth through the mid nineteenth centuries, death rates were much higher than today, and death could strike at any age. The rapid and unexpected approach of death, common when life expectancy was so low, meant in the past that many wills were written on the death bed or fairly shortly before death. In a study of late-nineteenth-century wills in Essex County, New Jersey, legal historian Lawrence Friedman found that at least one-fourth of wills from 1850 and 1875 were executed less than one month before death.[1] Overall, in 1850, 1875, and 1900, between approximately one-half and two-thirds of all wills were written less than a year before death. In more recent studies done in Montana (1933–1947), Ohio (1938), Wisconsin (1955), and Florida (1958), generally only about one-quarter of wills were written within a year of death.[2]

Over time, rates of parental death gradually declined. For example, in Massachusetts, the proportion of women who died leaving orphan children fell by 87 percent between 1830 and 1920.[3] The trend has continued in this century. In 1920 about one-sixth of children under seventeen in the United States had lost one or both parents, while by 1978, the figure had dropped to only about one-twentieth.[4] This historical trend of declining parental mortality, caused by improved sanitation, public health measures, and advances in medical treatment, can be seen in Table 7.2. Tables showing life expectancy at birth really only reflect the enormous decline in infant and childhood mortality rates

147

TABLE 7.1 **PERCENTAGE OF POPULATION AGED 65 AND OVER, 1900–2000**

Year	Percentage	Number (in millions)
1900	4.1	3.1
1910	4.3	4.0
1920	4.6	4.9
1930	5.4	6.7
1940	6.8	9.0
1950	8.1	12.4
1960	9.2	16.7
1970	9.8	20.1
1980	11.3	25.7
1990	12.7[a]	31.7[a]
2000	13.0[a]	34.9[a]

Sources: Percentages calculated from Bureau of the Census, *Historical Statistics of the United States, Colonial Times to 1970* (Washington: Government Printing Office, 1975) 10; projections from "Think about Disruptions," *New York Times,* April 14, 1985.
   [a]Projections.

over time, while they obscure trends in adult mortality. Hence we present a table of life expectancy at age twenty. Notice that life expectancy has risen significantly for all age groups. The accompanying figures for life expectancy at sixty-five point specifically to increased longevity among those who live to be old. This table reveals that most people die many years after their children are grown.[5]

Will writers, especially surviving spouses, do still leave significant shares of their estates to grown sons and daughters, but today these children are often in their fifties and sixties and are parents and grandparents themselves. In our 1979 sample of wills in Bucks County, the mean age of death for testators was 74.5 years. At that time, 89 percent of the Bucks County will writers were over 60 at death and thus unlikely to have minor children, whereas only 45 percent in 1890 were over 60 at the time of death.

Thus the demographic circumstances surrounding inheritance have changed greatly in this century. Because of increases in longevity, the passing of an inheritance has become almost the exclusive privilege of the elderly. The fact that testators live so long and die so old is potentially of tremendous importance to the study of inheritance in the twentieth century. It means that influences on the lives of the elderly and their relations to their children become relevant. The primary influence we focus upon in this chapter is the impact of public policies, largely governmental ones, on the relationship between generations. Pensions, social security, and ancillary programs have allowed the growth of old age homes, nursing homes, and retirement communities. Along with these have come new ideas about obligations between generations. Aging parents are viewed as less financially dependent upon their children; children, as relying less on parental inheritance to secure their place in society. We trace the development of these institutions and programs, link them to changes in family organization, and speculate about possible effects on inheritance.

There are, of course, considerable problems in determining the direct effects of these developments on wealth transmission. Also, the lack of supplementary research is sometimes a problem. Take social security, for example. Everyone acknowledges the importance of social security legislation. Economists debate its impact on savings and the distribution of wealth; some political scientists are interested in

BLE 7.2 **LIFE EXPECTANCY AT AGE 20 AND AGE 65 BY RACE AND SEX, 1900–1980**

	At age 20				At age 65			
	Male		**Female**		**Male**		**Female**	
Years	**White**	**Nonw.**	**White**	**Nonw**	**White**	**Nonw**	**White**	**Nonw**
1900–1902	42.2	35.1	43.8	36.9	11.5	10.4	12.2	11.4
1909–1909	42.7	33.5	44.9	36.1				
1919–1921	45.6	38.4	46.5	37.2				
1929–1931	46.0	36.0	48.5	37.2				
1939–1941	47.8	39.7	51.4	42.1	12.1	12.2	13.6	13.9
1949–1951	49.5	43.7	54.6	46.8	13.1[a]	13.5[a]	15.7[a]	15.7[a]
1960	50.1	45.5	56.2	49.9				
1970	50.3	44.7	57.4	52.2	12.8[b]	13.8[b]	16.4[b]	15.1[b]
1980	52.7	46.6	59.7	54.9	13.7[c]	13.8[c]	18.0[c]	17.6[c]
Gain from 1900 to 1980	10.5	11.5	15.9	18.0	2.2	3.4	5.8	6.2

Sources: Bureau of the Census, *Statistical Abstract of the United States, 1985,* 105th ed. (Washington: Government Printing Office, 70, table 104; *Sourcebook on Aging,* 2d ed. (Chicago: Marquis Who's Who, 1979).
[a] 1954 figures.
[b] 1968 figures.
[c] 1976 figures.

social security's bureaucracies and lobbies; sociologists and gerontologists discuss its impact on family relations. But historians have
written little.[6] To understand how social security has transformed
people's lives, it is necessary to know what things were like before its
enactment.

INSTITUTIONAL CHANGES

Retirement, Pension, and Social Security

The year Congress passed social security—1935—was a turning
point in the history of old age. Before social security, older people
were responsible for their own welfare, or their families were. Numerous states had family responsibility laws holding adult children ac-
countable for the support of dependent aged parents. These laws were
seldom enforced, largely because most adult children able to support
impoverished or helpless parents did so. The state acknowledged no
responsibility for the elderly. Since most American families did not accumulate large savings (and savings were earmarked for emergencies
or perhaps for the purchase of a house), few men could afford to give
up their role of breadwinner in favor of retirement.[7] In 1900 nearly
two-thirds of all men sixty-five and older were still in the work force.
Many of those not working were involuntarily retired, forced out by ill
health, physical incapacity, or the growing prejudice against older em-
ployees in the industrial labor force.[8] Nor was retirement widespread
among the well-to-do. The wealthy did not have to work, but there was
no ethic of retirement drawing them from employment. It was fairly
usual for a man merely to work less as he grew old, gradually turning
over more of his work to sons, partners, or assistants.[9]

Increasingly since 1935, however, retirement has been a major factor
in the lives of the elderly, rich and poor alike, and it has a complex
economic and social relation to their testamentary behavior. Compulsory retirement, which had been growing slowly but noticeably
since the late nineteenth century, expanded enormously in the years
after the passage of social security, until by 1971, only a quarter of the
men over sixty-five were still in the labor force. Whether by intention
or not, social security has served as a powerful tool in the manipulation

of the size of the labor market.[10] The over-sixty-five have been compelled or strongly influenced to leave the labor force, yet employers and society generally need feel no guilt because social security provides retiring workers a basic income. The tremendous post–World War II growth of private pension plans, encouraged by government regulations and tax benefits, further improves the economic outlook of those given the gold watch. And many older people now look forward to retirement.

Before 1935, when men planned their estates, they were essentially concerned with the financial security of their families after they died. Since 1935, estate planning has included planning for the retirement years as well. The gap between the end of work and the end of life has grown, in part because of the increasing popularity of early retirement and in part because of increasing longevity. As a result, the ratio of earning years to retirement years is approaching two to one.[11]

The elderly population has the most unequal wealth distribution of all age groups. It contains the greatest concentration of top wealthholders; but it also has a very large sector, usually on a fixed income, which is quite poor. Current estimates are that over half of households headed by someone sixty-five or older have no wealth, and this inequality of income distribution existed in the nineteenth century as well.[12] The poverty of these older people helps explain why so many adult decedents escape probate.

Despite the fact that Americans have known they would spend some part of their lives in retirement, many, perhaps most, have not planned for it.[13] They face long years of retirement with little or no savings, no assets beyond a modest furnished home, and a small monthly social security check.[14] Social security benefits have risen over the years. The average monthly benefit, in December 1979 dollars, has risen from 135 dollars in 1950, to 192 dollars in 1960, to 293 dollars in 1972, and to 294 dollars in 1979.[15] While social security coverage has become more adequate, it still does not keep all its recipients above the poverty line.

For many people in the lower income brackets, social security has acted to smooth their lifetime income profile, taking from them in their earning years and returning money to them in retirement. Government welfare programs and services, from unemployment insurance and social security to public education and federal home mortgage insurance, have probably brought more benefits to these people than the savings they might otherwise have accumulated had they not been paying taxes or withholding.

Middle and upper income groups, of course, usually begin retirement with income sources beyond social security—private pensions, insurance annuities, and interest and dividends from investments. Over the past fifty years, more and more elderly people have reported receiving payments from one or more of these sources. The growth in pensions has been substantial. While in 1920, no more than fifty-five thousand Americans worked in firms offering private pensions, by 1950, just under ten million workers had obtained coverage. And by 1970, thirty million, or about one-half the nonagricultural labor force were enrolled.[16] Because some retired people exited from the labor force before their employer adopted a pension plan, the number of retired workers receiving benefits, while also rising, has lagged behind these figures. A combined 1941/1942 survey of married couples receiving social security found 18 percent also receiving retirement pension income; by 1968, 30 percent were.[17]

There has also been a major increase in annuity funds for the retired. In 1940, 176 million dollars was paid in annuities; in 1980, over 10 billion dollars was paid. Life insurance and annuities form an important part of the retirement and estate-planning strategies of the middle and upper classes.[18] Finally, the proportion of older people getting income in the form of interest, dividends, and rents has risen. In 1941/1942, 43 percent of retired married couples got income from those sources; by 1968, 62 percent derived income from such sources, though nearly one-third of those got less than five hundred dollars per year.[19]

Since the 1940s retirement planning has become a growing service industry. Experts write many popular books and teach many courses that promote comprehensive retirement planning, often including "estate planning," a strategy whereby the retired couple's income-generating assets will continue generating income for the surviving spouse, usually assumed to be the wife, after the other dies and ultimately will pass to their children. The principal goal of these strategies, according to both the experts and surveys of consumers and retirees, is continued economic independence and a modestly comfortable standard of living. The old, in this era of social security, do not spend their savings; 47 percent of elderly consumers in a 1962 national survey reported they were saving for old age, as were 53 percent of a 1964 survey of affluent customers.[20]

Why do people save for their old age, not only when they are young, but after they retire? Why do they not deplete their savings? Because they wish to leave their children an inheritance? Two studies of consumer savings motives done in the late 1950s found that saving for children's education (among younger consumers) and for retirement were preeminent motives. Saving to provide an inheritance for children was not important.[21] We have found no comparable data on savings motives in the nineteenth century, but it seems highly unlikely that saving for children's college education and for retirement, particularly the latter, figured prominently in middle-class savings strategies. In Philip Cagan's late 1950s study of middle-class Consumer's Union members, the bequest motive came at the bottom of the list, with only 0.6 percent of respondents considering it their first priority. In a national study done in the early 1960s, only 4 percent of elderly respondents cited "providing an estate" as a savings objective.[22] Older people do face an uncertain lifetime, however. They simply do not know how much longer they will live. They must therefore control their spending and conserve their savings so as not to exhaust their retirement assets. Failure to do so may lead to real poverty or dependence upon children.[23] The desire to have enough money to remain independent appears to be a driving motive in the frugal behavior of the retired middle class.

In the postwar period, social security, retirement, and longevity are inextricably connected. Because social security payments are ostensibly derived from contributions from one's working years, social security helps the middle class maintain financial independence and a sense of dignity in retirement. Compulsory retirement removes people from the work force and reduces their monthly income. The combination of longer life expectancy and compulsory retirement means that people must plan for many more years of retirement than they did fifty or one hundred years ago. Those who do plan ahead and have funds set aside in insurance, annuities, pension plans, and other investment may be able to assure themselves comfortable retirement years, no matter how long they live, and may even be able to leave a handsome estate to their children.

One privilege of great wealth is privacy. For historians, this presents a problem. We do not have years of accumulated reports and surveys of the very wealthy to gain a clear picture of their motives. Nevertheless, it seems clear that the impact of social security on the savings and inheritance practices of the upper class is probably miniscule since the withholdings involved are such a small proportion of their wealth. Economists have found that social security has had an impact on life-cycle wealth, which is equity in one's home, durable and household inventory, demand deposits and currency, and the cash value of life insurance and pensions (less consumer debt). Typically, life-cycle wealth increases with advancing age. Life-cycle wealth, which is so important to most people, is, however, an insignificant portion of the wealthy's estates. Acquiring a retirement income and maintaining economic independence after age sixty-five are not the problems facing the wealthy. They depend on capital wealth, which comes from bonds and securities, corporate stock, savings deposits, business and investment real estate, and trust fund equity.[24] The upper class can educate their children while maintaining a luxurious lifestyle. They can provide generously for a surviving spouse and heirs and still have a large part of their estate left over to spend or save as they please. Aided by lawyers, bankers, and professional estate planners, they work to minimize inheritance taxation in order to pass on as much of their accumulated wealth as possible, using trusts, intervivos gifts, and tax-free charitable bequests and establishing philanthropic foundations for their heirs to control. Hence the priorities for saving among the very rich are different from other groups. At the highest levels of wealth, what testators are passing on is not just economic security and luxurious comfort but significant power in the form of control over corporations and philanthropic foundations.[25]

For most people, social security has provided the means to frugal but independent living in retirement. Its primary effect has been to redistribute from an individual's younger and middle earnings years to his or her old age, rather than from class to class. It has not had a major effect on wealth distribution in this country, and its direct economic impact upon inheritance is probably small.[26] Its indirect impact, however, may be greater. Keeping that in mind, let us examine the emergence of institutions for the elderly, one of the consequences of social insurance programs.

Old Age Homes, Retirement Communities, and Nursing Homes

The family was the most important social welfare institution of eighteenth- and nineteenth-century America. The ideal family was able to meet the needs of its members, young and old alike. In reality, however, families were frequently unable to care for or support all kin members.[27] Various public and private institutions—charitable societies, poorhouses, orphanages—grew up in response to the failure of individual families to care for their members. Certain family tasks have long been the province of the state, for example, the socialization of children through public education. Nonetheless, for a long time this society believed in the obligation of the family to care for all its members. Not until the twentieth century, under the pressure of extreme economic and social dislocation, did society acknowledge the need to provide systematic aid to families and to individuals without families. The care of frail, ill, unemployed, and widowed old people has been recast as a state responsibility. What people think children, parents, and grandparents owe each other has been modified. The ideal to which both generations now subscribe, one gerontologist remarks, is "one of 'closeness at a distance,' of basically independent existence."[28] Separate residence for elderly parents and their children is now affordable, thanks to social security, as well as desirable.

The first nonfamilial residences for the elderly (other than public almhouses) were old age homes, which began to appear in the early nineteenth century in American cities. Most were specifically designed to provide for impoverished, genteel ladies.[29] Their numbers grew over the course of the century, and the targets of their benevolence multiplied—men as well as women, blacks as well as whites, Catholics, Protestants, and Jews, but nearly all respectable old people who had fallen on hard times. Few well-to-do older people lived in such homes, although enough did that some homes charged admission or boarding fees. Others promised lifetime care for the aged in exchange for all or part of the resident's estate. By 1929 there were 1,215 old age homes in America, mostly sponsored by churches, benevolent societies, and fraternal organizations. Nearly half required no admission fee, and some would waive fees or lower them for the poor.[30]

Retirement communities, a much more recent phenomenon, were not begun until the 1920s when some religious, fraternal, and labor organizations purchased land in Florida to create supportive retirement communities for their members. The boom did not occur until after World War II, when significant numbers of elderly began receiving social security. Unlike old age homes, which were largely run by private charities, retirement communities were developed for paying customers and as business ventures. Private builders recognized the potential market for retirement homes among a growing portion of the American population, the middle- and upper-class elderly.[31] Growth has been astonishing. One 1981 survey of retirement communities containing over one hundred people found the population of these larger communities to be 667,000.[32] Residents of these communities tend to be younger, healthier, and wealthier than residents of old age homes (although retirement communities do age over time, as their residents move from young-old to old-old). Most retirement community residents clearly have enough money to leave an estate.

Nursing homes are also a twentieth-century phenomenon. They provide custodial and medical care for the frail, bedridden, and mentally incapacitated elderly. Advances in medicine in this century, especially since the 1940s, now allow people to survive to a very advanced age. These old-old people suffer increasing physical impairment which, while not fatal, destroys their capacity to live independent lives.[33] Adult children in the postwar period turned to nursing homes for the care of failing aged parents. Nursing homes grew in response to their demand. The federal and state governments also responded to complaints of people who found the cost of nursing home care for parents prohibitive (but who also found it impossible to offer that care in their own homes), and they responded as well to the need for care of the elderly who had no family or funds. In the 1950s and 1960s, public subsidies for nursing homes were liberalized. Lower costs to individuals thus increased demand.[34] Nursing home growth was vigorous in these years; indeed the rate of growth for nursing homes was greater in this period before the 1965 adoption of Medicare and Medicaid than afterward. Medicare and Medicaid, however, continued to stimulate nursing home growth. Between 1963 and 1973, there was an 11 percent increase in nursing home capacity. In 1963 the number of nursing home beds per hundred elderly was 2.9; in 1973, it was 5.2. In 1940 the total national expenditure on nursing home care was 33 million dollars; in 1950, 187 million dollars; in 1960, 526 million; in 1970, over 3 billion; and in 1976, 10.5 billion dollars.[35]

IMPACT ON FAMILY RELATIONS AND INHERITANCE

The clearest indication that demographic and institutional changes have indeed affected the family is in the transformation in residence patterns. The co-residence of older people and their grown children was far more prevalent a hundred years ago than it is today, as Table 7.3 illustrates. In the late nineteenth century, more than 60 percent of old people shared a home with one or more of their children; today, less than 15 percent do. Put another way, in 1880, only 25 percent of married old people lived alone; in 1975, 84 percent did. Part of the reason is that the timing of life-cycle events has changed. Men and women do not spend nearly their entire adult life raising children as they did in the eighteenth and much of the nineteenth centuries. They have fewer children than their ancestors did; and their children grow up, marry, and start families of their own when their parents are still middle-aged. Moreover, since World War II, children have often moved out of their parents' home even before they married.[36] Thus aging parents are no longer likely to share their home with married children.[37] Finally, there is the independence achieved by the elderly through social insurance programs and the availability of retirement, old age, and nursing homes.

What is less certain is the impact of all these developments on inheritance. The research at this point is very limited. Jeffrey Rosenfeld has studied the wills of the elderly in three varied residential settings in the New York metropolitan area from 1968 to 1971: a non–age-specific residential community, a retirement village, and the geriatric ward of a hospital. He found that people in the retirement village (56.4 percent) were more likely than others (33.7 percent in the community and 37.5 percent in the hospital) to leave bequests to friends in the village or to organizations, not just to their families. New emotional ties and friendships formed in the retirement community were acknowledged in wills. Those who spent time in the geriatric ward also exhibited a similar but less pronounced tendency to leave wealth to nonfamily members encountered in their last environment.[38]

TABLE 7.3 **LIVING ARRANGEMENTS BY PERCENTAGE OF THE POPULATION 65 AND OLDER, 1880–1975**

Arrangement	1880	1900	1962	1975
Old living with children	61	61	25	14
Married old living with spouse alone	25	29	79	84
Unmarried old living alone	9	11	48	66

Source: Daniel Scott Smith, "Historical Change in Household Structure of the Elderly in Economically Developed Societies," in *Aging: Stability and Change in the Family,* ed. Robert W. Fogel et al (New York: Academic, 1981), 100, 110.

One variable in the growing retirement community, nursing home, and old age home population that Rosenfeld did not investigate but that may support his thesis of declining inheritance to kin is the life care contract, which can take two forms: either the resident pays a large entrance fee—ranging, typically, from 15,000 to 75,000 dollars—and a monthly fee—ranging from 350 to 1,500 dollars, or the resident assigns all his or her current and future wealth to the home. In exchange, the resident is assured lifelong care. Residents maintain independent living as long as physically possible then receive unlimited nursing care in the same community at no extra cost.[39] This contract resembles a wager. Old people are gambling that the costs of caring for them in their remaining years will outrun their assets. By investing in a life care contract, they are insuring that they will never exhaust their own resources and thus become wards of the state or financial burdens on their children. While they are protecting their children from assuming the costs of their last days after they have exhausted their own funds, they are also depriving them of all or much of their prospective estate.

The life care contract is becoming increasingly popular. In 1976 there were approximately three hundred continuing care homes; three years later, there were about six hundred.[40] For many middle-class elderly, the security of knowing they will live in one community for the rest of their lives and not run out of financial resources, no matter how Methuselah-like their life span or how great the rate of inflation and the rise in medical costs, is worth the loss of estate-granting powers. Their children, who often make the decision with them, may also see the advantages. But life care is not carefree. Serious questions have been raised about the financial stability of life care contractees and about the adequacy of existing regulatory legislation controlling continuing care facilities. So far, five states have enacted laws concerning these institutions, and two states—New York and our case study state of Pennsylvania—now have statutes intended to ban life care contracts. Imprecise wording has, however, allowed institutions and individuals to bypass the law's intent and enter into a modified version of the contract.[41]

Litigation has also resulted from the life care contract. It tends to be of two sorts. In cases where living residents sue to break the contract, the courts have been sympathetic to residents who regret their decision and have generally allowed them to withdraw from the community *with* their assets or entrance fee, minus payment for services to date. In cases where heirs have sued to recover the assets the deceased contracted to the continuing care community, the court has upheld the contract. For example, in 1981 in the Pennsylvania case *In Re Estate of Musselman,* a woman residing in a continuing care facility who had signed a life care contract assigning her assets to the facility wrote a will leaving her ten thousand–dollar estate to kin and friends. After her death, the court upheld the life care contract rather than the will, and the heirs received nothing.[42]

At present we cannot tell the impact of life care contracts on inheritance since, almost by definition, elderly people who make life care contracts have no estate upon death, it having already been transferred to the home. Thus such people "disappear" from the ranks of testators. In 1979 in Bucks County, 17.4 percent of the testators could be identified as residing in a retirement community or nursing home at the time of death. Since the Pennsylvania prohibition of life care contracts did not affect contracts written before 1975 and because loopholes were found, we do not know how many potential testators residing in Bucks County institutions had vanished via life contracts. It is certainly possible that some did, for in Bucks County, with a population of roughly twenty-five thousand people over the age of seventy-five, there are currently nine life care communities with a capacity for 2,146 residents. The group whose bequest capacity would most likely be affected is the middle class, whose estates tend to be modest but sufficient to meet the requirements for life care. The institutionalized elderly are much less likely, however, to have children than the noninstitutionalized, and they are three times more likely never to have married. Many of those who choose to sign life care contracts may be the aged who have no children. Thus there may be no appreciable decline in bequests to children owing to life care contracts simply because many life care contracts involve elderly who have no children.[43]

Life care contracts, the high cost of medical care, and the greater availability of treatment for illness in old age may serve to eliminate some estates of the moderately well-to-do. Improved sanitation and medical care have increased the life span of the old but have not succeeded in keeping people healthy in old age. As in the past, the elderly suffer from chronic and acute illnesses. They are less well than other age groups and spend a greater proportion of their income on medication, doctor's visits, and hospitalization. The elderly, who comprise 11 percent of the population, occupy at least 30 percent of the hospital beds reserved for acutely ill patients. They have longer hospital stays than younger people, and they receive 25 percent of all prescriptions.[44] The extraordinarily high and ever-escalating cost of medical treatment, especially acute care in the last stages of life when sophisticated treatment and equipment are used, can bankrupt the elderly and wipe out any inheritance they hoped to pass on. The passage of Medicare and Medicaid in 1965 gave the aged access to more medical care. But, even with 80 percent of health expenses covered by Medicare, the elderly with acute health problems can accrue staggering bills in a short time. Even with Medicare, the elderly's per capita out-of-pocket health care expenditure in 1977 was nearly four times that of those under sixty-five.[45]

Another variable is the apparent tendency of parents today, especially middle-class mothers and fathers, to see their obligation to children in terms of education, of providing a start in life.[46] Holger Stub, author of a monograph on longevity, contends that "frequently, the economic sacrifices of parents in providing education is [*sic*] charged against what might have been a larger inheritance."[47] Middle-class parents frontload wealth transfers to children to provide opportunities, experiences, and skills. Hence the parental duty to provide for children decreases with age.

The popular estate-planning literature (more than the professional manuals of lawyers and tax accountants) reflects these attitudes. There is less emphasis on intergenerational wealth transmission and more on providing a pleasant retirement for the couple and a secure future for the surviving spouse, who most often is the wife. As one author counseled, "You don't have to pass all your principal on to your family."[48] Instead, the older couple should indulge themselves a little, in travel, little splurges, or whatever makes their last years more enjoyable. A bumper sticker seen recently on the back of a camper in the Grand Canyon, declaring, "We're Spending Our Children's Inheritance," is a humorous expression of the new ethic. As we discussed in Chapter Six, there is some indication that the very wealthy are leaving less to the next generation, and while the middle classes may be saving more, it does not seem to be for the purpose of intergenerational wealth transmission.

Sociologists have found in contemporary surveys on inheritance and wills that husbands tend to give their wives a much greater share of their estate than intestacy provides. In fact, most desire that their wives inherit everything.[49] As Chapter Five demonstrates, however, this trend is more complicated than the contemporary literature suggests. Although late-ninteenth-century testators frequently put tenure restrictions on spousal shares, thus demonstrating some vestigial dynastic concerns, most of these husbands also gave their wives larger shares than had their counterparts at the end of the eighteenth century. This improvement occurred before marked decreases in adult female mortality rates, the implementation of social insurance programs, and the institutional changes associated with them. Chapter Nine has a comparison between 1890s and 1980 testamentary patterns.

THE UNCERTAIN FUTURE OF INTERGENERATIONAL TIES

There is no consensus on the effects that social insurance and the developments associated with it have had on intergenerational relations. Before the enactment of social security there was much hand wringing in the periodical literature over the failure of families to provide economic support to the elderly.[50] After social security, hands were wrung over the failure of families to provide emotional support to the elderly. Undeniably, the old and their children seldom live together as they did in the previous century. Some view this as a clear indication of intergenerational family breakdown and as the cause for most of the emotional distress of the aged. Others, more positive, concede that co-residence is past but point out that grown children and their aged parents often do live nearby and keep in touch.[51] Co-residence in the past may have been more the product of economic necessity than of the desire for intergenerational closeness.

Some gerontologists who have investigated the family situation of the aged over the last forty years or so have concluded that families are still the major social support for their elderly members. As Ethel Shanas explains, "Family members respond to the needs of the elderly as best they can, either directly or by providing a linkage with bureaucratic institutions.[52] Shanas believes family ties and reciprocal helping strategies are as strong as in the past but that help is simply rendered in different ways. Instead of giving money to a widowed mother, or taking her into their home, for example, children may help her get signed up for social security, Medicare, or other benefits for which she qualifies.

Family historian Tamara Hareven, on the other hand, cautions that optimism about continuing reciprocal family ties may be misplaced: "The current involvement of the elderly with kin . . . represents a cohort phenomenon rather than a continuing historical pattern; the elderly cohort of the present has carried over into old age the historical attitudes and traditions that were prevalent when it was growing up earlier in this century, especially a strong reliance on relatives. It also has kin available because of the larger family size of earlier cohorts." [53] In the near future, the situation may shift. Gerontologist Gunhild Hagestad agrees with Hareven that the old "socially sanctioned mutual obligations" among generations in the family may fade away. Research on grandparenting, for example, has found little consensus among grandparents about the rights and duties of their role. Hagestad concludes, "Adults in the family now confront each other in relationships for which there is no historical precedent and minimum cultural guidance." [54]

So far, though, there is only limited evidence that greater longevity and lengthy retirement, increased independence and isolation of age groups from one another, and the escalating costs of medical care have diminished the parental practice of leaving bequests to children upon the death of the surviving spouse. These are relatively new phenomena and under researched. In Chapters Eight and Nine, the issue comes up again as we study how inheritance laws and testamentary behavior have changed in the twentieth century.

8

Inheritance Law and the
Unfinished Revolution

In 1969 a book came out entitled *Women and the Law: The Unfinished Revolution*.[1] The author, Leo Kanowitz, argued that, despite the enactment of the nineteenth-century married women's property acts and the adoption by eight states of a community property system, many laws still placed American women in a clearly disadvantageous position vis-à-vis men. His view, expressed at a time when the "second wave" of the feminist movement was just beginning to attract public attention, differed markedly from the attitudes commonly found in twentieth-century family law texts. There, especially in sections on marital property rights, it was not unusual to discover statements alleging that any remaining discrimination was minor and that wage-earning wives had, in the words of one author, "the best of both worlds" because they could save their salaries while their husband supported them. "The pendulum may have swung too far," in the woman's favor, wrote a second.[2] The review of federal and state laws made by Kanowitz and others, however, cast considerable doubt on these textbook generalizations about the situation of married women.[3]

As we noted in Chapter Four, the nineteenth century marital property acts and subsequent legal decisions essentially protected the property married women acquired from their own kin but were silent about their rights to assets derived partially or entirely from the labor they performed as wives, whether in the home or in a family business. Although the patrilineage may have been replaced by a more bilateral form of property descent, the man was still in charge of his nuclear family. The laws of most states required a husband to support his wife, but she in turn was to provide services. In his position as head of household, the man managed and controlled all the conjugal property. In community property states, this authority was put in the statutes. Wives ultimately could lay claim to one-half of community property when their husbands died, yet while alive, men could handle the wealth as they pleased. In common law states, women's situation was even more precarious. Assets acquired during a marriage, unless specifically put in the woman's name, became part of the husband's separate property, property to which wives often found themselves with no better than a one-third claim. It was this inequity in property law to which critics such as Kanowitz drew particular attention.

At many points during the twentieth century, the legislatures and the courts have been asked to intervene in familial affairs on behalf of married women. How inheritance rights have been altered, as a result of these interventions is the subject of this chapter. What especially interests us, though, is the relationship between these legal changes and the evolution of the women's movement.

STATE INHERITANCE LAWS IN 1890, 1935, AND 1982

A rough idea of the statutory transformations that occurred over the course of the twentieth century emerges from a comparison of state inheritance laws at intervals of approximately fifty years, beginning with 1890. The surveys for 1890 and 1982 were undertaken for this study and are found in Appendixes B and C. For 1935 we relied on a published survey of family law done by Chester G. Vernier.[4] It is fair to say that the most important modifications in the intestacy laws concern the spousal share. The changes in common law states, where there was no conjugal property per se, mainly involved the portion of a deceased spouse's separate estate a husband or wife could claim. In community property states, where half the conjugal property already belonged to the widow, the issue was a woman's right to will community property. In both types of jurisdictions there has been a move to exclude all kin aside from spouse and lineal descendants (children, grandchildren, great-grandchildren, etc.) from an intestate share of the estate.

Table 8.1 shows the rate at which laws limiting the value of the spousal share were replaced with legislation more favorable to widows and widowers. In common law states, the first improvements in a widow's portion were those transforming a life interest in realty to a fee simple or absolute right. In 1890 over two-thirds of the states followed

TABLE 8.1 **LIMITATIONS ON THE SPOUSAL SHARE IN THE STATE INTESTACY LAWS, 1890, 1935, and 1982**

Limitations	1890	1935	1982
Percentage of common law states (N = 42)			
Realty share for life, not forever	69.0	38.1	11.9
Share below half if there is a child or children	92.9	92.9	42.9
Percentage of community property states (N = 8)			
Wife unable to will her half of community property	50.0	25.0	0.0
Percentage of all states (N = 50)			
Decedent's kin shares equally with spouse when there are no children	80.0	80.0	60.0
Share is less when there are children from previous marriage	2.0	6.0	48.0

Sources: Appendices B and C and Chester G. Vernier, *American Family Laws* (1935; reprint, Westport, Conn.: Greenwood, 1971), vol. 3.

the old dower and curtesy pattern. It was the new states entering the union (see Table 4.1) that embraced the fee simple innovation first. This change generally resulted in greater sexual equality because, in the process of making the shares fee simple, widowers' portions were usually reduced to the same percentage as those widows received. The change was gradual though. By 1935, under 40 percent of the states retained life interests, and by 1982 they had become almost extinct.

The proportion of a decedent's estate that went to the spouse was slower to rise. As late as 1935, over 90 percent of common law states offered spousal shares lower than what would be awarded automatically in most community property jurisdictions, that is, one-half of the property acquired during marriage regardless of the number of children the decedent had.[5] By 1982, though, these relatively stingy descent and distribution statutes were in the minority (42.9 percent).

In 1890 the law of four out of the eight community property jurisdictions gave widows half of the community property, if they survived their husbands, while widowers received the entire estate. California and Idaho changed their statutes before 1935, but Nevada and New Mexico continued to discriminate against widows until fairly recently.

Both common law and community property jurisdictions have increasingly moved toward preferring the spouse over kin in their intestacy statutes. Although the majority of states, as of 1982, still allowed parents, or siblings, or even more distant relatives to inherit part of the estate of a married intestate decedent when no lineal descendants survived, the percentage had dropped significantly since 1935.

During the past one hundred years, many states have attempted to eliminate inheritance by the very distant relative, the so-called laughing heir. In the 1890s an estate would not be escheated (taken by the government) in most jurisdictions unless there were no next of kin. By 1982 nearly half of the states required intestate heirs to be within a certain degree of kinship, most often "grandparents or their issue," to prevent confiscation by the state. These limitations are, of course, not all that stringent, and it is still quite possible for a relative totally unknown to the intestate decedent to be the heir. Nevertheless, the laws do indicate a deterioration in the importance attached to consanguinity. Another example of this phenomenon relates to the nuclear family. Anglo-American law had always been unique because of the freedom it allowed testators to cut their children off without a cent. Except for Louisiana, states never put serious barriers in the way of disinheritance. A number of states did, however, specify that the testator should show "intent" to disinherit in the will. In 1890, 40 percent of the states had such stipulations. Less than a century later, fewer than 20 percent still had the requirement.

What about the proverbial old fool who, tricked by a fortune hunter, remarries shortly before death? Should that spouse be granted the same intestacy share that one of fifty years duration receives? Most states say yes. Inheritance laws have been slow to react to the new reality of serial monogamy. The only safeguard adopted by a number of states (48.0 percent) is a smaller spousal share when the decedent has children by a previous marriage. As Table 8.1 shows, such laws were rare in earlier periods.

Indisputably, then, the long-term trend in twentieth-century America, and elsewhere,[6] has been to make widows the equal of widowers as intestate heirs and to enhance the conjugal share at the expense of children and other blood kin. Life interest has been changed to absolute interest, and the proportion of the estate reserved for the spouse has increased in most jurisdictions. At the same time, the old protective legislation is disappearing. Dower and homestead exemptions had the disadvantage of being for life only, but in most jurisdictions, they were free from the claims of creditors and also provided a safeguard against the precipitious alienation of property by husbands.[7] The attack by the "modernizers" on life interest claims to realty began in the early nineteenth century. Homestead exemptions were one way states found to do away with dower yet insure widows and small children would not be left homeless. Support for them, however, has waned as well. In addition, the amount set aside by legislatures for a homestead allowance has not kept pace with inflation, so less than a fourth of the states in 1982 had exemptions that could cover the actual costs of an average house.

What is also obvious from Table 8.1 is that, while the trend is toward a conjugal orientation, the intestacy laws of many states as late as 1982 still gave a larger share to children than to spouses, and a majority of jurisdictions allowed relatives, in the absence of lineal descendants, to receive an inheritance equal to what a widow or widower got. The transformation in inheritance laws from lineal to conjugal has been slow and is still ongoing. The question is What has and is determining the pace of this change? Is it linked to the gradual evolution of the ideal of companionate marriage or have the alterations coincided with peaks of activity within the women's movement? To investigate this issue, we examine the history of inheritance law changes in our two case study states, Pennsylvania and California. But first, we need to review briefly the history of the struggle for women's rights in the twentieth century.

THE WOMEN'S MOVEMENT IN TWENTIETH-CENTURY AMERICA

During the nineteenth century, as we noted in Chapter Four, the women's movement concentrated much of its energy on the reform of property rights. Toward the end of the century, however, the focus shifted to suffrage, the issue that was to occupy center stage until the passage of the amendment permitting women to vote in 1920. This alleged single-mindedness has been criticized, retrospectively, by historians. Meaningful change in women's status could not be achieved, they have argued, unless gender roles in the family changed. Doubts have also arisen, however, about how effective making the family the center of the feminists' attack would have been.[8]

The traditional interpretation of feminism during the period from 1920 to the mid-1960s can be summed up by the word *dormancy*. Many women's rights supporters, so the story goes, believed after 1920 that the goals had been achieved and so retired from the movement. The remaining activists split into two groups. The National Women's Party (NWP), led by Alice Paul, pushed for an equal rights amendment (ERA), while others opposed that strategy on the grounds it jeopardized the protective labor legislation that had been won for female workers. Of these latter groups, the League of Women Voters (LWV) became the best known. The organization attracted a larger number of women than the NWP, but its members did not devote themselves to women's issues. The split over the ERA, as well as the less-than-soothing personality of Alice Paul, have often been credited with killing the movement.

Recent research has modified this picture somewhat.[9] Simply blaming the activists ignores the substantial opposition to feminist objectives present in the 1920s and after. Nor is it accurate to say that all significant work on women's rights by women's groups ceased in 1920. Important work was done throughout the 1920 by a variety of organizations. During the entire forty-year period, the NWP, whatever its limitations, kept the ERA and the concept of feminism alive, and the Women's Bureau continued to function. Although the LWV, the American Association of University Women, and other women's organizations rejected the title "feminist," that did not mean they also shunned all women's rights activities. For example, the LWV repeatedly surveyed the statutes on marital property law in each of the states. Still, it is true that there was no mass political movement to change further the status of women in America. Public events recorded in newspapers steadily declined between the 1920s and 1960. Instead, women's groups had, in Ethel Klein's words, "earned a place within the more traditional interest-group community." Their access to Congress grew, yet with a limited constituency and not much funding, the lobby could have very little clout. Thus the number of statutes passed concerning women did not grow.[10]

Why feminism surfaced as a movement in the 1960s is only beginning to be understood. Clearly, one strain of the women's liberation movement emerged out of the civil rights struggle and the campaign to end the Vietnam War.[11] Another important group, however, was older and had taken part in the more mainstream politics of the major parties, unions, and women's community organizations. Allegedly, John F. Kennedy's debt to female campaign workers played a role in his fateful decision to create the Presidential Commission on the Status of Women in 1961.[12] Soon every state had a commission, and among other things, these commissions began scrutinizing the state laws for discriminatory statutes. The National Organization for Women (NOW), started in 1966 by disgruntled participants at a conference of the state commissions, was instrumental in converting feminism into a mass movement. Large demonstrations such as the 1970 Women's Strike for Equality forced the public at large to take the demands of the women's rights activists seriously.[13] The ERA came to the fore as the favored instrument for equality, and Congress passed the amendment in 1972. Several states, Pennsylvania included, approved state ERAs. Battles in the states over ratification of the federal amendment followed. Demonstrations on all women's issues reached their peak numbers in 1975, and thereafter momentum for passage slowed as the conservative opposition to ERA and to another major feminist interest, reproductive freedom, increased. Still, institutional support for feminism and feminist organizations had grown enormously since 1960. The nomination of Geraldine Ferraro as the Democratic candidate for vice-president and the victories for comparable worth are examples indicating that the movement continued to be of importance in the 1980s despite the activities of a hostile federal administration and the proliferation of anti-feminist organizations.

The feminist push for marital property law reform has not garnered the press attention that the ERA or the abortion issue has received. Partially that is because the passage of the ERA would presumably effect most of the desired changes, although if what has happened with the state ERAs is any indication, the actual implications for property holding and inheritance rights would have to be hammered out case by case.[14] At any rate, property law reform, as distinct from the push for an ERA, has been a major concern of activists.

When state commissions and legal experts began combing the statutes for discriminatory property laws, in most states a number of inheritance rules were found to be unfair. Some discriminated against women, others against men. The discrimination against men arose because of the protective legislation that had been enacted to compensate for women's lack of control over conjugal property. The major ways the laws still discriminated against women in inheritance were often more indirect. By the 1960s most states had intestacy statutes that gave a widow the same proportion of her husband's estate as a widower received from his wife's. The discrimination occurred during marriage, when, as already noted, the law in both common law and community property states gave to the husband the right to manage and control household assets. His actions could result in the absence of anything to inherit. Furthermore, in common law states, almost all property acquired during marriage was assumed to be the husband's unless extraordinary measures were taken to identify it as belonging to the wife. This meant that the intestacy laws where the spousal share in a decedent's separate estate was less than half were usually unfair to wives, particularly those who had been contributing as homemakers in a long-standing marriage. Even wives who had been in the labor force rarely earned salaries commensurate with those paid men, and in addition, unlike their husbands, they were mandated in most states to perform certain household services that could interfere with working outside the home full time. These intestacy rules were covertly rather than overtly discriminatory.[15]

In community property states, the solution to the general problem of discriminatory property laws was comparatively straightforward. Most of those jurisdictions, in the early 1970s, as the federal government and the states passed equal rights legislation, granted wives equal control over community assets.[16] Common law states had two choices. They could wipe out gender-based work roles in the household and sex discrimination in employment to provide an equal chance to accumulate separate property, or they could admit to the concept of community property. Most states, through piecemeal legislation and court decisions, have taken small steps toward accomplishing the former rather than adopting the latter. The legal establishment in most common law states has voiced strong opposition to switching to a community property system.[17] So far, only in Wisconsin have women's groups triumphed over the lobbying efforts of lawyers and tax accountants and brought their state into the community property fold.[18]

THE WOMEN'S MOVEMENT AND
INHERITANCE LAW

Pennsylvania

In twentieth-century Pennsylvania, there have been two periods when the inheritance laws were overhauled. The first occurred in 1917 immediately before the passage of the Nineteenth Amendment, and the second took place in the 1970s, after the enactment of a state ERA. In 1915 the governor appointed the Commission to Codify and Revise the Law of Decedents' Estates, and the commission's recommendations were voted into law two years later. Under the new statutes, husband and wife received the same share of a deceased spouse's property, there being "no apparent reason," according to the commission, "why the reciprocal rights of husband and wife in each other's intestate estate should be so different." An absolute interest in one-third of the realty replaced the lifetime interest. The commission justified this change on the grounds that "it is a pure accident whether at the moment of a man's death his property consists of lands or stocks and bonds." The spouse's share of the estate was one-half if there was only one child, when before, for women, it had been one-third. "It seems unjust," the commission wrote, "where a man dies leaving a widow and one child, often a minor, that the single child should receive twice as much as its mother, and many cases of hardship have been observed in practice." The commission also retained a statute passed in 1909 providing that when the decedent had no children or lineal descendants, the spouse was entitled to the first five thousand dollars of the estate. This clause meant that the entirety of small estates went to the spouse when there were no children.[19]

These reforms did improve women's claims to conjugal property, but they fell far short of making them equal partners. The standard share, if a couple had children, was still one-third rather than one-half, and all assets acquired during marriage were assumed to be the husband's unless the wife took special measures to have something declared her property. In childless marriages, the collateral kin, nieces and nephews, could inherit as much from the decedent as the spouse.

Over fifty years passed before the intestacy laws governing the spousal share underwent further alteration. Women in the intervening period did make some gains in their rights to inherit property, but these were improvements brought about by individual agreements, not legislative action or judicial fiat. Specifically, it turns out that there was a significant growth in the number of married couples who held their homes as joint tenants with the right of the surviving spouse to inherit the whole.[20] Today it is common practice for spouses to purchase homes in this manner. To find out how prevalent the custom used to be, we sampled Bucks County deed books in 1890, 1920, 1940, 1960, and 1980. The results appear in Table 8.2.

In 1890 couples rarely bought houses together; not even 1 percent did so. Almost all property was in the name of an individual; four out of five times it was a man. The female buyers were a mixture of single women, widows, and wives. In the 1920s, the number of deeds belonging to married couples rose to 20 percent. By 1940 couples were the majority of buyers (54.8 percent), and in 1960 their share constituted almost 80 percent of the total. This percentage fell to 63.3 percent in 1980, although there might have been fewer married couples in the total population at that time. Also, the increase in unmarried couples purchasing realty as joint tenants with survivorship and tenants in common (a tenancy that gives the survivor only half of the property, not all of it) partially offsets the drop.

When married couples held their homes jointly, the house and property passed to the surviving spouse and circumvented the probate process (although, until recently, estate tax was levied on the value of one-

TABLE 8.2 **PERCENTAGE OF DEEDS IN WHICH THE BUYERS OF REALTY WERE COUPLES, 1890–1980, BUCKS COUNTY**

Year	N[a]	Married couple jointly with survivorship	Man and woman jointly with survivorship	Man and woman tenants in common
1890	245	0.4	0.0	0.0
1920	248	22.2	0.0	1.2
1940	241	54.8	0.0	0.8
1960	232	79.3	0.0	0.4
1980	226	63.3	4.4	2.7

Source: Land Deeds, Bucks County Courthouse, Doylestown.

[a]For each year we selected the first 250 deeds and then eliminated all buyers that were businesses, institutions, government agencies, or trustees, so the number varies slightly.

half of the home). The increase in the number of deeds set up in this way meant the spousal share of marital property was obviously rising throughout most of the twentieth century, even in periods—specifically 1920–1960—when very little was going on in the legislature or the courts to improve married women's power over property.

Political pressure for change in women's status resurfaced in the late 1960s, and by 1971 the citizens of Pennsylvania voted to add an ERA to the state constitution.[21] The Pennsylvania Commission for Women instituted its ERA Conformance Project to encourage further implementation of the ERA, focusing on bringing all state laws and statutes into line with the new constitutional guarantee.[22] The Homemaker's Committee of the National Commission on the Observation of International Women's Year was also active in Pennsylvania during the 1970s. Among its recommendations were that the spouse be given the entire estate of a decedent unless there were children living who were not of the marriage or parents and that inheritance or estate taxation on transfers between spouses be ended.[23] In 1978 the legislature did not agree to as generous a spousal share as had been suggested by women's groups, but they did pass a more conjugally oriented intestacy law that awarded the entire estate to spouses when (1) neither children nor parents survived or (2) the value of the estate came to twenty thousand dollars (changed to thirty thousand in 1980) or under and there were no children of the decedent from a previous marriage. Under all circumstances, the spouse received at least half of the estate.

The general problem of property acquired during marriage being considered the husband's property remains, however, and court decisions are only slowly changing the situation. Probably the biggest court victory in Pennsylvania to date on this issue was in the *DiFlorido* v. *DiFlorido* case,[24] and its particulars give some insight into the type of difficulties faced by married women in common law states. A Bucks County woman brought a suit against her ex-husband for return of jewelry she had inherited from her mother and for the value of half of the household goods and furnishings they had used during their ten-year marriage. The court of common pleas ruled in her favor, but her former spouse appealed the ruling, and the state supreme court agreed to review the case in 1974. The main issue revolved around the household goods and furnishings, Mr. DiFlorido claiming they had been bought with his funds. The court turned down his appeal. The opinion noted, "With the passage of the Equal Rights Amendment, this Court

has striven to insure the equality of rights under the law and to eliminate sex as a basis for distinction." [25] Household items can no longer
be assumed to belong to the husband. Rather, "It is likely that both
spouses have contributed in some way to the acquisition and/or upkeep
of, and that both spouses intend to benefit by the use of, the goods and
furnishings in the household." Thus the court considered household
goods joint property. This case, of course, concerned the division of
property at the time of a divorce, not at death; and it only involved
consumer durables, not all types of assets. Still, it is indicative of
a 1970s trend in common law courts toward carving out something
akin to community property without adopting the community property
system.

California

In California, as in Pennsylvania, legal changes beneficial to married women occurred in periods of intense feminist activity. The major
inequities in the descent and distribution laws were removed in the suf-
fragist era. The legislature voted in 1923 to give wives testamentary
power over their half of community property and to grant both widows
and widowers all of the community property when a spouse died intestate. As before, the spousal share of separate property was one-third if
the couple had more than one child, one-half if there was one child or
parents, and all if there were none of the above. [26]

The remaining problems California widows experienced as heirs
had to do with (1) different rules for widows and widowers in the probating of community property and (2) the control and management of
community property during the lifetime of the husband. Little happened in either of these areas until the women's liberation movement
gathered steam in the 1960s. California did not pass a state ERA, but
it did have an extremely active state Commission on the Status of
Women, which undertook a review of all California laws that conflicted with the proposed federal ERA. [27] The review drew attention to
the fact that, whereas when a wife died intestate her husband simply
took possession of all the community property, when a husband died
intestate his wife had to probate all the community property and live on
a court-ordered family allowance until the process was finished. Before
1965 she had even had to pay state inheritance tax on her husband's

share, an obligation a husband did not have to assume if his spouse died first. Women also had problems obtaining any intervivos control over community property as it was being accumulated. In the 1920s, California passed a state law recognizing the wife's interest as "present existing, and equal." Still, aside from laws passed requiring the wife's approval over the alienation of certain kinds of property and her right to manage property she earned, the husband as the head of household controlled the bulk of the resources. While this power was not directly connected to inheritance, it was instrumental in deciding what there would be to inherit. In 1975, after a year of legislative hearings on women's issues, these two discriminatory parts of the law were changed so that wives had the same privileges as husbands in the probate procedure and in managing community property.[28]

California, largely because of its community property system and the interpretations the courts have given it, has always had the reputation of being a particularly uxorious state. It is also, of course, a state with a very high divorce and remarriage rate. Perhaps the latter can explain the most recent change in the intestacy share granted spouses. In 1985 collateral kin, siblings and their issue, were put back as heirs to a decedent's separate property, sharing equally with the spouse when a decedent is childless. There are also some additions to intestacy rules, guaranteeing that the property of a predeceased spouse ultimately goes to his or her heirs rather than all to a decedent's subsequent spouse.[29]

FINISHING THE REVOLUTION

We began this chapter discussing the unfinished revolution in married women's inheritance rights. From our analysis of state intestacy laws in the twentieth century, it seems spousal shares have noticeably increased: life estates in realty have been replaced with absolute ownership, and the percentage of an estate going to a spouse rather than lineal or collateral heirs has risen. At the same time, protective legislation—dower, homestead exemptions—are disappearing. Part of this change can be attributed to the increasing importance of the conjugal bond in the family. Alterations in intestacy statutes mirror both the private decisions made by couples in buying realty as joint tenants and the greater willingness of Congress (as noted in Chapter Six) to vote marital exemptions into the federal estate tax code.

The close relationship in Pennsylvania and California between the passage of new inheritance and property laws favorable to married women and the activities of the feminist movement suggests, however, that more than just conjugal affections are required to change state law. State ERAs, women's commissions, and homemaker committees played a major role. Nationally, there is also some evidence to indicate a link between inheritance legislation and a strong women's movement. Comparing the spousal share in states that passed the ERA with that in the states that refused to ratify or rescinded ratification of the proposed amendment, we find that a majority (55 percent) of the former give the spouse in all situations at least one-half of an intestate's estate, while a much smaller proportion (37 percent) of the anti-ERA states are as generous to the widow or widower.[30]

Can we assume, then, that the revolution—or at least the part of it relating to equitable treatment of women under the laws of inheritance—is finished or nearly finished? Certainly most states have now eliminated statutes that explicitly give more inheritance privileges to one sex than to the other. A strict equal rights approach does have its limitations, though. Often protective legislation was the most overtly discriminatory, so that courts sometimes seem to have as many reverse discrimination cases before them as cases with women as defendants, as seemed to be the case in Pennsylvania after the passage of the state ERA. This does not mean that men had more to gain from the ERA than women. The cases involving discriminations against women, such as *DiFlorido* v. *DiFlorido,* usually involved greater stakes and potentially affected more people than those of male discrimination. It is simply that discriminatory laws against women are often subtler and tied into women's inferior economic position, childbearing responsibilities and their traditional role as childrearers. It is more difficult to strike down such laws under an equal rights clause than it is to turn aside a law that, for example, only gives widows, not widowers, an allowance during the probating of an estate. The small spousal share a hefty minority of common law states still give in intestacy cases is disadvantageous to women, even though there is no explicit discrimination, because so much of the property acquired during marriage falls into the husband's estate. Furthermore, almost all common law states still give the spouse election rights of no more than one-third of a testator's estate if they reject the legacy left them in the will. Under these circumstances it is difficult to say that all problems have been taken care of, particularly when surveys indicate married couples generally want *all* of their property to go to the survivor.[31]

The growing popularity of divorce has also reduced the likelihood that states will vote larger shares to widows and widowers. We alluded earlier to the dilemma of a spouse of fifty years receiving the same share as the spouse of one year. While inheritance laws have been binding the couple more closely together, the divorce laws are making the bond more easily dissolvable.[32] Intestacy laws that give a lesser share to spouses when the decedent has children from an earlier marriage, and statutes that dictate a different distribution for that part of a decedent's estate derived from a predeceased spouse, indicate awareness of the problem. Increased willmaking should be another by-product of serial monogamy. Testators have the power to give their spouses everything or no more than state election rights dictate. What wives and children do receive in contemporary times is the subject of the next chapter.

9

Testamentary Behavior in the Late Twentieth Century

Because the bulk of aggregate wealth today is transferred by will, it is impossible to gauge the exact effects of twentieth-century state policies without studying testamentary behavior. The federal estate tax made the government a major beneficiary of affluent decedents. Deductions, exemptions, and trust arrangements, as we have shown, gradually blunted the impact of the legislation. To halt a major state-supervised redistribution of wealth, a new quasi-private economy of foundations and trusts administered by banks, tax lawyers, accountants, and other professionals was created. Although most of the rich do not take full advantage of these estate-planning tools, the wealth of those who do is considerable enough to make it an important phenomenon. The IRS aggregates, however, provide little insight into what familial purposes estate tax avoidance maneuvers might be serving or why some of the rich use these devices and some do not. For this sort of information we must turn to the will samples. Because they cover all testators, not just the minority who filed estate tax returns, and because they extend back into time before such taxes were collected, these documents also put the testamentary choices of the twentieth-century affluent into perspective. The actual impact of social insurance on the wills of the elderly is a question mark as well. Likewise, the account of probate reforms in Chapter Eight does not tell us the degree to which testators have taken the same path as the legislators or have deviated from it.

It is our task in this chapter, then, to evaluate the effect of these initiatives of state capitalism on actual testamentary behavior. Wills probated in 1979 from our sample county of Bucks are the prime focus of the analysis, but the 1890s will sample from Bucks and samples from our community property jurisdiction, Los Angeles County, provide temporal and regional comparisons. How much and what kind of estate planning has been instituted because of estate taxation? Has social insurance made testators more likely to give shares and control of an estate to nonkin? And has the pressure for female equality with men enhanced the conjugal, as opposed to patrilineal, orientation of wills and erased all distinctions between sons and daughters as heirs?

THE IMPACT OF THE ESTATE TAX ON ESTATE PLANNING

Charitable bequests, the marital deduction, and trusts are the major estate-planning tools available to the affluent for the reduction or elimination of estate taxes.[1] Charitable gifts are totally exempt from taxation. Transfers to spouses, now also totally exempt, were, in the 1979 and 1980 period (the dates when the Bucks County and Los Angeles wills were probated) tax free only if the amount transferred was under 250,000 dollars. Otherwise the government limited the exemption to 50 percent of the estate. These richer testators could create a trust and give the spouse a life estate, thereby escaping one round of estate taxation.

Charitable deductions have risen the most dramatically. Although we know that during the past four decades an increasingly large percentage of the assets of multimillion-dollar estates has gone to philanthropy, sometimes in the form of a direct gift to an organization, sometimes in trust, and sometimes as an endowment for a general-purpose foundation, what has never been tested is how both the frequency and the value of charitable gifts in wills changes from what it had been before the passage of the federal estate tax legislation in the early twentieth century.

Table 9.1 shows the percentage of testators in late nineteenth and late twentieth century Bucks County and Los Angeles County who made charitable bequests in their wills. It also gives the percentage of "affluent" testators (those with estates exceeding 120,000 dollars and thus subject to tax in the 1979–1980 period) who contributed to charity.[2] Figures for 1890s testators are given for purposes of comparison. The numbers indicate that the proportion of testators giving to charity has increased slightly over time, going from 7.1 percent to

TABLE 9.1 **PERCENTAGE OF TESTATORS MAKING CHARITABLE BEQUESTS**

Place	Time	All testators	Affluent testators[a]
Bucks	1979	12.9	32.8
		(350)	(64)
Los Angeles	1980	10.1	15.9
		(495)	(126)
Bucks	1890s	7.1	8.0
		(351)	(75)
Los Angeles	1890s	8.0	7.0
		(327)	(100)

Note: Number of observations appear in parentheses below percentage.

[a] Affluent testators were those with $120,000 and above in total estate in the 1979–1980 data sets, $7,000 and above in total estate in the 1890s data. For a full explanation of choice of cut-off points, see Appendix A.

12.9 percent in Bucks County and from 8.0 percent to 10.1 percent in Los Angeles County. The big jump, however, was among the affluent testators. In the 1890s, bequests to charity were no more frequent among the affluent than among all testators, but in the 1979–1980 period, the affluent were much more likely to make such legacies. Being liable for estate taxation seemed to increase the charitable impulse. Not only are the twentieth-century percentages in the affluent testator column higher than those in the column for all testators (particularly in Bucks in 1979, where the percentage of testators who made charitable legacies was only 12.9 percent while among those with wealth exceeding 120,000 dollars the proportion grew to nearly one-third), but in comparing the 1890s percentages with the more recent ones, notable increases are also evident. In Pennsylvania the percentage tripled, and in California it doubled. These temporal comparisons are important. Percentage differences between wealth groups in the 1979 and 1980 samples could be due simply to the fact that richer people have more extra money to dispense to charities, not that estate taxation has driven them to contribute. The 1890s figures, however, suggest that in the earlier sample the rich had been much less motivated to will assets to philanthropic organizations.

In the nineteenth century, charitable giving at death, if one had heirs, was to some extent discouraged. Many states had laws limiting the percentage that could be transferred to charities. California allowed no more than one-third, and Pennsylvania stipulated that all such gifts had to be put into wills thirty days before death.[3] With the advent of the estate tax and the availability of the charitable exemption, such barriers to giving slowly disappeared. Today only Georgia, Mississippi, and Ohio set a maximum on the proportion of an estate than can be bequeathed to a philanthropic or religious organization. A few other states have other restrictions on such testamentary gifts.

There is some reason to believe, however, that other factors in addition to the state-sponsored incentive of a deduction may account for increases over time in charitable bequests. The vast majority of those at risk to pay estate taxes give little or nothing to charity in their wills, yet some of those who have no tax liability nevertheless make such legacies. In the 1979 Bucks County sample, those estates worth less than 120,000 dollars contributed to charity almost the same percentage of their aggregate worth as did those estates valued over 120,000 dollars and subject to estate tax. The first group gave 1.68 percent, and the other willed 1.86 percent.

At the same time, many of those with estates over 120,000 dollars who made charitable gifts gave relatively small amounts. Figure 9.1 shows a scatterplot comparing this group's charitable bequests with the size of their estates. As the plotting shows, there is no discernible direct correlation between the two variables. The size of the gift did not necessarily follow the size of the estate, and the correlation is not statistically significant at an acceptable level (significance level of .439). This scatterplot actually excludes one outlier. The largest estate in the augmented sample of 388 was valued at over 9 million dollars, and about 62 percent of it was willed to charity. Had that estate been included, the correlation results would have registered a strong positive relationship, even though the scatterplot would have shown essentially the same picture. With probate data, a very large estate can distort a correlation coefficient, so that it does not reflect the majority of cases. Of course monetarily what that one testator did may be of greater importance than the actions of all the rest.

The charitable deduction clearly works rather erratically. Based on our research and that of others, it seems that most of the aggregate amount given by wealthy decedents to charity comes from a few of the superrich donating the bulk of an estate to a charity or foundation.[4] Why do they do it? The necessary information is not available to test

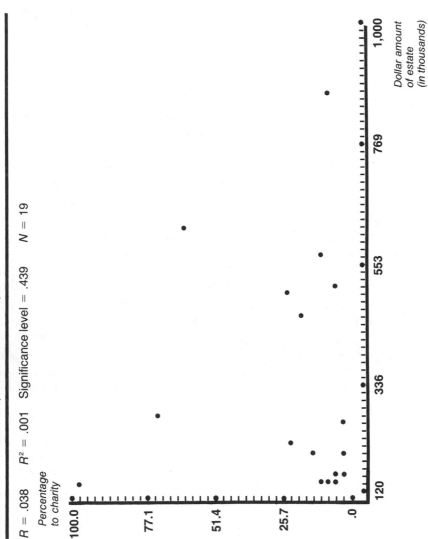

FIGURE 9.1 **PERCENTAGE OF ESTATE GIVEN TO CHARITY BY AFFLUENT TESTATORS, BUCKS COUNTY, 1979**

$R = .038$ $R^2 = .001$ Significance level $= .439$ $N = 19$

the hypothesis, but it may be that changes in the family have played a role here. Fertility has declined, leaving more testators with what might be called the Howard Hughes problem, no lineal descendants. The volatility of marriage has perhaps left others with the John Paul Getty dilemma: plenty of heirs, but none of whom they like or like them. The possibilities for promoting charitable giving through fiscal means, therefore, are limited. Recall, as well, that in Chapter Six, we found the government probably loses more in estate tax revenue by this deduction than charities gain in bequests.

Making full use of the marital deduction is another way of saving one's estate from the taxman. A marital deduction of 50 percent was instituted in 1948 to give spouses in common law states the same tax advantage as those in community property jurisdictions. In 1976 the law was liberalized further to allow the whole of an estate under 250,000 dollars to be transferred to a spouse tax free. Thus to take full advantage of the deduction those married testators with estates between 120,000 and 250,000 dollars would transfer the entire estate to their spouse, while those with assets over 250,000 dollars would have bequeathed at least 50 percent. For those whose estates fell below the 120,000-dollar level, the deduction was of little importance because they would not have been subject to an estate tax anyway.

It is interesting to see what the Bucks County testators in the common law state of Pennsylvania did with the deduction. Table 9.2 shows the percentage of an estate one spouse, usually the husband, bequeathed to another for three different estate groups: those under 120,000 dollars, those between 120,000 and 250,000 dollars, and

TABLE 9.2 **PERCENTAGE OF ESTATE BEQUEATHED TO SPOUSE, BUCKS COUNTY, 1979**

Percentage[a]	Estate below $120,000[b] (N = 85)	Estate $120,000–$250,000 (N = 9)	Estate over $250,000 (N = 7)
Under 50	27.1	44.4	57.1
50	2.4	0.0	0.0
Over 50	7.1	11.1	28.6
100	63.5	44.4	14.3

[a]Percentage of estate given absolutely without limits, such as life only or during widowhood or minority of children.

[b]The wealth categories in this table correspond to the cut-off points for affluent and nonaffluent in Table 9.1.

TABLE 9.3 **PERCENTAGE OF ESTATE BEQUEATHED
TO SPOUSE, BUCKS COUNTY, 1890s**

Percentage[a]	Estate below $7,000 (N = 111)	Estate of $7,000 or more[b] (N = 35)
Under 50	63.9	74.3
50	2.7	8.6
Over 50	2.7	5.7
100	30.6	11.4

[a]Percentage of estate given absolutely without limits, such as life only or during widowhood or minority of children.
[b]Adjusted figures; see Appendix A for explanation.

those over 250,000 dollars. For purposes of comparison, we have also included, in Table 9.3, figures on what 1890s married testators, again mainly males, did back when there was no estate tax. The tables indicate that many more testators in 1979 gave their spouses over 50 percent of their estate than had in the late nineteenth century. The testamentary choices of those in the 1979 sample with estates under 120,000 dollars, however, cast some doubt on whether the temporal changes were due largely to the marital deduction or other causes. Although those with estates below 120,000 dollars derived no particular tax advantage from the marital deduction, almost two-thirds of these testators gave their wives their entire estates, a much higher percentage than that observed for testators who had taxable estates. The marital deduction was used fully by less than half of those who might have benefited from it. Among married testators in the 120,000–250,000-dollar bracket, nearly 50 percent gave less than their entire estate forever to their spouse, yet among the over-250,000-dollar group, 57.1 percent gave under 50 percent.

While testators used the marital deduction, clearly other kinds of concerns, apart from immediate tax benefits, went into deciding the proportion of the estate a husband would leave to a wife. In some cases, there might be a tax benefit to not bequeathing all the estate to a spouse, but seldom could there be a clearcut disadvantage to giving one-half. Those who gave less than one-half usually gave substantially less or they gave the entire or a large part of the estate for *life only*. The treatment of wives we explore in more depth later in the chapter, when we examine the relationship between the movement for equal rights for women and testamentary behavior.

Trusts, the most complex instruments rich men and women have at their disposal for reducing the estate tax burden, have, however, been around for centuries and fully recognized by law in most of the United States since the early ninteenth century, long before estate taxes were levied. The relative power of trustee versus beneficiary has varied, as has the stipulation of how long the beneficiary was to enjoy the legacy.[5] Estates granted for life or during widowhood only were, and are, common. Table 9.4 indicates that trusts were actually employed as frequently, or possibly more frequently, in the late nineteenth century as in the twentieth. In Bucks County in the 1890s, nearly 30 percent of the testators mentioned trusts in their wills, while among married affluent testators, the percentage was double that figure. In newly settled Los Angeles County during the same period, trust devices appear much less often. Only a fifth of affluent testators used them. In the following century, Los Angeles, grown to a metropolis, still could not equal the trust usage practiced in turn of the century Bucks County but did increase the levels over what they had been in the 1890s, particularly among affluent married testators. Bucks County in 1979 also nearly matched the 1890s proportion of affluent married testators who employed trust devices, although among all testator groups its 10.6 percent fell far below the earlier 29.3 percent.

Table 9.5 suggests that much of the difference between Bucks and Los Angeles in the late nineteenth century was due to the disparity in the percentage of trusts made for spouses, 34.8 percent of married testators in the former and only 5.1 percent in the latter. Both married

TABLE 9.4 **PERCENTAGE OF TESTATORS USING TRUSTS**

Place	Time	All testators	Affluent testators[a]	Affluent married testators
Bucks	1890s	29.3	45.3	58.8
		(351)	(75)	(34)
Los Angeles	1890s	12.5	20.0	20.9
		(327)	(100)	(67)
Bucks	1979	10.6	26.6	55.6
		(350)	(64)	(18)
Los Angeles	1980	16.0	42.1	53.3
		(495)	(126)	(60)

Note: Number of observations appear in parentheses below percentage.
[a] For the description of affluent, see Table 9.1.

TABLE 9.5 **PERCENTAGE OF TESTATORS IN 1890s SAMPLES WITH DIFFERENT TYPES OF TRUSTS**

Type	Bucks 1890s	Los Angeles 1890s
All testators		
N	351	327
None	70.7	87.5
For spouse	16.2 (34.8 of married testators only)	2.7 (5.1 of married testators only)
For female heirs	8.3	6.7
For male heirs	5.7	6.7
Other: charity, etc.	3.7	.9
Affluent testators[a]		
N	75	100
None	54.7	79.1
For spouse	24.0 (53.0 of married testators only)	7.0 (10.5 of married testators only)
For female heirs	20.0	11.0
For male heirs	12.0	12.0
Other: charity, etc.	6.7	2.0

Note: Columns may exceed 100 percent because some testators had more than one type of trust.

[a] For the description of affluent, see Table 9.1.

male and married female testators are included in these figures, but as in both Pennsylvania and California, only married women who had separate property transferred to them by inheritance or gift could make wills, married men outnumbered them as testators by a ratio of over four to one. Wives were also less likely to encumber a husband's estate with a trust arrangement. Almost all of those settling trusts on heirs were male. We have seen, in earlier periods, that men in frontier regions have often given wives more power over property than they would enjoy when the area matured. Those who peopled the new Anglo communities in Los Angeles County followed this pattern.

Aside from legacies to spouses, trusts were not widely used by testators in either locale. Trusts for female and for male heirs, whether daughters and sons, sisters and brothers, more distant kin, or nonkin, were rare, and almost all were for guardianship purposes. Most often these testators wanted a trustee to manage the estate of minor children or aged siblings. There is no clear pattern of female or male heirs being the preferred objects of trusts. Apart from tying up the wife's share of an estate, grand dynastic designs were not much in evidence.

Turning to the twentieth century, when tax considerations become an additional incentive for the affluent to draw up trusts as part of an estate-planning strategy, only with spouses did the practice become common (Table 9.6). Spousal bypass trusts involve putting part or all of a bequest to a husband or wife in a trust. The spouse receives income from the trust during life, but at death the estate reverts to someone named, in most of the cases we noted, by the settlor of the trust, not the beneficiary. The great advantage is that the spouse's lifetime estate is not taxable when that spouse dies. (The marital deduction that a spouse could take might also be put in a trust, but taxes on that could not be escaped.) Of affluent married testators in Bucks County, 44.5 percent created spousal bypass trusts, and nearly a third in Los Angeles did so. Wives made them for husbands, but mainly they were drawn up by men for their wives. Wealth was more important

TABLE 9.6 **PERCENTAGE OF TESTATORS IN THE 1979–1980 SAMPLES WITH VARIOUS TYPES OF TRUSTS**

Type	Bucks 1979	Los Angeles 1980
All testators		
N	350	495
None	89.4	84.0
Spousal bypass	4.6 (13.2 of married testators only)	4.4 (10.9 of married testators only)
Generation skip	2.3	1.0
Intervivos	0.3	3.8
Charitable	1.1	1.4
Guardian/caretaker	2.3	5.5
Affluent testators[a]		
N	64	126
None	73.4	57.9
Spousal bypass	12.5 (44.5 of married testators only)	16.7 (31.7 of married testators only)
Generation skip	7.9	4.0
Intervivos	1.6	14.3
Charitable	3.1	1.6
Guardian/caretaker	3.1	6.3

Note: Columns may exceed 100 percent because some testators used more than one type of trust.

[a] For the description of affluent, see Table 9.1.

than age in indicating who might use this device. One might expect that life estates would be the chosen device only of elderly men in their seventies and eighties who expected their wives shortly to follow them to the grave. While testators over the age of sixty-five were slightly more likely to use bypass trusts than were those under that age, the difference was not dramatic (23.7 percent to 17.4 percent).

Generation skipping, until recently, was another means of avoiding taxes. As explained earlier, any lifetime trusts where the beneficiary had no or limited powers of appointment over the successor to his or her property would not be taxed when that beneficiary died. Thus a testator could give a lifetime estate to a child and name a grandchild as ultimate owner of the property (the remainderman). The child's legacy would not be taxed when he or she died. A generation (or two or three if a testator wanted to make a great-grandchild, or even a great-great-grandchild, the remainderman) managed to skip the estate tax. Table 9.6 indicates that whatever the advantages of generation skipping, it was not a device much favored by affluent testators in Bucks County or Los Angeles; less than 8 percent in the former and only 4 percent in the latter created them.[6] Since 1983 it is no longer possible to set up this kind of trust.

Intervivos trusts are a mixed bag of legal tricks. The irrevocable intervivos trust could save taxes. With this type of arrangement, a settlor while alive puts some of his assets into a trust or several trusts for the benefit of heirs. The settlor cannot revoke the trust or make changes in it after it is created. At death these trusts are not considered part of the settlor's wealth and, therefore, the estate is smaller and taxed at a lower rate. Irrevocable intervivos trusts were exceedingly rare in our samples, no more than one or two in both Bucks County and Los Angeles. We have said much already about the reluctance of the affluent to engage in lifetime giving,[7] and these results give further support to that generalization. It was another kind of intervivos trust, the living trust, that showed up more often, although only in California, not in Pennsylvania. In a living trust, all assets or almost all assets are put in a trust. The settlor is his or her own trustee and can alter any provision of the trust instrument at any time. Over one in ten of the affluent Los Angeles County testators made such arrangements, but they did not do it for tax purposes. The IRS treats estates that are part of a living trust the same as a regular estate. These trusts are created to escape the jurisdiction of the probate court and expedite the settlement of the estate.

Charitable trusts, like irrevocable intervivos trusts, could reduce the tax burden as well as serve dynastic purposes. As we already explained, any charitable trust is completely tax exempt. Nonvoting stock in a company owned by the settlor can be given to the trust, leaving the actual running of the enterprise to lineal heirs, who can control the business even though they do not inherit all of it. Alternately, a charitable front-end annuity trust can give a philanthropic organization income for a set number of years, at the end of which the corpus of the trust can pass to the settlor's heirs tax free. There are no examples of these type of trusts in either the California or Bucks County samples.

Finally, there are the guardianship and caretaker trusts used to protect and manage the wealth of minors, the aged, and the infirm. Many testators were over eighty, and they set up arrangements whereby banks would manage an estate for minor grandchildren, an aged spouse, siblings, or, sometimes, even themselves. They were completely revocable, however, and no tax saving would be realized. As Table 9.6 indicates, there was almost no relationship between the affluence of a testator and the creation of this type of trust.

Taking all the trusts together, it appears that in both Bucks and Los Angeles counties, a little more than 20 percent of affluent testators (those at risk to pay estate taxes) used a trust device designed to lower the rate. Although trusts were more common among the wealthy in Los Angeles than in Bucks, the difference in frequency can be almost entirely attributed to living trusts and guardianship trusts, neither of which produced tax savings. The small number of generation-skipping trusts perhaps explains why Congress was able to close this loophole at a time when sentiments against progressive estate taxation were quite strong. Comparisons with other studies suggest that throughout the twentieth century, trust usage has seldom climbed higher than 15 percent of the testate population and that most trusts have been either for wives or for guardianship purposes.[8]

The underutilization of dynastic devices points up the way capitalism has changed and continues to change. Less than 3 percent of the testators in the 1979–1980 samples (Table 9.7) transferred all or part of a business or a farm in their wills, down markedly from the 14 percent (19 percent if only male testators are counted) in the 1890s. Even in midwestern farm communities, three-fourths of family farms in the late nineteenth and first half of the twentieth century did not make it through two generations, and close-knit ethnic groups are disproportionally responsible for the persistence that did occur.[9] The family firm, already frequently liquidated rather than bequeathed when nineteenth-

TABLE 9.7 **PERCENTAGE OF TESTATORS TRANSFERRING BUSINESS OR FARM IN A WILL**

Place	Time	All testators	Male testators
Bucks	1979	3.0	8.6
		(336)	(175)
Los Angeles	1980	2.2	4.5
		(495)	(193)
Bucks	1890s	11.6	17.7
		(351)	(216)
Los Angeles	1890s	15.3	19.3
		(327)	(218)

Note: Number of observations appear in parentheses below percentage.

century corporate forms and financial networks became available, has almost disappeared from estates today. Once the bulk of wealth takes the form of financial assets, concern about its preservation seems to be less intense.

Apparently, the main way that estate taxation has affected estate planning and the drawing up of trusts has been in respect to spouses. The tradition of the lifetime estate for the wife was prolonged, it seems, by the instituting of a tax. Now that transfers to husbands and wives are completely tax free, it will be interesting to see what happens to spousal trusts. There is some reason to believe that desire to control what happened to the wealth awarded spouses was at least an element in the setting up of these trusts. For example, testators with wealth below 120,000 dollars sometimes created them. Then there were the testators who put the marital-deduction half of the estate in trust even though it would have to be taxed at the death of the spouse. Finally, the tendency for testators to go beyond what the law required in these trusts and restrict the spouse's appointment power and her or his ability to dip into the principal suggests motives other than just tax saving. Apparently it was more acceptable to tie up an estate bequeathed to a spouse than one going to lineal heirs.

THE EFFECTS OF SOCIAL INSURANCE

One of the most distinctive characteristics of state capitalism in twentieth-century America has been the government's assumption of responsibilities formerly thought to belong to the family. Pension plans, social security, and Medicare enable the elderly to be more independent, and as discussed in Chapter Seven, some social science observers contend that intergenerational ties and extended family relations have consequently been weakened. One indicator of the reliance of family members upon one another has been the percentage of the elderly who reside with children and other kin. In the late nineteenth century more than 70 percent of those sixty-five and over lived with family members (aside from spouses), while one hundred years later the proportion had shrunk to less than a quarter.[10] Some of those now on their own live in retirement communities, where, it is hypothesized, peer-group friendships may come to rival kin relations.[11]

Of the sixty-five and over testators in our 1979 Bucks County sample, a little less than 11 percent could be identified as residing with children or kin. Two-thirds occupied their own households, although some of those may have had children living with them; 4.7 percent had moved to retirement communities; and 12.7 percent lived in nursing homes. It was impossible to determine the living arrangements of the remaining 3.7 percent. These Bucks County residency patterns reflect the nation as a whole. Whether there has been a true diminishing of family feeling is still being debated,[12] but it is apparent that certain material links have been severed. The issue that we are interested in is whether testamentary behavior has also been affected by the independence of the aged.

We considered two measures of the degree to which testators have switched their loyalties from kin to nonkin. First, we calculated how many testators today, compared with before the advent of mass pension and social security programs, alienated part or all of their estates from their kin by bequests to charity or to nonrelatives. Table 9.8 shows the results from our samples in Bucks County and Los Angeles County. In Pennsylvania there was little increase over the century; about one in five testators made bequests to other than kin in the 1890s and in 1979. In California there was some change. During the 1890s the proportion was similar to that for Bucks County, but in 1980 the percentage had risen to 30. As the theories about kin estrangement are mainly concerned with widowed or unmarried testators who have children, we looked at the percentages for that subgroup. As one might expect, fewer gave bequests to nonkin and charities, but otherwise the pattern was the same as for the sample as a whole: no change in Bucks County over time but a notable jump in California.

TABLE 9.8 **PERCENTAGE OF TESTATORS MAKING BEQUESTS TO NONKIN AND CHARITIES**

Place	Time	All testators	Unmarried with children
Bucks	1979	20.3 (350)	12.2 (156)
Los Angeles	1980	30.3 (495)	20.7 (140)
Bucks	1890s	18.2 (351)	10.1 (89)
Los Angeles	1890s	20.8 (327)	10.5 (76)

Note: Number of observations appear in parentheses below percentage.

Did residence patterns have any influence on testators making these bequests? To find out, we had to control for wealth, marital status, number of children, sex, age, and religion. We performed a probit analysis on the 1979 Bucks County data set (information on residence was not available for the 1980 Los Angeles County sample, unfortunately) to determine the probability of a testator bequeathing some portion of his or her estate to nonkin or a charity. Our findings are reported in Table 9.9. Most of the coefficients have the expected signs. Wealth enhances the probability of such bequests, while being married and number of children reduce the likelihood. Age and sex are not significant at an acceptable level. Indicating a religious affiliation greatly increased the probability that bequests would be made, but there is a measurement problem with that variable. We frequently knew the testator had a religious affiliation because he or she made a charitable contribution in his or her will. The coefficients of the variables used to test the importance of residence also have all the right signs. That is, living in retirement homes and nursing homes increased the probability, and living with children and kin decreased it. The problem is the results are not significantly different from zero (significance levels of .905, .845, and .949, respectively).

Second, we calculated another measure of the closeness of testators and their relations by comparing the proportion who chose nonkin or professionals as executors and trustees in the 1890s and in the late twentieth century. The percentages in Table 9.10 suggest no increase in such appointments over time. On the contrary, nineteenth-century testators named outsiders more frequently than did those writing wills in

1979 and 1980. The former showed a marked reluctance to nominate daughters and other female kin to execute an estate (more on this point below), thereby shrinking the number of eligible family members. This may have resulted in more nonrelatives being called in. Another unanticipated finding was that unmarried testators (essentially, widows and widowers) chose professionals and nonkin as executors *less* often than did the sample as a whole. In the twentieth century, it was not widows and widowers disenchanted with their adult offspring who most often resorted to outsiders. Rather, it appears to have been married testators who wanted to aid or replace a spouse as executor.

There was a definite trend within the outsider group itself toward substituting professionals for nonkin. During the 1890s in both counties, only about 1 percent of the testators chose as executor or trustee someone who could be readily identified as a lawyer or other professional, whereas in the 1979–1980 samples, about 15 percent selected such people.[13]

The results as a whole, then, are inconclusive. In Pennsylvania there seemed to be no change over time in the proportion of testators who

TABLE 9.9 **DETERMINANTS OF TESTATORS' BEQUESTS TO NONKIN AND CHARITABLE INSTITUTIONS, BUCKS COUNTY, 1979**

Independent variable	Maximum likelihood estimate	Significance level (for *t* test)
Constant	−1.774	.007
Wealth	0.004	.000
Number of children	−0.414	.000
Age at making will	0.009	.106
Religious affiliation[a]	1.759	.000
Married testators[a]	−1.064	.002
Women testators[a]	−0.070	.756
Residence[a]		
Living with child/kin	−0.024	.949
Living in nursing home	0.057	.845
Living in retirement community	0.058	.905

Note: Probit analysis: $N = 343$; -2 the log likelihood ratio $= 146.0472$; significance level $= .000$. Percent predicted correctly: 88.9 percent. Rank order correlation, predicted versus actual $= .611$. The dependent variable is dichotomous: if a testator made a bequest to a nonkin member or a charitable institution, it was coded 1; and if no such legacy was given, it was coded 0.

[a]Dummy variables. Indications of having a religious affiliation, being married, or being a woman resulted in a code of 1. Other cases received a 0. With residence, each of the choices—living with child/kin, living in a nursing home, and living in a retirement community—was coded 1; and the reference category—living on one's own or with spouse—was coded 0.

TABLE 9.10 **PERCENTAGE OF TESTATORS APPOINTING NONKIN AND PROFESSIONALS AS EXECUTORS AND TRUSTEES**

Place	Time	N	Nonkin and professionals only	Nonkin and professionals with relative	Total
		All testators			
Bucks	1979	348	17.8	4.9	22.7
Los Angeles	1980	459	32.0	2.7	34.7
Bucks	1890s	345	32.5	8.7	41.2
Los Angeles	1890s	312	29.5	5.4	34.9
		Unmarried testators with adult children			
Bucks	1979	155	11.6	5.7	17.3
Los Angeles	1980	135	14.8	3.6	18.4
Bucks	1890s	87	21.8	8.0	29.8
Los Angeles	1890s	66	22.7	10.5	33.2

bequeathed property to nonfamily members, while in Los Angeles there was an increase. Possibly, Southern California, a retirement mecca, is in the vanguard, and the change we have detected there gradually will spread elsewhere. The probit analysis performed on the Bucks County 1979 sample indicated that living in a retirement community raised the likelihood of testators making legacies to nonrelatives, but the findings were not statistically significant. At this point, the number of retirement home residents in these samples is too small to make reliable inferences about their testamentary behavior. Moreover, the comparison between nineteenth-century and twentieth-century testators' choices of executors and trustees does not support the notion that the use of children and other relatives in these positions has declined over time. Increased employment of professionals has occurred, but they have mainly replaced nonkin or spouses not lineal or collateral kin.

THE INFLUENCE OF THE WOMEN'S MOVEMENT

One result of the ongoing changes in twentieth-century probate law detailed in the last chapter is that women now write a greater proportion of the wills than they did at the turn of the century. They, in fact, write as many or more than men. In the 1890s, 38.5 percent of the testators in Bucks and 33.3 percent in Los Angeles County were women. California was no higher because married women did not have the right to will their half of community property if a spouse survived. In the 1979–1980 samples, the percentages were 50.0 (Bucks) and 58.8 (Los Angeles). Another result is that the share to which children or other kin can lay claim has diminished with the shift in inheritance statutes from a lineal to a conjugal orientation. Social scientists have argued a similar transformation has taken place in testamentary behavior. They point to evidence from surveys showing that the vast majority of husbands wish to go beyond the intestacy laws of their states and will everything to their spouses. Wives, in only slightly smaller proportions, express similar sentiments when asked their testamentary preferences. Rising divorce rates do not seem to have affected these responses.[14]

Have wills become more conjugally oriented in the twentieth century and do they lead or follow the trend in intestacy legislation and dower? In Table 9.11 we show the share married male testators in late-nineteenth- and twentieth-century Bucks County and Los Angeles County left their wives.[15] Clearly, in both periods there was greater dissatisfaction with intestacy arrangements in the common law jurisdiction of Bucks County than in the California community property

TABLE 9.11 **MARRIED MALE TESTATORS' BEQUESTS TO WIVES COMPARED WITH INTESTACY PROVISIONS**

	Percentage from			
	Bucks		Los Angeles	
Bequest compared to intestacy	1979 (N = 77)	1890s (N = 120)	1980 (N = 86)	1890s (N = 128)
More than intestacy	51.9	34.2	3.5	27.3
Same	15.6	3.3	59.3	34.4
Less	18.2	5.0	22.1	11.7
More but time limit[a]	11.7	49.2	7.0	16.4
Same but time limit[a]	1.3	2.5	2.3	5.5
Less but time limit[a]	1.3	5.8	5.8	4.7

[a]For life, widowhood, during minority of child, or for a term of years. The time limit had to be beyond that specified in the intestacy law for a bequest to be placed in one of these categories.

county of Los Angeles. In Bucks during the 1890s, few of the male testators (3.3 percent) emulated the Pennsylvania statutes when making legacies to their wives; instead, one-third increased the wife's share. Most (49.2 percent), however, gave the wife more than the intestacy provisions designated, but only for lifetime use. In the twentieth century, Bucks husbands also frequently disagreed with the share set aside under the intestacy statutes. Over half gave more than intestacy, and the number leaving some portion for life only declined sharply. In contrast, Los Angeles testators showed more enthusiasm for the intestacy arrangements, one-third in the 1890s and nearly 60 percent in 1980 following intestacy prescriptions in their wills. Also during the 1890s in Los Angeles, restrictions on the length of time property could be held were much less frequent than in Pennsylvania, although by the twentieth century they were comparable. the relative popularity of the California intestacy laws among testators suggests one reason why new states coming into the union favored the community property system over the common law.

The dissatisfaction with Pennsylvania intestacy arrangements in the 1890s may have had something to do with the fact that the law in regard to widows remained about what it had been in colonial times.[16] If a decedent had children, a widow received a third of the personalty forever and one-third of the realty for life. If there were no children but there were kin, she was left one-half of the personalty. Only if there were no other heirs did she get all of her husband's assets. Apparently, by the 1890s many men felt a third was insufficient. They might also have wished to give more than one-half to their spouse rather than have a distant relative be an equal partner in the estate. Instead of skimping on the share, they preferred to limit the duration of the bequest. In this case, it seems the law clearly lagged behind popular male sentiments. The change in statutes, however, did not come until 1917. This legislation allowed the spouse, whether wife or husband, one-third of the estate (both realty and personalty) forever if the decedent had more than one child. When there was just one child or no children or only other relatives, then the spouse received one-half of the estate. The sum of five thousand dollars (later raised to twenty thousand, then, thirty thousand was also added to the legacy of the wife or husband when collateral rather than direct lineal descendents inherited. In cases of small estates or where much of the wealth had been transferred before death, this amount could constitute the entire estate. For larger estates, the spouse only received it all when the decedent had no relatives. The 1917 law, then, with its increased share if only one child survived and the lump sum when collaterals inherited, did improve somewhat the proportion wives received. The end to the life estate was also of significance because it was at odds with male testamentary behavior. The Pennsylvania intestacy provisions were fairly representative of the kind of statutes passed in common law states during the first half of the twentieth century.

In the community property state of California, there was more congruence between the intestacy statutes and what male testators left their wives. In the 1890s a widow received half of the husband's estate as her community property share. Any separate property he might have had previous to the marriage or received by inheritance or gift was also half hers unless the decedent had more than one child, in which case, she was awarded one-third. Of course, if he had no kin, she got all the separate and community assets. Although wives' rights were inferior to those of husbands, who owned all the community property when the spouse died, married women fared better than their counterparts in common law jurisdictions. These comparatively generous terms for widows obviously fit in with the circumstances and sentiments of the Anglo population that had invaded Los Angeles County in the late nineteenth century. By 1980 the intestacy law had undergone further changes, allowing both spouses to inherit all community property in the absence of a will. Rights in separate property remained the same. For those who have only community property, giving a wife the entire estate is the same as following the intestacy provisions, and for most people community property is the only type of asset held. Consequently only 3.5 percent of the men in Table 9.11 are recorded as leaving their spouse more than the intestacy share. In contrast, the intestacy law operative during most of the twentieth century in Bucks County was the 1917 statute described above, and therefore, over half of the husbands in the 1979 sample opted to give their wives more in their wills.[17]

Did the testamentary alterations equalize the situation of women in Bucks and Los Angeles counties and thus compensate for the latter's more generous intestacy law? It seems unlikely, given that only about 50 percent of probates were testate and that the percentage of testators who gave more than intestacy in Bucks County in no way made up for the discrepancy. If one just considers testators, it also does not seem possible that Bucks could have made up for the more favorable terms in the California county because only one-third bequeathed more to their wives in Bucks while not that much smaller a proportion (27.3 percent) gave more in California. The gap may have narrowed in the late twentieth century. We can make some direct comparisons between the percentage of testators in each county that gave their entire estate to the spouse forever. Table 9.12 indicates that among the testates, Los Angeles had many more than Bucks (44.3–24.6 percent) who willed their entire estate to the spouse in the 1890s, but in the late twentieth century the percentage in Bucks was slightly higher (55.1–48.0 percent). All of these percentages, however, fell below the figures in surveys reporting the proportion of men intending to leave everything to their wives in their wills. Something, perhaps a lawyer, seems to have come between these intentions and the actual bequest. It is also important to note that affluent testators were much less likely to dispose of their estates in this manner.[18]

Among the general testate population it seems giving spouses a lifetime interest in property became less frequent during the course of the twentieth century (see Table 9.13).[19] In the 1890s, over 60 percent of the Bucks husbands put some time restriction on their legacy or on part of their legacy to the wife. Some of these men simply invoked the standard life interest provision on the widow's third of realty, but others

TABLE 9.12 **PERCENTAGE OF MARRIED MALE TESTATORS WHO GAVE THE ENTIRE ESTATE TO THE WIFE**

Place	Time	All married male testators	Affluent married male testators[a]
Bucks	1979	55.1 (89)	26.7 (15)
Los Angeles	1980	48.0 (98)	22.9 (35)
Bucks	1890s	24.6 (134)	11.1[b] (34)
Los Angeles	1890s	44.3 (140)	26.3 (57)

Note: Only bequests that were forever are included. Those who gave the wife the entire estate for life or widowhood are not counted as 100 percent legacies here. Number of observations appear in parentheses below percentage.

[a] For the description of affluent, see Table 9.1.

[b] An adjusted figure. For reasons and method of adjustment, see Appendix A.

TABLE 9.13 **PERCENTAGE OF MARRIED MALE TESTATORS WHO PUT TIME LIMITATIONS ON A BEQUEST TO THE WIFE**

Place	Time	All married male testators	Affluent married male testators[a]
Bucks	1979	20.2	53.3
		(89)	(15)
Los Angeles	1980	20.4	48.6
		(98)	(35)
Bucks	1890s	61.9	71.0
		(134)	(31)
Los Angeles	1890s	22.9	40.0
		(140)	(55)

Note: Limitations are instances where part or all of bequest was for life or (in a few cases) for widowhood, during minority of child, or for term of years. Number of observations appear in parentheses below percentage.

[a] For the description of affluent, see Table 9.1.

went further. In California, where there were no lifetime interests in the intestacy statutes, under a quarter of the testators included such restrictions, although among affluent testators the proportion jumped up to 40 percent. In the later twentieth century we might expect such passages to disappear, but they do not. In Bucks County they declined to one-fifth, which is also where they remained in Los Angeles County. The enactment of the estate tax no doubt prolonged the life of this device because property so devised escaped the federal levy. Since the Economic Recovery Act of 1981, spousal bypass trusts or life estates only give tax saving for multimillionaires because all transfers to spouses are tax free and tax credits so generous.

In the 1979 Bucks County sample, it is clear that, while affluent testators who were at risk to pay estate taxes were the main clients for life estates, 18 percent of husbands whose wealth was below 250,000 dollars, and who thus could have passed an estate to a wife tax free, chose to tie up the bequest for life and name the ultimate beneficiary themselves. We also found some testators putting the marital deduction in a trust, another practice that was not instituted for tax-saving purposes. The desire to manage a wife's inheritance from the grave has certainly diminished, but it has not completely disappeared.

The comparison of the shares husbands left their wives with the conditions they placed on the property in the two counties suggests that more is now bequeathed to wives than in earlier periods and that time restrictions have been reduced. Improvements are much more dramatic in the common law state of Pennsylvania, however, than in California, where from the beginning community property law gave wives a greater proportion of the husband's estate. Pennsylvania's statutes consistently lagged behind testamentary behavior in regard to spousal portions. Now the laws of the state have changed to allow the spouse to inherit no less than half of the estate and to receive it all if it amounts to less than thirty thousand dollars or neither issue nor parents of the decedent survive. These changes only happened, however, once the current movement for marital property reform was well underway.

In addition to the share of the estate inherited, we used another indicator of a wife's status in the probate process: her role in administering the estate of her deceased husband. Did the earlier trend not to appoint wives continue or change direction once again? Table 9.14 shows the percentage of wives named as sole executrix, designated as joint appointee, or excluded from administering the estate. The choices of all testators and just affluent testators appear. The results are a bit confusing. In Bucks County, it seems, as we might expect, that the trend has been reversed. Male testators regardless of wealth appointed their wife executrix much more often in the late twentieth century than they had at the turn of the century. Southern Californians, however, actually

TABLE 9.14 **WIVES AS EXECUTRIXES**

Place	Time	*N*	Wife alone	Wife and another	Wife excluded
		Percentage of married male testators			
Bucks	1979	89	64.0	7.8	28.2
Los Angeles	1980	91	49.5	5.5	45.0
Bucks	1890s	134	30.6	11.2	58.2
Los Angeles	1890s	133	72.2	8.4	19.4
		Percentage of affluent married male testators[a]			
Bucks	1979	15	46.7	26.7	26.7
Los Angeles	1980	34	44.1	2.9	53.0
Bucks	1890s[b]	33	18.2	12.1	69.7
Los Angeles	1890s	55	65.5	7.2	27.3

[a] For the description of affluent, see Table 9.1.
[b] Adjusted; see Appendix A.

grew less "uxorious"; the percentage who named the spouse declined over the ninety-year period. In the 1890s Los Angeles husbands named their wife as *the* or one of the executors over 80 percent of the time, while in 1980 the proportion dropped to 55 percent. Among the affluent the drop over time was only slightly lower (72.7–47.0 percent). What was happening in Los Angeles that was different from what occurred in Bucks? Age could be a factor. The 1890s Los Angeles sample was younger. One-third of the testators were under fifty when they wrote their wills, and half were under sixty.[20] Yet in controlling for age by comparing only those husbands who had adult children, we found the same difference between the two 1890s samples. In Bucks 72 percent excluded their wives from being executrixes, and in Los Angeles only 23 percent did so. We do know that in Bucks more testators used children and kin as executors than did their counterparts in the West. Possibly the reason was that their relatives lived two thousand miles away or resided in Europe. Wives, in contrast, were more likely to be on the spot.

In the twentieth century, Los Angeles County husbands used professionals more often than Bucks County testators. Among affluent married men in Los Angeles, for example, 35 percent named a professional as sole executor. Bucks County male testators who appointed lawyers, bankers, or other professionals as executor or trustee also tended to name their own wife as well. The concentration of professionals and financial institutions in major metropolitan areas may lead to heavier reliance on their services.

Up to this point, we have considered only wives. How did daughters fare? Did the earlier improvement in their situation vis-à-vis male heirs continue, or was there little difference between the late nineteenth and the late twentieth centuries in that regard? From the standpoint of explicit legal restraints leading testators to give less to daughters or put restrictions on their control or ownership of property, the important changes had occurred. Essentially what remained, therefore, to inhibit equal treatment of children regardless of sex were dynastic sentiments about the patrilineage and the belief that women were incompetent to handle financial affairs.

Comparisons between how testators with both sons and daughters chose to distribute their estates reveal little firm evidence of differences in treatment (see Table 9.15). In California in the 1890s a greater number of testators left more than intestacy mandated to daughters than to

TABLE 9.15 **COMPARISON OF SHARES GIVEN CHILDREN BY TESTATORS WITH BOTH SONS AND DAUGHTERS**

N	Bucks 1979 107		Los Angeles 1980 116		Bucks 1890s 99		Los Angeles 1890s 111	
Division[a]	Sons	Daughters	Sons	Daughters	Sons	Daughters	Sons	Daughters
More than intestacy	16	12	15	14	17	18	10	18
Same	41	42	76	74	20	20	34	30
Less	45	44	21	23	52	49	55	49
Some more, some less	5	9	4	5	10	12	12	14

[a]Because there were few life estates given, the "more than intestacy but for life only," "same as intestacy but for life only," and "less than intestacy and for life only" divisions are lumped into the "more than intestacy," "same as intestacy," and "less than intestacy categories," respectively.

sons (18 to 10). No such pattern appears in Bucks in the same period, suggesting that migration patterns (daughters perhaps moving more often with parents than sons) may account for the California results. The Bucks County 1979 sample shows sons more often getting more (16 to 12), but the difference disappears if one adds the category "some more, some less" than intestacy to it. Apparently, these testators were more likely to single out a particular daughter for special treatment than they were a son. If we limit the comparison to just affluent testators, the numbers get rather small, and no real trend emerges either. Those who have studied wealthy testators in present-day America have noted some slight bias in favor of male heirs. Our numbers may be too small and our information on intervivos transfers too restricted, especially for California, to pick that bias up.[21]

Time restrictions and power over the administration of the estate are other ways testators can discriminate among heirs. There does not seem to have been much recourse to life estates for either sons or daughters. In all the samples, the percentage fell below 5 percent except for Bucks County in the 1890s, when testators tied up the estates of sons 10.3 percent and daughters 11.4 percent of the time. With executorship, however, there are significant differences that to some extent diminish over the course of the century but do not disappear. In Table 9.16 are the percentage of testators who had adult sons and excluded them from executorship compared with those who had adult

TABLE 9.16 **PERCENTAGE OF TESTATORS EXCLUDING ADULT SONS VERSUS ADULT DAUGHTERS FROM EXECUTORSHIP**

Place	Time	Excluding sons	Excluding daughters
Bucks	1979	45.1	55.0
		(153)	(182)
Los Angeles	1980	59.5	68.8
		(195)	(186)
Bucks	1890s	39.0	84.0
		(136)	(132)
Los Angeles	1890s	69.8	75.5
		(116)	(106)

Note: Number of observations appear in parentheses below percentage.

daughters and excluded them. The tendency in all periods was for daughters to be excluded more often than sons. In Bucks County the gap narrowed substantially over time, but in Los Angeles it did not. In the 1890s Southern Californian mothers actually excluded sons more often than they did daughters. Fathers favored sons but not in the proportion that those in Bucks County did. This behavior fits with the results on inheritance shares in Table 9.15, and it resulted in only a small gap between the treatment of sons and daughters, which the latter were unable to close in the twentieth century. Were mothers better "feminists" than fathers? It seems they were. While in the samples other than Los Angeles in the 1890s, mothers excluded more daughters than sons, the gap was less than with the male testators. These findings on executorship reinforce the notion that the biggest problem women have in dominating economic activities in contemporary America is not so much one of ownership but of control. They are not picked to manage resources as often as men are, even if the resources are in their names.

THE STATE, THE FAMILY, AND WILLS

Testamentary behavior in the late twentieth century differs in important respects from what went before, and government policy has definitely influenced some of those changes. The estate tax is largely responsible for the creation of professional estate planning, which in turn has produced an elaborate network of charities and foundations and a complex law on trusts. Now, more testators make charitable bequests, and a whole variety of trust instruments appear in wills. Testators, however, are very selective in the estate-planning devices they use. More affluent testators give to charity, but what they give is not very much, certainly not enough to justify the 100 percent exemption that exists on such bequests. Trusts are employed, but probably no more often than in the nineteenth century, and as then, they are not part of any elaborate dynastic strategy to preserve wealth through the generations. As corporate capital in the form of financial assets, rather than capital in the form of a family firm, is what is passed between generations in wills, concern about dissolution of the patrimony has ebbed. Rather, what we see in the trusts being drawn up are short-term strategies giving spouses more than intestacy shares and yet reserving to the testator the power of ultimate disposition of the legacy. These testamentary preferences are reflected in the recent tax "reforms" whereby generation-skipping trusts were no longer exempted from tax, yet much larger exemptions were allowed so that testators could bequeath assets outright to heirs.

The impact of social insurance, specifically, the degree to which it has made the elderly independent from the younger generation and thus less likely to will property to them and choose them to administer estates, is more difficult to assess. The percentage of testators who made bequests to nonkin and charities increased over time in Los Angeles, but the rise in Bucks was only a couple of percentage points. We know of course that there may have been other reasons why charitable giving rose. Multivariate analysis, where the effects of wealth and other variables are held constant in order to measure the impact of residence, proved inconclusive because there were insufficient numbers of testators who could be identified as living in retirement communities, nursing homes, and with kin. Most testators seemed to be living on their own, and that gave us no clue as to the regularity with which they had contact with children and relatives. The percentage of nonkin acting as executors and trustees actually declined. Nonkin had played a significant role in earlier periods, mainly because male testators would not entrust estate management to wives and daughters. That changed in the twentieth century. Also of note is that it was friends and acquaintances rather than people serving in a professional capacity (as lawyer, bank officer, accountant, etc.) that were being appointed less often. Professional participation in will making was growing, particularly in Los Angeles.

When we consider the influence of the women's equal rights movement on testamentary behavior, the historical differences between the two counties we have studied become most apparent. The California county looks as if it were "born modern." Under community property law, married women in 1890s Los Angeles automatically received much more of the husband's estate than did their counterparts in the common law jurisdiction of Pennsylvania. Life estates also showed up much less often in the California wills than those of Bucks in the 1890s. These Los Angeles husbands seldom excluded their wives from executrixship either. In fact, the 1980 Los Angeles husbands actually named their wives less often, and the affluent put more time restrictions into their bequests to spouses than they had in the late nineteenth century. This reversal of the trend one might expect was probably the result of more reliance on professional advice and the presence of estate taxes. At any rate, the immigrant nature of Los Angeles at the turn of the century meant regional differences in treatment of spouse exceeded temporal differences. When relatives were half a continent or more removed, testamentary patterns seemed to change markedly. They did in the early colonization period and in Los Angeles in the 1890s. The question is, of course, whether this behavior is characteristic of all newly relocated populations and still holds despite modern communication and transportation systems. The fact that other researchers working on patterns of women's work in the late nineteenth century find that Los Angeles conforms to the national norm lends support to the notion that what was going on had to do with relocation rather than some basic change in spousal relations.[22]

In these late-twentieth-century wills, spouses are of overriding importance, although the desire to control their bequests by granting life only estates remained strong among the affluent. While professionals have made their mark on wills, the numerous tax-avoidance devices they have created are underused. Testators are disinclined to engage in long-term strategies for preserving familial wealth. This reluctance reflects the changing functions of the family unit and reminds us of the problems inherent in relying upon it as the vehicle for societal saving, investment, and economic planning.

Conclusion

Inheritance, the Family, and Capitalism

In this book we have looked at an economic process, inheritance, and studied how it was affected over time by the changing composition and organization of capital and the family. As we are dealing with America, the analysis began rather abruptly in the seventeenth century, when the colonial family (or, more accurately, household heads) controlled almost all capital and when a modification of the English common law stressing both the patrilineage and testamentary freedom governed inheritance practices. Our investigation ended in the late twentieth century, when corporate forms, state regulation, and community property innovations had combined to alter the way wealth was transmitted. Three centuries of intestacy law and testamentary behavior have allowed us to measure the varying commitment of wealthholders to the conjugal tie, the lineage, the broader kin network, and friends and charitable organizations in the community. In some areas, continuity was more striking than change.

A prominent characteristic of the American inheritance system throughout the centuries has been its steady focus on the nuclear family. Despite almost complete testamentary freedom, Americans have whenever possible limited their substantial bequests to spouse, sons, and daughters. Generally, of testators who have children, 90 percent or more have passed up legacies to relatives, friends, and charities. State intestacy laws gave daughters precedence over collateral male kin and often forbade the willing of the bulk of an estate to charities. The exceptions have been few. The colonial period saw more bequests to kin, but mainly they were legacies to sons-in-law. As married women gained more property rights, these gifts decline. In the twentieth century, fiscal policy made charitable contributions more attractive to affluent testators. The rich, when faced with a choice of filling the coffers of private organizations or those of the state, preferred the former. In many instances these charitable bequests fit in nicely with dynastic aims because they increased the after-tax shares inherited by the decedent's heirs. It is difficult, therefore, to attribute the rise in legacies of this type to a growth in eleemosynary impulses or community spirit.

Theories that the new independence enjoyed by the elderly through the existence of social insurance (pensions, social security, Medicare) have resulted in a weakening of the intergenerational bond and closer relations with nonkin could not be proven with our data. Many of these developments may still be too recent to make a clear impact on behavior. While a jump in inheritance by friends could not be documented, it does appear that increased longevity and escalating medical costs are driving more of the elderly into life care contracts with old age homes. In that sense, there has been a noticeable channeling of resources from lineal heirs to those ouside of the family.

There has also been some continuity in the use of elaborate strategies to perpetuate wealth within the family over many generations. The mechanisms have changed, but the market for them has remained both tiny and fairly constant. Neither primogeniture, entail, nor the strict family settlement, all favored English dynastic tools, enjoyed much popularity in America. Many colonies rejected primogeniture, preferring to give the eldest son a double share of realty or personalty rather than all of the realty. Seldom did testators entail land. Both practices ended with the Revolution. While these devices suited the aristocracy of England, who for the most part were landlords, they served the purposes of Americans less well. In the colonies there were fewer of the super rich, and many of them had mercantile fortunes, not landed ones. Even among the agrarian interests primogeniture and entail were of limited use, for land was much more available in America. Only among large tobacco planters did entail become common, and they entailed slaves as well as realty.

The emergence of trusts kept dynastic strategists employed in the nineteenth century because these legal instruments could be used to conserve financial assets as well as realty. Most trusts, though, were used for guardianship purposes or to limit the autonomy of widows. Long-term estate planning in the twentieth century is a creature of tax policy. Schemes such as generation skipping have dramatically reduced estate tax liability. Trust and foundation wealth today is immense, yet fears about wealth concentration are seldom heard, perhaps because most of the funds are managed by professionals rather than the superrich themselves, and complete information about family holdings is hard to come by. Ironically, the emergence of the most efficient methods of estate preservation ever are coincident with a decline in a lineal orientation, so few of the wealthy take complete advantage of the powerful dynastic tools at their disposal. Still, more attention needs to be paid to trusts and foundations than has been the case in the recent past, for, even if only a small percentage of the superrich are involved, the amount of assets is considerable.

The consistent underuse of elaborate estate-planning technique does not mean that throughout their history Americans have been unconcerned with the lineage. The passing of physical property, often the family farm, was of central importance in early America. Colonists, if they could, avoided liquidation of production capital. They favored one, two, or sometimes even three sons while frequently widows, daughters, and any remaining boys had to be satisfied with less than intestacy rules would have given them.

Gradually, during the nineteenth century, there was a major change. By the end of the century, even in a farm community such as our case study county of Bucks, only a minority of testators passed on a family business or farm. Instead they liquidated, and children more often received cash shares. Except among the rich, there were no noticeable differences between what sons and daughters inherited. In the twentieth century, even among the affluent, detectable discrimination had disappeared. Thus, in the early American period, the lineage was central in inheritance, but it was an abbreviated lineage. Testators were concerned with passing on the means of production to the next generation but did not attempt to go much further. With the growth of financial institutions and corporate forms in the nineteenth century, wealthholders found it easier to convert physical property into liquid assets. The transferance of a viable business was no longer necessary. Sibling shares became more equal, and widows' portions became more generous, and the sense that inheritance shaped the economic structure faded.

Change over time is also quite apparent in the treatment accorded the widow as heir, although it is more a curvilinear than linear trend. Because of coverture, men owned 85–90 percent or more of property well into the nineteenth century. While a husband gained absolute rights to his wife's personalty upon marriage and lifetime rights to his wife's realty, a widow received only a third of her husbands' estate, the realty portion being also for life. The intestacy rules followed English precedents, although some innovations in testamentary behavior and dower are not immediately copied.

At the time America was colonized, English men were growing more restrictive with their widows, directing that personalty and realty be surrendered if they remarried, giving them a quarterly allowance rather than a lump sum, and eliminating them from the execution of their estates. Dower shrank from one-third of both personalty and realty to just one-third of realty. Initially, colonists did not adopt these innovations. Testators tended to make their widows executrixes and frequently gave them shares larger than the intestacy laws would have awarded them. "For widowhood" clauses were rare. In the latter part of the eighteenth century, however, more and more husbands bequeathed mainly food and lodging to their wives until they remarried or died and had others than the spouse handling their estates. Married women's claims to their husbands' estates seem to have reached their lowest point around 1800.

The first improvement in women's situation came in the form of marriage settlements that gave married women control and testamentary power over property they had inherited. By the mid-nineteenth century, the states, under strong political pressure, began passing married women's property acts that gave all women these rights, not just those whose husbands agreed to a settlement. By the end of the century the impact of this legislation could be seen in the growth in the percentage of women who were testators and in the proportion of probated wealth belonging to them. A bilateral system had replaced the patrilineage.

The married women's property acts did little to improve the share a wife received from her intestate husband's estate, however. While many of the states entering the union from the mid-nineteenth century on joined as community property states or enlarged the spousal intestacy share, the majority of jurisdictions clung to the common law thirds. The testamentary behavior of husbands and the growth of joint tenancy agreements between spouses during the twentieth century indicated a growing desire to make inheritance more conjugally oriented, but it took the reemergence of the feminist movement in the late 1960s to effect widespread statutory change. Battles are still being fought to recognize conjugal property in common law states. Complicating the situation is the growing volatility of marriage and the appearance of nonprobate property, pensions, social security, and the like. Still, the vast majority of married couples, when surveyed, want the surviving spouse to inherit the entire estate.

While from the mid-nineteenth century on, one might say there was an upward and onward trend for married women as heirs, earlier there were two discontinuities that require explanation. First, there was, by contemporary English standards, a definite generosity toward wives in the wills of early colonial settlers. Second, we recorded the same tendencies among the Americans and Western Europeans who poured into Los Angeles in the late nineteenth century. They were much more likely than their counterparts in established communities on the East Coast to give large portions to their wives and name them executrixes. There seems to be something about newly settled regions that temporarily strengthens the conjugal tie. Apparently, such moves mean sons and daughters as well as collateral kin are in less abundance. Migrants tend to marry later and have fewer children. Also a certain percentage may not move with their parents, and another group may move away after their parents' initial migration, movers being known to be more at risk to move once again. Under such circumstances, the marital relationship might, in earlier times, temporarily have taken precedence over that of the lineage.

By the later eighteenth century the colonists reverted to the pattern that had emerged earlier in England. More and more male testators prevented their widows from owning property absolutely and excluded them from executrixship. They devised the most dependent form of legacy for these women: room space and provisions supplied by children. It may be that the growth in financial assets and the more frequent alienation of property made the intestacy share of the one-third of personalty forever more than husbands wanted to give and that the dower third in land for life tied up realty for too long a time. We know at least that the trend does not seem to be due to a shortage of land or a surplus of sons because it was the richer testators who were most likely to give the spouse less than intestacy and place time restrictions on legacies.

What is the significance of these trends in the law of inheritance and in testamentary behavior? For one thing, our findings cast doubt on the belief, still current in some economic and political circles, that parental desires to perpetuate family fortunes would, if only such disincentives as estate and inheritance taxes were removed, play an important role in capital formation. It has been a very long time, our figures indicate—well over a century—since the wills of any sizeable number of wealthholders showed signs of special estate planning or lifetime saving for a child or children. When fathers were trying to pass on a family firm or farm, then some type of strategy was usually apparent. These strategies, however, contained elements that would not be particularly attractive to most contemporary families. "Estate planning" largely consisted of skimping on the wife's share of the estate and treating daughters and some sons inequitably. Family members also were bound together by a series of obligations that would be difficult to enforce today. Once physical wealth could be converted more easily into cash and financial assets, inheritance became more egalitarian among the majority of wealthholders, but capital also became less concentrated and less often channeled directly into production. Elaborate trust devices existed and still exist to perpetuate the new forms of wealth down through the generations, but like the earlier dynastic device, entailing, they are not widely used. In the past, very few of even the superrich were sufficiently motivated by dreams of lineal glory to put into operation elaborate dynastic strategies. What data are available on intergenerational wealth transfers by the rich in the twentieth century suggest dissaving rather than saving. Consequently the theory that lower estate taxes will benefit capital formation because the wealthy will once again be inspired to save for their lineal descendants, and thus posterity, seems improbable. The biographies of the contemporary superrich suggest that desire to deprive the government of its estate tax revenue rather than love of lineage motivates a larger share of complex estate planning schemes. ¦

Our findings also point to the role women and the women's movement have played in the development of capitalism. The type of family capitalism that evolved in both England and America depended on propertied women agreeing to surrender ownership and control over their assets when they married. The husband's ability to command not only his resources but those of his wife was the keystone of family capitalism. Nor did widowhood necessarily restore women's economic powers unless their husbands gave them more than their intestacy thirds. From the data we have studied, it was more likely by the later eighteenth century that a husband gave his widow less. The notion that women silently accepted this treatment is belied by the numerous court cases brought by widows willed less than dower and by the growth in marriage settlements in the late eighteenth and early nineteenth century. When the women's movement began, the first major issue became property law reform.

The married women's property acts, even more than the earlier abolition of primogeniture, made family capitalism, as it had been practiced, untenable as the organizational structure for the economy. The family firm had too many chiefs and, at least legally, too many equal partners. In such a situation, corporate forms had a great attraction because they separated ownership from management. Financial corporations facilitated the liquidation of firms, and, along with other types of corporate ventures, provided investment opportunities for the resultant capital. Women could own property equally with men but still not control it. While they were certainly major factors leading to the establishment of corporate capitalism, the need to distribute risk, raise large amounts for capital goods, and the like have probably been somewhat overrated. As long as there was enough corporate wealth to found banks, insurance companies, and other financial institutions, family capital could stretch pretty far. One has only to think of the Ford Motor Company in the 1930s. More attention should be paid to the problem of using the family, with its recruitment of executives by accident of birth and its underuse of female members, as management. The family was and is a rather small and unstable unit for the supervision of large amounts of money and labor. The financial independence of women or even the threat of independence increased that instability. Corporate forms, in addition to their other advantages, pointed a way out. Not only has the inheritance process been affected by changes in the family and the economy, but in some instances, it has promoted them.

Appendixes

Samples of Probate Records from Bucks County, Pennsylvania, and Los Angeles County, California

This book relies heavily on a series of probate record samples from Bucks County, Pennsylvania, and Los Angeles County, California. We discussed in the introduction the reason for choosing these two counties. The method of sampling was the one usually employed in studies of testamentary behavior. In each time period, we included every probate case in Bucks County and every testamentary case in Los Angeles County.

For Bucks County we wanted will data sets of about 350 observations, figuring that we would need at least that many to analyze testamentary behavior. To estimate probate participation and probated wealth, we also created separate data sets for all the administrations (intestates) filed between the two dates in which the wills in the sample had been filed. We did stratified sampling for the 1979 data on wills to get enough affluent testators, and we added additional cases to the colonial wills because there were a number of cases where wealth information was lacking. Bucks County probate files included, aside from the will or administration, an estate inventory that gave appraisals of the decedent's personal wealth (all wealth aside from realty). Estate accounts showing the worth of all personal and real property sold and the debts owing by the decedent were also available for decedents for all but the colonial period. The 1979 data set had the most complete wealth information, because a Pennsylvania state form had to be filled out listing all assets.

The probate dates of the respective samples are:

1. March 1, 1685, through December 31, 1755. This produced 871 probate files: 374 wills, 374 administrations, and 123 missing or

illegible probate cases. We added 13 additional observations to the will data set because of the large number of cases with missing information; these 13 cases we excluded when estimating probate participation and probate wealth, but we used them in the chapters on testamentary behavior. Thus in many of the tables the dates for the colonial sample read "1685 to 1756."

2. January 1, 1791, through December 31, 1801: 352 wills, 352 administrations, and 9 missing or illegible cases.

3. March 21, 1891, through May 29, 1893: 351 wills, 410 administrations, and 12 missing or illegible cases.

4. January 2 through May 29, 1979: 350 wills, 220 administrations, and 25 missing cases. We added 38 additional testate estates with wealth exceeding 60,000 dollars to the will data set to augment the affluent group. We only used these in the testamentary behavior chapters when we did calculations for the subgroup affluent. Because we eventually defined affluent as 120,000 dollars and over, only those additional estates that level or above were used.

Our microfilm copies of these probate files came from the Registrar's Office, Bucks County Courthouse, Doylestown, Pennsylvania.

For Los Angeles County we only collected data on wills because the main purpose of these samples was to see if the testamentary patterns of decedents in community property states differed from those in common law states like Pennsylvania. The periods covered by the two samples from Los Angeles are:

1. November 16, 1898, through August 3, 1900: 327 wills. These records included supporting materials indicating the testators' age and wealth.

2. March 10 through 26, 1980: 495 wills with no supporting materials. We collected more observations for this data set because we had to make our estimates of affluency from internal evidence and we wanted to be certain to have enough for analysis of that subgroup.

We obtained these probate files on microfilm from the Civil Processing Division, Los Angeles County Courthouse, Los Angeles. Some of the 1980 files are located in the courthouse complex, while others are in the branch court offices. The 1890s files are in the archives of the County Hall of Records.

ESTIMATION OF THE PROBATE AND TESTATE POPULATION

In the introduction we made estimates of the proportion of Bucks County men and women whose estates were probated and who wrote wills in the various time periods (Table I.1), and we also calculated the percentage of the Los Angeles County population in 1980 that was testate (Table I.2). We derived those percentages in the following way.

Population information for Bucks County in the colonial period is difficult to come by. The first citation in Greene and Harrington is for 3,012 taxables in 1751.[1] We assumed the female taxpayers included in the figure and the unpropertied males over twenty-one excluded from the estimate canceled one another out. Based on calculations that have been made about colonial growth rates and death rates, we chose model West mortality level 9 $r = 20$ as the appropriate life table describing the Bucks County population in 1751.[2] According to that table for males, about 50 percent of the population was over twenty-one, so the total male population stood at about 6,000. The death rate was 25.6 per thousand, and 38 percent of those deaths were of men over twenty-one. Consequently we may estimate that in 1751 roughly 58 adult male Bucks County residents died a year. In that year, 21 wills and administrations were probated. An additional 4 may be assumed from the 123 estates that were probated, but that have disappeared from the records or are illegible, if we suppose that the same percentage (3 percent) of them are from 1751 as are the nonmissing. We estimate total number of male probated estates, then, at 25. Of the probate population in 1751, 46.5 percent was testate, meaning altogether 12 male testates. We may assume that the female population was approximately 10 percent smaller than the male because of greater male in-migration. That would mean 5,400 females with a death rate of 23.26 per thousand, 40 percent of it adult. There was one Bucks County female whose testate estate was probated in 1751. We used the same procedure to calculate the figures for the 1790s except that 1790 census figures were available.[3] Because the ratio of males under sixteen to those over sixteen in the census was relatively high, we chose model West mortality level 9 $r = 25$ to estimate the size of the adult decedent population for the 1790s.

For the 1890s there were manuscript death registers for Bucks County.[4] We used an average of the deaths for 1894–1896 because there were no figures for 1891–1892 and the ones for 1893 seemed incomplete. For the 1979 sample there are printed mortality figures for Bucks County; the same is true for the Los Angeles County sample in 1980.[5]

DEFINING AFFLUENT TESTATORS

For all the will samples except Bucks County and Los Angeles County in 1979 and 1980, we labeled "affluent" the estates falling into the top third in wealth. In the colonial (1685–1755) Bucks County sample, the top one-third were those estates where personal wealth (personalty) amounted to 220 pounds Pennsylvania currency or more. If personal wealth was the same proportion (43.6 percent) of total wealth (realty plus personalty) in the sample as a whole as it was in the forty-seven cases where we do know the total wealth amount, then the top one-third had total wealth of 500 pounds Pennsylvania currency or over. Converted into pounds sterling, this meant estates of roughly 300 pounds and over fell into the affluent category. After checking other studies of colonial wealth, we were satisfied that the cut-off point of 220 pounds personalty was a plausible one for eighteenth-century Pennsylvania.[6] In the 1790s (1791–1801), the top third held personal wealth of 500 pounds Pennsylvania currency or more. If personal wealth was the same proportion (46.4 percent) in the sample as a whole as it was in the 254 probate cases where we do know the total wealth amount, then the top one-third had total wealth of 1,000 pounds or over.

In the 1890s samples from Bucks County and Los Angeles County, there were enough observations with total wealth to use that rather than just personalty in determining the cut-off point of 7,000 dollars. The top third in the Bucks County sample had 6,900 dollars or more, while in Los Angeles it was 7,400 dollars. These both seemed close enough to make 7,000 dollars the cut-off point for each sample. Again, we referred to other wealth studies, and 7,000 dollars seemed plausible as the lower limit for affluence.[7]

In the twentieth century, the cut-off point was more or less predetermined by the estate tax law. We chose total gross wealth of 120,000 dollars or more because at that level most people had to be concerned about estate and inheritance taxes, and the impact of fiscal policy on testamentary behavior is one of the major questions we were asking of the twentieth-century data. As it turned out, estates of 120,000 dollars or more constituted the top 16 percent of the 1979 Bucks County sample. For the Los Angeles County 1980 sample, it was impossible to obtain wealth figures, and we had to rely on internal evidence. We defined as "affluent" testators who bequeathed realty beyond their residence, substantial shares of stocks and bonds, or money amounts exceeding 120,000 dollars. Of the Los Angeles 1980 sample, 25 percent fell into the affluent category.

We made one further adjustment in the Bucks County 1890 will sample. When a testator gave his or her entire estate to a spouse, often the estate was not inventoried, and consequently the value of the estate is unknown. This situation resulted in a lot of cases with wealth missing and, therefore, the affluent group was smaller than it should have been. Thus we made an adjustment. There were 9 cases where the wealth variable was known among the 37 cases where testators gave everything to their spouses. Only 1 of those 9 (or 11.1 percent) had wealth over 7,000 dollars. We assumed that the same ratio existed for the 28 wealth-unknowns. In those tables where we show treatment of spouse by the affluent, the greater-than-intestacy column has been increased by 3 observations.

B

Inheritance Laws 1890

	Spouse's Share If There Is No Will and									
	(1) Children		(2) No children, but parents		(3) No children, no parents, but other heirs		(4) Spouse takes all		(5) Spouse's share if he/she disregards will	
	Real	Personal	Real	Personal	Real	Personal	Real	Personal	Real	Personal
Common law states										
Alabama										
Wife	⅓ for life[b]	½ if 1 child; child's share if 2–4; ⅕ if 4[c]	½ for life	All	Same		No next of kin		Intestate share	
Husband	All for life	½	Same		Same		Same as wife		No provision	
Alaska										
Wife	⅓ for life	½	All		Same		No children[f]		⅓ for life	None
Husband	All for life	½	All		Same		Same as wife		All for life	None
Arkansas										
Wife	⅓ for life	⅓	½ for life	½	Same		No provision		Intestate share	
Husband	No provision		Same		Same		Same as wife		No provision	

(6) Homestead exemption	(7) Barriers to disinherit- ing children	(8) Spouse's kin in succession	(9) Escheat when no	(10) Illegitimate child's rights[a]	(11) Married women's testamentary capacity
$2,000 or 160 acres[d]	None	No	Next of kin	Inherits from and trans- mits to mother; trans- mits to mother's kin	All property rights upheld
Same as wife				If father acknowledged child, child inherits from father[e]	May make a will
$2,500 home, lived in; 160 acres rural; ¼ acre urban	None[g]	No	Next of kin	Inherits from mother and her kin; transmits to mother	All property rights upheld
					May make a will
$2,500; 160 acres rural or not <80 acres "with- out regard to value"; 1 acre urban	Must show intent	No	Next of kin	Inherits from and trans- mits to mother	All property rights upheld
					May make a will

	Spouse's Share If There Is No Will and									
	(1) Children		(2) No children, but parents		(3) No children, no parents, but other heirs		(4) Spouse takes all		(5) Spouse's share if he/she disregards will	
	Real	Personal	Real	Personal	Real	Personal	Real	Personal	Real	Personal
Common law states										
Colorado										
Wife	½	½	All	All	Same		No children		½	½
Husband	Same as wife		Same as wife		Same		Same as wife		Same as wife	
Connecticut										
Wife	⅓ for life of lands owned at death	⅓	½ for life of lands owned at death	½	Same		Ancestral estate in realty; no siblings and representatives of ancestor from whom lands decended		⅓ for life of lands owned at death	⅓ for life
Husband	Same as wife		Same as wife		Same		No next of kin		Same as wife	
Delaware										
Wife	⅓ for life	⅓	½ for life	½	Same		Life estate if no next of kin; never in fee		⅓ for life	None
Husband	All for life if children of the marriage	All	½ for life	All	Same		No provision	Always	All for life	None

(6) Homestead exemption	(7) Barriers to disinherit- ing children	(8) Spouse's kin in succession	(9) Escheat when no	(10) Illegitimate child's rights[a]	(11) Married women's testamentary capacity
$2,000	None	No	Lineal an- cestors and issue	Inherits from and trans- mits to mother; trans- mits to mother's kin	All property rights upheld May make a will
$1,000 home, lived in; for life of survivor and minority of children	None	No	Next of kin	No provision	All property rights upheld May make a will
None	None	No	Next of kin	Transmits to mother	All property rights upheld May make a will

	Spouse's Share If There Is No Will and									
	(1) Children		(2) No children, but parents		(3) No children, no parents, but other heirs		(4) Spouse takes all		(5) Spouse's share if he/she disregards will	
	Real	Personal	Real	Personal	Real	Personal	Real	Personal	Real	Personal
Common law states										
Florida										
Wife	⅓ for life	⅓ if > 1 child; ½ if 1 child	⅓ for life, or all in fee	All	Same		No children		⅓ for life	½ if 1 child; ⅓ if > 1 child
Husband	Child's share		All	All	Same		Same as wife		No provision	
Georgia										
Wife	⅓ for life of lands owned at death; or child's share of entire estate if < 5 children; ⅕ if 5 or more children		All	All	Same		No children		⅓ for life	None
Husband	Child's share		Same as wife		Same		Same as wife		No provision	
Hawaii										
Wife	⅓ for life	⅓	½	½	Same		No descendants of brother(s) or sister(s)		Same as intestacy	
Husband	Same as wife		Same as wife		Same		Same as wife		Same as wife	
Illinois										
Wife	⅓ for life	⅓	½	½	Same		No next of kin		⅓ for life	⅓
Husband	Same as wife		Same as wife		Same		Same as wife		Same as wife	

(6) Homestead exemption	(7) Barriers to disinherit- ing children	(8) Spouse's kin in succession	(9) Escheat when no	(10) Illegitimate child's rights[a]	(11) Married women's testamentary capacity
Dwelling house; 160 acres rural	None	Yes	Next of kin	Inherits from and transmits to mother	All property rights upheld
					May make a will
$200; 50 acres + 5 acres for each child under 16 rural; $500 urban with no acreage limitation; for life of survivor and minority of children	None	No	Next of kin	Inherits from and transmits to mother and her children; transmits to mother's kin	All property rights upheld
				Father may legitimate child	May make a will
Homestead for life	None	No	Next of kin	Inherits from mother; transmits to mother	May make a will
$1,000 home, lived in; for life of survivor and minority of children	None	No	Next of kin	Inherits from mother and her kin; transmits ½ to mother, ½ to her children and their descendants	All property rights upheld
					May make a will

	Spouse's Share If There Is No Will and									
	(1) Children		(2) No children, but parents		(3) No children, no parents, but other heirs		(4) Spouse takes all		(5) Spouse's share if he/she disregards will	
	Real	Personal	Real	Personal	Real	Personal	Real	Personal	Real	Personal
Common law states										
Indiana										
Wife	½ if 1 child; ⅓ if > 1 child, in estate valued at $10,000 or less; ¼ if $20,000 or less; ⅕ if $20,000; may not devise if remarries	⅓ if > 1 child; ½ if 1 child	¾; all if estate is valued at < $1,000	¾	All	All	No children or parents		⅓	$500 in articles + ⅓
Husband	⅓	⅓	Same as wife		Same as wife		Same as wife		⅓	⅓
Iowa										
Wife	⅓	⅓	½	½	Same		No ancestors and their lineal descendants		⅓	⅓
Husband	Same as wife		Same as wife		Same		Same as wife		Same as wife	

(6) Homestead exemption	(7) Barriers to disinherit- ing children	(8) Spouse's kin in succession	(9) Escheat when no	(10) Illegitimate child's rights[a]	(11) Married women's testamentary capacity
$600	None	No	Next of kin	Inherits from and transmits to mother and her kin	All property rights upheld
				If father has no legitimate heirs in the U.S., he may acknowledge the child and child inherits	May make a will
Whole homestead for life in lieu of distributive share of realty; $500; 40 acres rural; ½ acre urban	None	Yes	Next of kin	Inherits from and transmits to mother	All property rights upheld
				If father acknowledged child or if paternity was "notorious," child inherits from father; if paternity "is proven" and recognition is mutual, father inherits from child	May make a will

	(1) Children		(2) No children, but parents		(3) No children, no parents, but other heirs		(4) Spouse takes all		(5) Spouse's share if he/she disregards will	
	Real	Personal	Real	Personal	Real	Personal	Real	Personal	Real	Personal

Spouse's Share If There Is No Will and

Common law states

Kansas

Wife	½	½	All	All	Same		No children		Intestate share	
Husband	Same as wife		Same as wife		Same		Same as wife		Intestate share	

Kentucky

Wife	⅓ for life	⅓	⅓ for life	½	Same		No lineal ancestors and issue		Intestate share	
Husband	All for life of children of marriage	All	None	All	Same		Same as wife		Intestate share	

Maine

Wife	⅓ for life	⅓	½ for life	½	Same		No next of kin		Intestate share	None
Husband	Same as wife		Same as wife		Same		Same as wife		Intestate share	None

(6) Homestead exemption	(7) Barriers to disinheriting children	(8) Spouse's kin in succession	(9) Escheat when no	(10) Illegitimate child's rights [a]	(11) Married women's testamentary capacity
160 acres rural; 1 acre urban; for widowhood	None	No	Lineal ancestors and issue	Inherits from and transmits to mother; transmits to mother's kin; if father acknowledged child or paternity was notorious, child inherits from father; if recognition was reciprocal, father inherits from child; but mother and her heirs take preference	All property rights upheld
					May make a will
$1,000, for life of survivor and minority of children	None	Yes	Next of kin	Inherits from and transmits to unmarried mother	Must have a separate estate by deed or devise
					May devise separate estate
$500; home lived in; for life of widow and minority of children	Must show intent	No	Next of kin	Inherits from and transmits to mother and her kin; if father acknowledges child, child inherits from and transmits to father	All property rights upheld
					May make a will

	(1) Children		(2) No children, but parents		(3) No children, no parents, but other heirs		(4) Spouse takes all		(5) Spouse's share if he/she disregards will	
	Real	Personal	Real	Personal	Real	Personal	Real	Personal	Real	Personal
Common law states										
Maryland										
Wife	⅓ for life	⅓	⅓ for life	½	Same		No kindred	No sibling or issue	⅓ for life	⅓
Husband	All for life if children of the marriage	All for life	All for life	All	Same		Same as wife	No children	No provision	
Massachusetts										
Wife	⅓ for life	⅓	$5,000 in fee; ½ for life in residue	$5,000; ½ the excess over $10,000	Same		No kindred		Intestate share	$10,000; income of ⅓–½ of excess
Husband	All for life if children of the marriage	½	$5,000 in fee; all for life in residue	All	Same		Same as wife		All for life if children; ½ for life if none	½
Michigan										
Wife	⅓ for life	⅓ if > 1 child; ½ if 1 child	½	All to $1,000; ½ the residue	Same		Siblings and issue		⅓ for life	Intestate share to $5,000; ½ intestate share in residue
Husband	All for life if children by present marriage; nothing if wife has children by former marriage	⅓ if > 1 child; ½ if 1 child	½	No provision	Same		Same as wife		Intestate share	No provision

Spouse's Share If There Is No Will and

(6) Homestead exemption	(7) Barriers to disinherit-ing children	(8) Spouse's kin in succession	(9) Escheat when no	(10) Illegitimate child's rights[a]	(11) Married women's testamentary capacity
$100	None	In lands only	Real: no heirs; personal: relations within the 5th degree	Inherits from mother and her illegitimate children; transmits to her illegitimate children; if there are none, to her, or her kin	All property rights upheld
					May make a will
$800; for widowhood and minority of children	Must show intent	No	Next of kin	Inherits from mother and maternal ancestors; transmits to mother and her kin	All property rights upheld
					May make a will
$1,500; 40 acres rural; 1 lot urban; to widow and children as long as in use as a residue	Must show intent	No	Next of kin	Inherits from and transmits to mother; transmits to mother's kin	All property rights upheld
				If father acknowledges child, child inherits from father	May make a will

	(1) Children		(2) No children, but parents		(3) No children, no parents, but other heirs		(4) Spouse takes all		(5) Spouse's share if he/she disregards will	
	Real	Personal	Real	Personal	Real	Personal	Real	Personal	Real	Personal
Common law states										
Minnesota										
Wife	⅓	⅓	All	All	Same		No children		⅓	⅓
Husband	Same as wife		Same as wife		Same		Same as wife		Same as wife	
Mississippi										
Wife	Child's share		All	All	Same		No children		Child's share; ½ if no children	
Husband	Same as wife		Same as wife		Same		Same as wife		Same as wife	
Missouri										
Wife	⅓ for child's life; share or, all the property, real and personal, that came to the husband from the wife if children are by earlier marriage		All the property that came to the husband from the wife, or ½ husband's		Same		No descendants of parents or siblings		Intestate share	
Husband	No provision		No provision		Same		Same as wife		No provision	

Spouse's Share If There Is No Will and

(6) Homestead exemption	(7) Barriers to disinheriting children	(8) Spouse's kin in succession	(9) Escheat when no	(10) Illegitimate child's rights[a]	(11) Married women's testamentary capacity
Dwelling house and 80 acres rural; 1 lot in urban area with > 5,000 population; ½ acre if urban area with < 5,000 population; to survivor if no children; to survivor for life if children	Must show intent	No	Next of kin	Inherits and transmits to mother	All property rights upheld
				If father acknowledged child, child inherits from and transmits to father	May make a will
$2,000 home, lived in; 160 acres rural	None	No	Next of kin	Inherits from mother and her children; inherits from mother's kin if there are no legitimate heirs; if father acknowledged child, child inherits from father	All property rights upheld
					May make a will
160 acres or $1,500 rural; 18 sq. rd. or $3,000 urban population > 40,000; 30 sq. rd. or $1,500 urban population > 10,000 but < 40,000; 5 acres or $1,500 urban population < 10,000; for life of widow, minority of children	Must show intent	Yes	Next of kin	Inherits from and transmits to mother	All property rights upheld
					May make a will

| | Spouse's Share If There Is No Will and | | | | | | | | |
| | (1) Children | | (2) No children, but parents | | (3) No children, no parents, but other heirs | | (4) Spouse takes all | | (5) Spouse's share if he/she disregards will | |
	Real	Personal	Real	Personal	Real	Personal	Real	Personal	Real	Personal
Common law states										
Montana										
Wife	⅓ if > 1 child; ½ if 1 child		½	½	Same		Siblings		⅓ for life if child; or may elect to take ½ in fee if no children	Intestate share
Husband	Same as wife		Same as wife		Same		Same as wife		⅔	⅔
Nebraska										
Wife	⅓ if > 1 child; ½ if 1 child		½	½	Same		No next of kin		Intestate share	
Husband	Same as wife		Same as wife		Same		Same as wife		Intestate share	
New Hampshire										
Wife	Choice of ⅓ for life or ⅓ in fee	⅓ if > 1 child; ½ if 1 child	½ for life as dower or ½ in fee	½	Same		Never; it escheats		Intestate share	
Husband	Choice of all for life or ⅓ in fee if children of the marriage; ⅓ for life if wife has children by former marriage	⅓ if > 1 child; ½ if 1 child	½	½	Same		Same as wife		Intestate share	

(6) Homestead exemption	(7) Barriers to disinheriting children	(8) Spouse's kin in succession	(9) Escheat when no	(10) Illegitimate child's rights[a]	(11) Married women's testamentary capacity
$2,500; 160 acres rural; ¼ acre urban	Must show intent	No	Next of kin	Inherits from and transmits to mother; transmits to mother's kin	All property rights upheld
				If father acknowledged child, child inherits from father	May make a will
$2,000; 160 acres rural; 2 lots urban	Must show intent	No	Next of kin	Inherits from and transmits to mother; transmits to mother's kin	All property rights upheld
				If father acknowledged child, child inherits from and transmits to father	May make a will
$500; for life of survivor, minority of children	Must show intent	No	Next of kin	Inherits from and transmits to mother; transmits to mother's kin	All property rights upheld
					May make a will

	Spouse's Share If There Is No Will and									
	(1) **Children**		**(2)** **No children,** **but parents**		**(3)** **No children,** **no parents,** **but other heirs**		**(4)** **Spouse takes all**		**(5)** **Spouse's share** **if he/she** **disregards will**	
	Real	**Personal**	**Real**	**Personal**	**Real**	**Personal**	**Real**	**Personal**	**Real**	**Personal**
Common law states										
New Jersey										
Wife	⅓ for life	No provision	Same		Same		No provision		Intestate share	
Husband	All for life if children of marriage	No provision	Same		Same		No provision		Intestate share	
New York										
Wife	⅓ for life	⅓	⅓ for life	½	⅓ for life	$2,000 + ½	No provision	Siblings and issue	⅓ for life	No provision
Husband	All for life if children of marriage	⅓	None	½	None	$2,000 + ½	Same as wife		All for life	No provision
North Carolina										
Wife	⅓ for life	⅓ if < 2 children; child's share if > 2 children	⅓ for life	½	Same		No next of kin		Intestate share	
Husband	All for life if children of the marriage	All	None	All	Same		Never	Always	No provision	

(6) Homestead exemption	(7) Barriers to disinheriting children	(8) Spouse's kin in succession	(9) Escheat when no	(10) Illegitimate child's rights[a]	(11) Married women's testamentary capacity
$1,000; for life of widow, minority of children	None	No	Next of kin	Transmits to mother	All property rights upheld May make a will
$1,000, home lived in; for life of widow, minority of children	None	No	Next of kin	Transmits to mother and her kin	All property rights upheld May make a will
$1,000, home lived in; for life of widow, minority of children	None	No	Next of kin	Inherits from mother if she has no legitimate child; transmits to mother; inherits from and transmits to illegitimate children of mother If father legitimated child, child inherits from and transmits to father	All property rights upheld May make a will

| | Spouse's Share If There Is No Will and | | | | | | | |
| | (1) Children | | (2) No children, but parents | | (3) No children, no parents, but other heirs | (4) Spouse takes all | | (5) Spouse's share if he/she disregards will | |
	Real	Personal	Real	Personal	Real Personal	Real	Personal	Real	Personal
Common law states									
North Dakota									
Wife	⅓ if > 1 child; ½ if 1 child		½	½	Same	No siblings		No provision	
Husband	Same as wife		Same as wife		Same				
Ohio									
Wife	⅓ for life	½ to $400; ⅓ of the excess	All for life if lands came by descent, devise, or gift; all in fee otherwise	All	Same	If property came by descent, devise, or gift, no relative of the blood of ancestor from whom property came; otherwise, no children		⅓ for life	Intestate share
Husband	Same as wife		Same as wife		Same	Same as wife		Same as wife	
Oklahoma									
Wife	⅓ if > 1 child; ½ if 1 child		½	½	Same	No siblings		No provision	
Husband	Same as wife		Same as wife		Same	Same as wife		No provision	

(6) Homestead exemption	(7) Barriers to disinherit- ing children	(8) Spouse's kin in succession	(9) Escheat when no	(10) Illegitimate child's rights[a]	(11) Married women's testamentary capacity
Home, lived in; 160 acres rural; 1 acre urban; for life of survivor, descent to children	Must show intent	No	Next of kin	Inherits from and transmits to mother; transmits to mother's kin	All property rights upheld
				If father acknowledged child, child inherits from and transmits to father	May make a will
$1,000; for widowhood, minority of children	None	No	Next of kin	Inherits from and transmits to mother and her kin	All property rights upheld
					May make a will
60 acres with improvements rural; 1 acre with improvements urban, home, lived in; for the life of survivor, minority of children	Must show intent	No	Next of kin	Inherits from and transmits to mother; transmits to mother's kin	All property rights upheld
				If father acknowledged child, child inherits from and transmits to father; father preferred to mother	May make a will

	(1) Children		(2) No children, but parents		(3) No children, no parents, but other heirs		(4) Spouse takes all		(5) Spouse's share if he/she disregards will	
	Real	Personal	Real	Personal	Real	Personal	Real	Personal	Real	Personal
Common law states										
Oregon										
Wife	⅓ for life	½	All		Same		No children		⅓ for life as dower	No provision
Husband	All for life if children of the marriage	All	Same as wife		Same		Same as wife		All for life	No provision
Pennsylvania										
Wife	⅓ for life	⅓	½ for life	½	Same		No next of kin		As though husband died intestate	
Husband	All for life	Child's share	All for life	All	Same		Same as wife		Same as wife, or all for life	Same as wife
Rhode Island										
Wife	⅓ for life	⅓	⅓ for life	½	Same		No next of kin		⅓ for life	No provision
Husband	All for life if children of the marriage	All	None	All	Same		Same as wife		All for life if children of marriage	No provision

Spouse's Share If There Is No Will and

(6) Homestead exemption	(7) Barriers to disinheriting children	(8) Spouse's kin in succession	(9) Escheat when no	(10) Illegitimate child's rights[a]	(11) Married women's testamentary capacity
None	None	No	Next of kin	Inherits from and transmits to mother	All property rights upheld May make a will
$300	None	No	Next of kin	Inherits from and transmits to mother; if none to her other illegitimate children	All property rights upheld May make a will
None	Must show intent	Yes	Next of kin	Inherits from and transmits to mother	All property rights upheld May make a will

	Spouse's Share If There Is No Will and									
	(1) Children		(2) No children, but parents		(3) No children, no parents, but other heirs		(4) Spouse takes all		(5) Spouse's share if he/she disregards will	
	Real	Personal	Real	Personal	Real	Personal	Real	Personal	Real	Personal
Common law states										
South Carolina										
Wife	⅓	⅓	½	½	Same		No next of kin		⅓ for life	No provision
Husband	Same as wife		Same as wife		Same		Same as wife		No provision	
South Dakota										
Wife	⅓ if > 1 child; ½ if 1 child		½	½	Same		No siblings		No provision	
Husband	Same as wife		Same as wife		Same		Same as wife			
Tennessee										
Wife	⅓ for life	Child's share, but no more than ⅓	⅓ for life	All	Same		No next of kin		Intestate share	
Husband	All for life	All	Nothing	All	Same		Same as wife		All for life	All

(6) Homestead exemption	(7) Barriers to disinherit-ing children	(8) Spouse's kin in succession	(9) Escheat when no	(10) Illegitimate child's rights[a]	(11) Married women's testamentary capacity
$1,000; for life of survivor, with descent to children	None	No	Next of kin	Father may not devise more than ¼ of his estate, real and personal, to an illegitimate child, if he has a wife or legitimate children	All property rights upheld
					May make a will
$5,000; 160 acres rural; 1 acre urban	Must show intent	No	Next of kin	Inherits from and transmits to mother; transmits to mother's kin	All property rights upheld
For life of survivor, with descent to children				If father acknowledged child, child inherits from and transmits to father	May make a will
$1,000; for life of widow, with descent to children	None	No	Next of kin	Inherits from and transmits to mother; transmits to children of mother if she is deceased; if none, transmits to mother's kin	All rights to real property upheld; personalty cannot be used to pay husband's antenuptial debts
					May make a will of real property

			Spouse's Share If There Is No Will and							
	(1) Children		(2) No children, but parents		(3) No children, no parents, but other heirs		(4) Spouse takes all		(5) Spouse's share if he/she disregards will	
	Real	Personal	Real	Personal	Real	Personal	Real	Personal	Real	Personal
Common law states										
Utah										
Wife	⅓ for life as dower; ⅓ of residue in fee simple if > 1 child; ½ if 1 child *h*	⅓ if > 1 child; ½ if 1 child	⅓ for life as dower; ½ of residue in fee simple	½	Same		No siblings		No provision	
Husband	⅓ if 1 child; ½ if 1 child		½	½	Same		Same as wife		No provision	
Vermont										
Wife	⅓ for life of lands owned at death	⅓	⅓ real for life; or $2,000 + ½ the residue of entire estate in fee		Same		No next of kin		⅓ for life	⅓
Husband	All for life if children of the marriage	No provision	All for life, or $2,000 + ½ the residue of entire estate in fee		Same		Same as wife		All for life if issue of the marriage; ⅓ for life if no issue	Nothing if children of the marriage; ⅓ if no children
Virginia										
Wife	⅓ for life	⅓	⅓ for life	½	Same		No next of kin		Intestate share	
Husband	All for life if children of the marriage	All	Nothing	All	Same		Same as wife		All for life if children of the marriage	No provision

(6) Homestead exemption	(7) Barriers to disinherit- ing children	(8) Spouse's kin in succession	(9) Escheat when no	(10) Illegitimate child's rights[a]	(11) Married women's testamentary capacity
$1,000 + $500 if wife and $250 for each child or other dependent family member	Must show intent	Yes	Next of kin	Inherits from and transmits to mother; transmits to mother's kin	All property rights upheld
				Edmunds-Tucker law of 1877 made it impossible for a child to inherit from intestate father	May make a will
$500; for life of widow and minority of children	Must show intent	No	Next of kin	Inherits from and transmits to mother; transmits to mother's kin	All rights to personalty upheld; May control rents and profits of realty May make a will
$2,000; for widowhood, minority of children	None	Yes	Next of kin	Inherits from and transmits to mother and her kin	All property rights upheld May make a will

	Spouse's Share If There Is No Will and									
	(1) Children		(2) No children, but parents		(3) No children, no parents, but other heirs		(4) Spouse takes all		(5) Spouse's share if he/she disregards will	
	Real	Personal	Real	Personal	Real	Personal	Real	Personal	Real	Personal
Common law states										
West Virginia										
Wife	⅓ for life	⅓	⅓ for life	All	Same		No next of kin		⅓ for life	⅓ if children; ½ if none
Husband	All for life	⅓	All for life	All	Same		Same as wife		All for life	⅓ if children; ½ if none
Wisconsin										
Wife	⅓ for life	Child's share	All	All	Same		No children		⅓ for life	⅓
Husband	All for life if children by the marriage	No provision	Same as wife		Same		Same as wife		No provision	
Wyoming										
Wife	½	½	$10,000 + ¾		Same		Siblings and their issue		Intestate share	
Husband	Same as wife		Same as wife		Same		Same as wife		Same as wife	

(6) Homestead exemption	(7) Barriers to disinherit- ing children	(8) Spouse's kin in succession	(9) Escheat when no	(10) Illegitimate child's rights [a]	(11) Married women's testamentary capacity
$1,000; for life of the survivor, minority of children	None	Yes	Next of kin	Inherits from and transmits to mother	All property rights upheld
					May make a will
Dwelling house and 40 acres rural; ¼ acre urban; for widowhood, with descent to children	Must show intent	No	Next of kin	Inherits from and transmits to mother; transmits to mother's kin	All property rights upheld
				If father acknowledged child in writing, child inherits from father	May make a will
$1,500; 160 acres rural; for life of survivor and minority of children	None	No	Grand-parents and issue	Inherits from and transmits ½ to mother, ½ to children of mother; if no children, all to mother; if no mother, to mother's kin	All property rights upheld
					May make a will

	Spouse's Share If There Is No Will and								
	(1) Children		(2) No children, but parents		(3) No children, no parents, but other heirs		(4) Spouse takes all		(5) Spouse's share if he/she disregards will	
	Real	Personal	Real	Personal	Real	Personal	Real	Personal	Real	Personal
Community property states[j]										
Arizona										
Wife	½ community; ⅓ separate		All community; ½ separate	All community; all separate	All		No parents		Intestate share of community; none of separate	
Husband	Same as wife		Same as wife		All		Same as wife		Same as wife	
California										
Wife	½ community; ⅓ separate if > 1 child; ½ separate if 1 child		½ community; ½ separate		Same		Siblings and their grandchildren		½ community; none of separate	
Husband	All community; ⅓ separate if > 1 child; ½ if 1 child		All community; ½ separate		Same		All of community in all cases; same as wife for separate		All community; none of separate	
Idaho										
Wife	½ community; ⅓ separate if > 1 child; ½ separate if 1 child		½ community; ½ separate		Same		No siblings		½ community; none of separate	
Husband	All community; ⅓ separate if > 1 child; ½ separate if 1 child		All community; ½ separate		Same		Same as wife		All community; none of separate	

(6) Homestead exemption	(7) Barriers to disinheriting children	(8) Spouse's kin in succession	(9) Escheat when no	(10) Illegitimate child's rights[a]	(11) Married women's testamentary capacity
$4,000	None	No	Lineal ancestors and issue	Inherits from and transmits to mother and her kin	All property rights upheld except to wages
			Same as wife		May make a will of separate property
Dwelling house and land on which it is situated	Must show intent or equal advancement	Yes, for community; no, for separate	Next of kin	Inherits from and transmits to mother; transmits to mother's kin	All property rights upheld except to wages
				If father acknowledged child, child inherits from father	May make a will of separate property
$5,000	Must show intent	Yes, for community; no, for separate	Next of kin	Inherits from and transmits to mother; transmits to mother's kin	Separate property is that acquired before or after marriage by gift, bequest, devise, or descent
				If father acknowledged child, child inherits from father	May make a will of separate property

	Spouse's Share If There Is No Will and								
	(1) Children		(2) No children, but parents		(3) No children, no parents, but other heirs		(4) Spouse takes all		(5) Spouse's share if he/she disregards will	
	Real	Personal	Real	Personal	Real	Personal	Real	Personal	Real	Personal
Community property states[j]										
Louisiana										
Wife	½ community; none of separate		Same		Same		Next of kin		No provision	
Husband	Same as wife		Same		Same		Same as wife		Same as wife	
Nevada										
Wife	½ community; ⅓ separate if > 1 child; ½ separate if 1 child		All community; ½ separate		Same		No next of kin		½ community; no provision on separate	
Husband	All community; ⅓ separate if > 1 child; ½ separate if 1 child		Same as wife		Same		Same as wife		All community; no provision on separate	

(6) Homestead exemption	(7) Barriers to disinherit- ing children	(8) Spouse's kin in succession	(9) Escheat when no	(10) Illegitimate child's rights[a]	(11) Married women's testamentary capacity
$2,000; 160 acres	Must show 1 of 10 reasons[j]	No	Next of kin or natural child	If mother acknowledged child and if she had no legitimate child, child inherits from mother; if she had legitimate child, the illegitimate child receives only "a moderate alimony."	Spouses may choose to have no partnership; then wife has all prop- erty rights; or she may hold, but not manage, separate property
				If father acknowledged child and left no kin or wife, child inherits from father; transmits to par- ent who acknowledged child	May make a will
$5,000; descends to le- gitimate children only	Must show intent	No	Next of kin	Inherits from and trans- mits to mother; trans- mits to mother's kin	Separate property is that acquired before or after marriage by gift, bequest, devise, or descent
				If father acknowledged child, child inherits from father	May make a will of sep- arate property

| | Spouse's Share If There Is No Will and | | | | | | | | | |
| | (1) Children | | (2) No children, but parents | | (3) No children, no parents, but other heirs | | (4) Spouse takes all | | (5) Spouse's share if he/she disregards will | |
	Real	Personal	Real	Personal	Real	Personal	Real	Personal	Real	Personal
Community property states[j]										
New Mexico										
Wife	½ community; ¼ separate		All		Same		No children		½ community; none of separate	
Husband	Same as wife		Same as wife		Same		Same as wife		Same as wife	
Texas										
Wife	½ community; ⅓ separate life	½ community; ⅓ separate	All community; ½ separate	All community; all separate	Same		No siblings or their descendants		No provision	
Husband	Same as wife		Same as wife		Same		Same as wife		Same as wife	
Washington										
Wife	½ community; ⅓ separate if > 1 child; ½ separate if 1 child	½ community; ½ separate	All community; ½ separate	All community; all separate	Same		No siblings		½ community; none of separate	
Husband	Same as wife		Same as wife		Same		Same as wife		Same as wife	

(6) Homestead exemption	(7) **Barriers to disinherit- ing children**	(8) **Spouse's kin in succession**	(9) **Escheat when no**	(10) **Illegitimate child's rights**[a]	(11) **Married women's testamentary capacity**
$1,000; for minority of sons and until marriage of daughters	None	Yes	Lineal ancestors and issue	Inherits from and transmits to mother; transmits to mother's kin	All property rights upheld
				If father acknowledged child, and child acknowledged father, child inherits from and transmits to father, if father had no legitimate child	May make a will
200 acres rural; lot or lots to $5,000 urban, without reference to value of the improvements; home lived in	None	No	Siblings and descendants	Inherits from and transmits to mother; inherits personalty from mother's kin	Separate property is that acquired before or after marriage by gift, devise, or descent
					May make a will of separate property
$1,000	None	No	Next of kin	Inherits from and transmits to mother; transmits to mother's kin	All property rights upheld
				If father acknowledged child, child inherits from and transmits to father	May make a will

[a] Transmission when illegitimate child died intestate, without surviving spouse or issue.

[b] If no qualifier, widow's share is in lands owned during marriage.

[c] If no qualifier, assume an absolute estate.

[d] If no qualifier, homestead is an absolute estate.

[e] If parents married, child became legitimate and inherited as such.

[f] "No children" means no children or their lineal descendants.

[g] Does not include children born after the making of a will or posthumous children, who inherited as though parent died intestate.

*h*This dual provision for widows in Utah resulted from the overlapping jurisdiction of the territorial assembly, which provided for the widow's fee simple share, and the U.S. Congress, which provided for the widow's life estate. In *Ane Kundsen, Respondent,* v. *Julius Hannberg and Others* (1892), the Utah Supreme Court allowed a widow the benefit of both statutes (see 8 Utah 203).

*i*Community property states' shares in the table pertain to the half belonging to the decedent. The spouse automatically received the other half.

*j*In Louisiana, a parent could disinherit a child for one (or more) of ten reasons: if child raised hand or actually struck parent; if child was cruel to parent or guilty of a crime or grievous injury; if child attempted to kill parent; if child accused parent of a capital crime, except in high treason; if child refused sustenance for parent, and could afford it; if child neglected to care for insane parent; if child refused to ransom parent in captivity; if child used act of violence or coercion to prevent parent from making a will; if child refused to become security for parent to get parent out of prison, having the means; if minor child married without consent.

Inheritance Laws 1982

	Spouse's Share If There Is No Will and					
	(1) Children by earlier marriage[a]		(2) Children by present marriage[b]		(3) No children but parents[c]	(4) No children, no parents, but other heirs[d]
	1+	1	1+	1		
Common law states						Common law states
Alabama	½		$50,000 and ½ balance		$100,000 plus ½ balance	All
Alaska	⅓	½	All		All	All
Arkansas	Same as column 2		Realty ⅓ life; personalty ⅓		All if married 3+	All if married 3+
Colorado	½		$25,000 and ½		All	All
Connecticut	½		$50,000 and ½		$50,000 and ¾	All
Delaware	½ personalty, all realty life		$50,000 and ½ personalty and ½ realty life		$50,000 and ½ personalty, and ½ realty life	All
Florida	½		$20,000 and ½		All	All
Georgia	Same as column 2		⅓ or child's share, whichever larger		All	All
Hawaii	Same as column 2		½		½	All
Illinois	Same as column 2		½		All	All

(5) Spouse's share if he/she elects to disregard existing will[e]	(6) Spouse's homestead exemption[f]	(7) Barriers to disinheriting children[g]	(8) Spouse's kin in line of succession[h]	(9) Escheat when no[i]
⅓	$6,000 or 160 acres	None	No	Grandparents or their issue
⅓	$27,000	None	No	Grandparents or their issue
Realty ⅓ life, personalty ⅓	$2,500 or 80 acres rural; ¼ acre city	Must show intent	Yes	Deceased spouse's heirs
½	$20,000	None	No	Lineal ancestors and issue
⅓ life	None	None	No	Next of kin
⅓ or $20,000, which-ever is less	None	None	No	Next of kin
30%	Whole home, no limitation	None	Yes	Kin of deceased spouse
Nothing	$5,000	None	No	Next of kin
⅓	$5,000	None	No	Great grandparents and their issue
½ if no child; ⅓ if child	$7,500	None	No	Next of kin

	(1) Children by earlier marriage[a]		(2) Children by present marriage[b]		(3) No children but parents[c]	(4) No children, no parents, but other heirs[d]
Spouse's Share If There Is No Will and						
	1+	1	1+	1		
Common law states						Common law states
Indiana	⅓		⅓	½	¾	All
Iowa	Same as column 2		$25,000 or ⅓		$50,000 and ½	$50,000 and ½
Kansas	Same as column 2		½		All	All
Kentucky	Same as column 2		Personalty ½, realty ⅓ life		Personalty ½, realty ⅓ life	Personalty ½, realty ⅓ life
Maine	½		$50,000 and ½		$50,000 and ½	All
Maryland	Same as column 2		$15,000 and ½		$15,000 and ½	All
Massachusetts	Same as column 2		½		$50,000 and ½	$50,000 and ½
Michigan	½		$60,000 and ½		$60,000 and ½	All
Minnesota	⅓		½		All	All
Mississippi	Same as column 2		Child's share		All	All

(5) Spouse's share if he/she elects to disregard existing will*e*	(6) Spouse's homestead exemption*f*	(7) Barriers to disinheriting children*g*	(8) Spouse's kin in line of succession*h*	(9) Escheat when no*i*
⅓; ⅓ personalty and ⅓ realty life if children by earlier marriage	None	None	No	Next of kin
⅓	Whole homestead for life in lieu of inherited share of realty	None	Yes	Surviving spouse or issue
½	Whole homestead; minority of children	None	No	Kin, 6 degrees removed
Personalty ½; realty ⅓ life	$5,000	None	Yes	Deceased spouse's kin
⅓	$6,500	None	No	Grandparents and their issue
⅓ if child; ½ if none	None	Must show intent	Yes	Stepchildren and issue
⅓ if child; $25,000 and ½ if no issue or kin	$40,000	None	No	Next of kin
½ intestate share	Whole homestead for widowhood or minority of children or $13,500	None	No	Grandparents and their issue
½ if no child or 1 child; ⅓ if 1+ children	Whole homestead in life	None	No	Next of kin
Child's share up to ½ less value of own estate	$30,000	None	No	Next of kin

	Spouse's Share If There Is No Will and						
	(1) Children by earlier marriage[a]		**(2)** Children by present marriage[b]		**(3)** No children but parents[c]	**(4)** No children, no parents, but other heirs[d]
	1+	1	1+	1		
Common law states						
Missouri	Same as column 2		$20,000 and ½		$20,000 and ½	All
Montana	⅓	½	All		All	All
Nebraska	⅓	½	All		All	All
New Hampshire	½		$50,000 and ½		$50,000 and ½	All
New Jersey	½		$50,000 and ½		$10,000 and ½	All
New York	$4,000 and ⅓		$4,000 and ⅓	$4,000 and ½	$25,000 and ½	All
North Carolina	Same as column 2		$15,000 and ⅓	$15,000 and ½	$25,000 and ½	All
North Dakota	⅓	½	All		All	All
Ohio	$10,000 and ⅓		$30,000 and ½		All	All
Oklahoma	Child's share		⅓	½	½	½
Oregon	Same as column 2		½		All	All
Pennsylvania	½		$30,000 and ½		$30,000 and ½	All

(5) Spouse's share if he/she elects to disregard existing will*e*	(6) Spouse's homestead exemption*f*	(7) Barriers to disinheriting children*g*	(8) Spouse's kin in line of succession*h*	(9) Escheat when no*i*
½ if no child; ⅓ if child	$7,500	None	No	Kin 9 degrees removed
⅓	$40,000	None	No	Next of kin
⅓	$6,500	None	No	Grandparents and their issue
⅓ if child; $20,000 and ½ if heirs; $10,000 plus $2,000 per years married if no heirs	$5,000	Must show intent	No	Siblings and grandchildren
Intestate share	None	None	No	Next of kin
Intestate share up to ½	$10,000	None	No	Great grandparents and issue
Intestate share up to ½	Whole homestead for widowhood or minority of children	None	No	Next of kin
⅓	$80,000	None	No	Grandparents and issue
Intestate share	$1,000	None	Yes	Stepchildren or their lineal descendants
Intestate share	Homestead for widow or minority of children	Must show intent	No	Next of kin
¼	$15,000	None	No	Grandparents and issue
⅓	None	None	No	Grandparents and issue

	Spouse's Share If There Is No Will and					
	(1) Children by earlier marriage[a]		**(2)** Children by present marriage[b]		**(3)** No children but parents[c]	**(4)** No children, no parents, but other heirs[d]
	1+	**1**	**1+**	**1**		
Common law states						**Common law states**
Rhode Island	Same as column 2		Personality ½; realty all life		$50,000 and ½ personalty and all realty life	$50,000 and ½ personalty and all realty life
South Carolina	Same as column 2		⅓	½	½	½
South Dakota	Same as column 2		⅓	½	$100,000 and ½	$100,000 and ½
Tennessee	Same as column 2		⅓	½	All	All
Utah	⅓	½	All		All	All
Vermont	⅓		Personalty ⅓; realty ⅓	½	$25,000 and ½	$25,000 and ½
Virginia	Same as column 2		Personalty ⅓; realty all		All	All
West Virginia	Same as column 2		Personalty none; realty ⅓ life		All	All
Wisconsin	Same as column 2		$25,000 and ⅓	$25,000 and ½	All	All
Wyoming	Same as column 2		½		$20,000 and ¾	$20,000 and ¾

(5) Spouse's share if he/she elects to disregard existing will[e]	(6) Spouse's homestead exemption[f]	(7) Barriers to disinheriting children[g]	(8) Spouse's kin in line of succession[h]	(9) Escheat when no[i]
Realty ⅓ life plus $25,000 if no issue	None	None	No	Great-grandparents and issue
Realty ⅓ life or realty ⅙	$1,000	None	Yes	Stepchildren
$100,000 or ⅓, whichever greater	$30,000	None	No	Next of kin
⅓	$5,000	Child must be 15	No	Grandparents and issue
⅓	$5,000	None	No	Grandparents and issuc
Realty ⅓ if children; realty ½ if no children	$30,000	None	No	Next of kin
⅓ if children; ½ if none	$5,000	Must show intent	No	Next of kin
Realty ⅓ life	$5,000	None	Yes	Kin of deceased spouse
⅓ minus other property from estate	$25,000	Must show intent	No	Next of kin
½; ¼ if children by previous marriage	$6,000	None	No	Grandparents and issue

	Spouse's Share If There Is No Will and				
	(1) Children by earlier marriage[a]		**(2)** Children by present marriage[b]		**(3)** No children but parents[c]	**(4)** No children, no parents, but other heirs[d]
	1+	**1**	**1+**	**1**		
Community property states[j]						
Arizona	Separate, ½; community, none		All		All	All
California	Same as column 2		Separate, ⅓ Community, all	Separate, ½	Separate, ½; community, all	All
Idaho	Separate, ½; community, all		Separate, $50,000 and ½; community, all		Separate, $50,000 and ½; community, all	All
Louisiana	Community, ½ for widowhood; separate, none		Community, ½ for widowhood; separate, none		Community, all; separate, none	Community, all; separate, none
Nevada	Same as column 2		Separate, ⅓ Community, all	Separate, ½	Separate, ½; community, all	Separate, ½; community, all
New Mexico	Same as column 2		Separate, ¼; community, all		All	All
Texas	Same as column 2		Separate personalty, ⅓; separate realty, ⅓ life; community, ½		Separate, ½; community, all	Separate, ½; community, all
Washington	Same as column 2		Separate, ½; community, all		Separate, ¾; community, all	Separate, ¾; community, all

(5) Spouse's share if he/she elects to disregard existing will[e]	(6) Spouse's homestead exemption[f]	(7) Barriers to disinheriting children[g]	(8) Spouse's kin in line of succession[h]	(9) Escheat when no[i]
⅓	$50,000	Must show intent	No	Grandparents and their issue
None	None	Must show intent or show advancement already given	Yes	Next of kin
⅓	$25,000	None	No	Grandparents and issue
None	$15,000	Must show child attempted to kill parent or married against wishes	No	Next of kin
None	$75,000	None	No	Sibling's grandchildren
None	$20,000	None	No	Next of kin
None	$10,000 and 200 acres	None	No	Next of kin
None	$20,000	None	No	Grandparents and issue

[a]Decedent's issue are not all by surviving spouse. Given the divorce rate, this situation is likely to increase over time. As with column 2, some states make distinctions regarding personal property and realty and number of children. Personal property is almost always given absolutely, but realty is sometimes given for life or widowhood only. Some community property states also make a distinction between the separate property of a decedent and the decedent's half of community property.

[b]Decedent's children are all by surviving spouse. See other comments in note *a*.

[c]Generally, parents are the next in line for succession if there are no lineal descendants. For other comments, see note *a*.

[d]The other heirs are usually brothers and sisters and their descendants, although in some states it goes further before spouse inherits everything. In Arkansas, a couple must be married for over three years for the spouse to receive all of the estate. For other comments, see note *a*.

[e]In most states, spouses have some recourse if a decedent tries in a will to disinherit them completely. Some of the distinctions discussed in note *a* also apply here.

[f]In many states the spouse receives the use of the home for life or during the minority of children even though the spouse might not actually own it. Usually there is a dollar or acre amount to this exemption. Only in a few states is it large enough to cover the entire cost of an average house or farm. Nevertheless homestead exemptions are the most substantial of the special allowances given spouses.

[g]In most states, simply omitting a child from the will effectively disinherits him or her. In other states, it is necessary to indicate that omission is not an oversight but that there was a clear intention to disinherit. Only in Louisiana are there serious barriers to disinheritance. In that state, a child must have attempted parricide or married against the wishes of the parent.

[h]In some states, the children, kin, or heirs of a predeceased spouse are eligible to inherit if there are no blood kin.

[i]Some states limit how far the kinship tie can take inheritance in intestacy cases in order to eliminate the laughing heir. The most usual limitation is grandparents and their issue. Others go back further to great-grandparents and their issue. The majority of states, however, do not stop until all next of kin or lineal ancestors and issue are run through, and a few even tack on affinal relations.

[j]Community property states' shares in the table pertain to the half belonging to decedent. The spouse automatically receives the other half.

Notes

INTRODUCTION

1. Laurence J. Kotlikoff and Lawrence H. Summers, "The Role of Intergenerational Transfers in Aggregate Capital Accumulation," *Journal of Political Economy* 89 (1981): 706–732 suggest the 80 percent figure by tallying up bequests, life insurance, college support payments, and trusts. This paper is part of a debate over whether capital accumulation occurs primarily through life-cycle savings or intergenerational transfers. The authors' professed concerns, in other words, are over capital formation, not inequality; but their findings have some unintended implications for the rationality of the system.
2. For example, Lester Thurow, *Generating Inequality* (New York: Basic Books, 1975); John Brittain, *Inheritance and the Inequality of Material Wealth* (Washington: Brookings Institution, 1978); and M. P. Allen, "The Perpetuation of Wealth: A Simulation Model," in *Modeling the Distribution and Intergenerational Transmission of Wealth,* ed. James D. Smith (Chicago: University of Chicago Press, 1980), 139–158.
3. Economists in main-line journals seldom express the argument as crudely as it is set down here, but it is the underlying logic behind Kotlikoff and Summers, "Intergenerational Transfers," and most of the other work done on the link between savings and bequests, some of which is discussed in detail in Chapter Six. Shriller versions come out in the publications of the American Enterprise Institute by authors such as George Wagner. For the long intellectual history behind the debate on inheritance, see Ronald Chester, *Inheritance Wealth, and Society* (Bloomington: Indiana University Press, 1982).
4. This is something of a recasting of the way capitalistic forms are often analyzed. We believe, however, that it provides more systematic criteria for determining basic changes in people's relationship to property.
5. On the nature of late eighteenth- and nineteenth-century corporations and the type of economic endeavors that found the form most congenial, see Winifred B. Rothenberg, "The Emergence of a Capital Market in Rural Massachusetts, 1730–1838," *Journal of Economic History* 45 (1985), 781–808; Peter Dobkin Hall, *The Organization of American Culture 1700–1900: Private Institutions, Elites and the Origins of American Nationality* (New York: New York University Press, 1982), chaps. 1–6; Ronald E. Seavoy, *The Origins of the American Business Corporation, 1784–1855* (Westport, Conn.: Greenwood, 1982); J. Van Fenstermaker,

The Development of American Commercial Banking: 1782–1837, Kent State University Bureau of Economic and Business Research Publication no. 5 (1965); Naomi R. Lamoreaux, "Banks, Kinship, and Economic Development: The New England Case," *Journal of Economic History* 46 (1986), 647–668; Hendrik Hartog, *Public Property and Private Power: The Corporation of the City of New York in American Law, 1730–1870* (Chapel Hill: University of North Carolina Press, 1983), passim; Philip Scranton, *Proprietary Capitalism: The Textile Manufacture at Philadelphia 1800–1885* (Cambridge: Cambridge University Press, 1983), 188–189, 310–311; Paul F. Paskoff, *Industrial Evolution: Organization, Structure, and Growth of the Pennsylvania Iron Industry* (Baltimore: Johns Hopkins University Press, 1983), passim; and Viviana A. Rotman Zelizer, *Morals and Markets: The Development of Life Insurance in the United States* (New York: Columbia University Press, 1979), chaps. 1–3. There has been some debate over the degree to which corporations, even in the twentieth century, are still controlled by family interest. Adolf A. Berle Jr. and Gardiner C. Means, *The Modern Corporation and Private Property* (New York: Macmillan, 1932) and, later, Robert Larner, *Management Control and the Large Corporation* (New York: Dunellen, 1970) present the standard view that a professional managerial class has more or less taken over in most business sectors. Philip H. Burch, Jr., in *The Managerial Revolution Reassessed: Family Control in America's Large Corporations* (Lexington, Mass.: Heath, 1972), contends that the family is still paramount. What he actually seems to have proven, however, is that there continue to be a number of extremely wealthy families with financial assets spread over corporate America rather than that they exert dynastic control over most large enterprises.

6. On the mediating activities of the nineteenth-century American government in areas that touched the family and its property, see Michael Grossberg, *Governing the Hearth: Law and the Family in Nineteenth Century America* (Chapel Hill: University of North Carolina Press, 1985); Morton Keller, *Affairs of State: Public Life in the Late Nineteenth Century 1880– 1900* (Cambridge, Mass.: Harvard University Press, 1977); and Stephen Skowronek, *Building a New American State: The Expansion of National Administrative Capacities, 1877–1920* (New York: Cambridge University Press, 1982). On the growth of the state and its welfare functions during the late nineteenth and early twentieth century, see Ann Shola Orloff and Theda Skocpol, "Why Not Equal Protection? Explaining the Politics of Public Social Spending in Britain, 1900–1911, and the United States, 1880–1920," *American Sociological Review* 49 (1984): 726–750; and Michael Mann, "The Changing Finances and Functions of the State 1815–1914," draft of a chapter from *The Sources of Social Power,* vol. 2, *A History of Power since the Industrial Revolution* (Cambridge University Press forthcoming). On current developments, see Mary Ann Glendon, *The New Family and the New Property* (Scarborough: Butterworth, 1981).

7. For a recent summary by a historian of the theories for the fertility decline, see Robert V. Wells, *Uncle Sam's Family: Issues in and Perspectives on American Demographic History* (Albany: State University of New York Press, 1985), chap. 2.
8. Daniel Scott Smith, "Family Limitation, Sexual Control, and Domestic Feminism in Victorian America," *Feminist Studies* 1 (1973): 40–57.
9. Mary Beth Norton, *Liberty's Daughters: The Revolutionary Experience of American Women 1750–1800* (Boston: Little, Brown, 1980); Nancy Cott, *The Bonds of Womanhood: Women's Sphere in New England 1780–1835* (New Haven, Conn.: Yale University Press, 1977); Carl Degler, *At Odds: Women and the Family in America from the Revolution to the Present* (New York: Oxford University Press, 1980); Robert V. Wells, "Demographic Change and the Life Cycle of American Families," *Journal of Interdisciplinary History* 2 (1971): 273–82; and Daniel Blake Smith, *Inside the Great House: Planter Family Life in Eighteenth-Century Chesapeake Society* (Ithaca, N.Y.: Cornell University Press, 1980) all see signs of the domestic ideology beginning in the later eighteenth century. On its evolution in the nineteenth century, see D. S. Smith, "Family Limitation"; Degler, *At Odds;* and Mary P. Ryan, *Cradle of the Middle Class: The Family in Oneida County, New York, 1790–1865* (New York: Cambridge University Press, 1981). Two studies of divorce at the end of nineteenth and the early twentieth century—Elaine T. May, *Great Expectations: Marriage and Divorce in Post-Victorian America* (Chicago: University of Chicago Press, 1980) and Robert L. Griswold, *Family and Divorce in California, 1850–1890* (Albany: State University of New York Press, 1982)—suggest the roots of its demise.
10. Two pioneering studies on these acts done in the 1960s were never published: the 1960 Radcliffe dissertation of Elizabeth Bowles Warbasse, "The Changing Legal Rights of Married Women, 1800–1861," and Kay Ellen Thurman's LL.M. dissertation, "The Married Woman's Property Acts" (University of Wisconsin Law School, 1966). Recent work has had a happier fate; see Suzanne Dee Lebsock, "Radical Reconstruction and the Property Rights of Southern Women," *Journal of Southern History* 43 (1977): 195–216; Peggy A. Rabkin, *Fathers to Daughters: The Legal Foundations of Female Emancipation* (Westport, Conn.: Greenwood, 1980); Norma Basch, *In the Eyes of the Law: Women, Marriage, and Property in Nineteenth-Century New York* (Ithaca, N.Y.: Cornell University Press, 1982); Linda E. Speth, "The Married Women's Property Acts, 1839–1865: Reform, Reaction, or Revolution?" in *Women and the Law: A Social Historical Perspective,* ed. D. Kelly Weisberg (Cambridge, Mass.: Schenkman, 1982), 2:69–92; Richard Chused, "Married Women's Property Law: 1800–1850," *Georgetown Law Journal* 71 (1983): 1359–1425; and idem, "The Oregon Donation Act of 1850 and Nineteenth Century Federal Married Women's Property Law," *Law and History Review* 2 (1984): 44–78. See also Kathleen Elizabeth Lazarou, "Concealed under Petticoats: Married Women's Property and the Law of

Texas, 1840–1913" (Ph.D. diss., Rice University, 1980) and Leo Kanowitz, *Women and the Law: The Unfinished Revolution* (Albuquerque:
University of New Mexico Press, 1969) for what happened in states
adopting the community property system. On legal scholars' and law
schools' earlier neglect of marital property reform, see John D. Johnston,
Jr., "Sex and Property: The Common Law Tradition, the Law School
Curriculum, and Developments toward Equality," *New York University
Law Review* 47 (1972): 1033–1092. Legal history has also been slow to
provide an economic context for family and probate law; on this point,
see Michael Grossberg, "Republican Domestic Relations: Three Themes
in the Creation of an American Family Law, 1790–1870," paper delivered at the 1984 summer seminar of the Legal History Program, University of Wisconsin, Madison.

11. Community property law became the system of those states influenced
    heavily by either the Spanish or the French and of those located in the
    West: Arizona, California, Idaho, Louisiana, Nevada, New Mexico,
    Texas, and Washington. Wisconsin converted to the community property
    system in a series of bitterly fought-over acts in the mid-1980s.

12. Richard B. Morris, *Studies in the History of American Law* (1930; re-
    print, New York: Octagon, 1958); Julius Goebel, Jr., "King's Law and
    Local Custom in Seventeenth-Century New England," *Columbia Law Re-
    view* 31 (1931): 416–448; and David Grayson Allen, *In English Ways:
    The Movement of Societies and the Transferral of English Local Law and
    Custom to Massachusetts Bay in the Seventeenth Century* (Chapel Hill:
    University of North Carolina Press, 1981).

13. George L. Haskins, "The Beginnings of Partible Inheritance in the Ameri-
    can Colonies," *Yale Law Journal* 51 (1942): 1280–1315; C. Ray Keim,
    "Primogeniture and Entail in Colonial Virginia," *William and Mary
    Quarterly,* 3d ser., 25 (1968): 545–586; and Stanley N. Katz, "Republi-
    canism and the Law of Inheritance in the American Revolutionary Era,"
    Michigan Law Review 76 (1977): 1–29.

14. In the first studies of early American communities by social historians
    such as John Demos, Philip Greven, and Kenneth Lockridge, the focus
    was completely on the transmission of land from father to sons. In recent
    studies, daughters, wives, and personalty are given more attention; see
    Toby Ditz, "Daughters and Inherited Property in Rural Connecticut,
    1750–1820," paper delivered at the 1982 meeting of the Social Science
    History Association, Bloomington Ind.; Lois Green Carr and Lorena S.
    Walsh, "Woman's Role in the Eighteenth Century Chesapeake," paper de-
    livered at the Conference on Women in Early America, Williamsburg,
    Vir., November 5–7, 1981; Lois Green Carr, "Inheritance in the Colo-
    nial Chesapeake" (Paper delivered at the U.S. Capitol Historical Society,
    Washington, D.C., March 1985); Gail S. Terry, "Women, Property, and
    Authority in Colonial Baltimore County, Maryland: Evidence from the
    Probate Records, 1660–1759" (Paper presented at a conference, The Co-

lonial Experience: The Eighteenth-Century Chesapeake, Peabody Library, Baltimore, September 12–14, 1984); Jean Butenhoff Lee, "From Parent to Child: Descent of Land and Slaves in Charles County, Maryland 1732–1783," ibid.; James Deen, "Patterns of Testation: Four Tidewater Counties in Colonial Virginia," *American Journal of Legal History,* 16 (1972): 154–176; D. B. Smith, *Inside the Great House,* 245; Linda E. Speth, "More Than Her 'Thirds': Wives and Widows in Colonial Virginia," in *Women, Family, and Community in Colonial America: Two Perspectives* (New York: Haworth, 1983), 16; Joan R. Gunderson and Gwen Victor Gampel, "Married Women's Legal Status in Eighteenth-Century New York and Virginia," *William and Mary Quarterly,* 3d ser., 39 (1982): 122–123; and John E. Crowley, "Family Relations and Inheritance in Early South Carolina," *Histoire sociale/Social History* 17 (1984): 47–50.

15. Richard R. Powell and Charles Looker, "Decedents' Estates: Illumination from Probate and Tax Records," *Columbia Law Review* 30 (1930): 919–953; Allison Dunham, "The Method, Process, and Frequency of Wealth Transmission at Death," *University of Chicago Law Review* 30 (1963): 241–285; Lawrence Friedman, "Patterns of Testation in the Nineteenth-Century: A Study of Essex County (N.J.) Wills," *American Journal of Legal History* 8 (1964): 34–53; Olin L. Browder, Jr., "Recent Patterns of Testate Succession in the United States and England," *Michigan Law Review* 67 (1969): 1303–1360; William H. Newell, "The Wealth of Testators and Its Distribution: Butler County, Ohio, 1803–1835," in *Distribution and Intergenerational Transmission of Wealth,* ed. J. D. Smith, 95–138.

16. See James D. Tarver, "Intra-Family Farm Succession Practices," *Rural Sociology* 17 (1952): 266–271; Sonya Salamon, "Ethnic Differences in Farm Family Land Transfers," ibid. 45 (1980): 290–308; Mark W. Friedberger, "The Farm Family and the Inheritance Process: Evidence from the Corn Belt 1870–1950," *Agricultural History* 57 (1983): 1–13; Kathleen Neils Conzen, "Peasant Pioneers," in *The Countryside Transformation* eds. Steven Hahn and Jonathan Prude (Chapel Hill: University of North Carolina Press, 1985), 259–292.

17. Marylynn Salmon, *Women and the Law of Property in Early America* (Chapel Hill: University of North Carolina Press, 1986) and Linda K. Kerber, *Women of the Republic* (Chapel Hill: University of North Carolina Press, 1980).

18. Norton, *Liberty's Daughters* and Salmon, *Women and the Law of Property.*

19. Salmon, *Women and the Law of Property,* Chused, "Married Women's Property Law."

20. See Terry, "Women, Property, and Authority"; Carr and Walsh, "Women's Role"; Deen, "Patterns of Testation"; D. B. Smith, *Inside the Great*

House; Gunderson and Gampel, "Married Women's Legal Status"; and Crowley, "Family Relations and Inheritance."

21. Richard A. Easterlin, "Population Change and Farm Settlement in the Northern United States," *Journal of Economic History* 36 (1976): 45–75; and idem, "Factors in the Decline of Farm Family Fertility in the United States," *Journal of American History* 63 (1976): 600–612. For a recent critique of this theory and a discussion of alternatives, see William A. Sundstrom and Paul A. David, "Old-Age Security Motives, Labor Markets, and Farm Family Fertility in Antebellum America," *Working Paper, Stanford Project on the History of Fertility Control* 17 (1985).

22. Marvin Sussman, Judith N. Cates, and David T. Smith, *The Family and Inheritance* (New York: Russell Sage, 1970), 1.

23. Friedman, "Patterns of Testation" and Browder, "Recent Patterns of Testate Succession."

24. Paul L. Menchik, "The Importance of Material Inheritance: The Financial Link between Generations," in *Distribution and Intergenerational Transmission of Wealth,* ed. J. D. Smith, 159–186.

25. Robin Barlow, Harvey E. Brazer, and James N. Morgan, *Economic Behavior of the Affluent* (Washington: Brookings Institution, 1966), 97–112; Carl S. Shoup, *Federal Estate and Gift Taxes* (Washington: Brookings Institution, 1966) 17; and Thurow, *Generating Inequality,* 140–141.

26. Powell and Looker, "Decedents' Estates"; Dunham, "Wealth Transmission"; Cates, and Smith, eds., *Family and Inheritance,* 89; and Rita J. Simon, William Rau, and Mary Louise Fellows "Public versus Statutory Choice of Heirs: A Study of Public Attitudes about Property Distribution at Death," *Social Forces* 58 (1980): 1265–1267.

27. Jeffrey P. Rosenfeld, *The Legacy of Aging: Inheritance and Disinheritance in Social Perspective* (Norwood, N.J.: Ablex, 1979).

28. Dunham, "Wealth Transmission at Death" and Carr, "Inheritance in the Colonial Chesapeake."

29. Among the most interesting theories are those advanced by Lee J. Alston and Morton Owen Shapiro, "Inheritance Laws across Colonies: Causes and Consequences," *Journal of Economic History* 44 (1984): 277–287; and Bernard Farber, *Family and Kinship in Modern Society* (Glenview, Ill.: Scott Foresman, 1973).

30. James Lemon, *The Best Poor Man's Country: A Geographical Study of Early Southeastern Pennsylvania* (New York: Norton, 1972), 199; and Diane Lindstrom, *Economic Development in the Philadelphia Region 1810–1850* (New York: Columbia University Press, 1978), 132, 142, 169. On the early history of the county, see W. W. H. Davis, *The History of Bucks County, Pennsylvania* (Doylestown, Pa.: Democratic Book and Job Office Printing, 1876).

31. Barry Norman Checkoway, "Suburbanization and Community: Growth and Planning in Postwar Lower Bucks County, Pennsylvania" (Ph.D. diss., University of Pennsylvania, 1977).

32. Robert Fogelson, *The Fragmented Metropolis: Los Angeles, 1850–1930* (Cambridge, Mass.: Harvard University Press, 1967); Richard Griswold del Castillo, *The Los Angeles Barrio, 1850–1890* (Berkeley and Los Angeles: University of California Press, 1979); Barbara Laslett, "Social Change and the Family: Los Angeles, California, 1850–1870," *American Sociological Review* 42 (1977): 268–291; and Frederic Cople Jaher, *The Urban Establishment: Upper Strata in Boston, New York, Charleston, Chicago, and Los Angeles* (Urbana: University of Illinois Press, 1982), 577–709. According to Fogelson, *Fragmented Metropolis,* 80–82, the nonwhite population of Los Angeles in 1900 was 4.3 percent of the total population, and the white foreign-born segment (which included those born in Mexico) was 18 percent. In the will sample for Los Angeles County, however, only 9.2 percent could be identified as foreign born or having a Hispanic or Asian surname. In the 1980 will sample, only 4.6 percent could be so identified.

33. For previous use of the terms *family capitalism* and *corporate capitalism,* see Rosabeth Moss Kanter, "Families, Family Processes, and Economic Life: Toward Systematic Analysis of Social Historical Research," *American Journal of Sociology,* 84 suppl. (1978): 5317–5318.

34. Daniel Scott Smith, "Underregistration and Bias in Probate Records: An Analysis of Data from Eighteenth-Century Hingham Massachusetts, *William and Mary Quarterly,* 3d ser., 32 (1973): 104, finds that between 1726 and 1786 in the community he studied, 54 percent of men and 7 percent of women went through probate, and 36 percent of men and 6 percent of women left wills. Kenneth A. Lockridge, *Literacy in Colonial New England* (New York: Norton, 1974), 128, believes 25–35 percent of men left wills in New England and 5 percent of women. Alice Hanson Jones, *Wealth of a Nation to Be* (New York: Columbia University Press, 1980), 45, bases her estimates on wealthholders rather than decedents, so she excludes married women, the poor, and all unfree people. Her estimates of the proportion going through probate for Pennsylvania-Delaware-New Jersey (64 percent) and the South (68 percent) therefore are high. To make them comparable to our figures and those of Smith and Lockridge, the Middle Colonies estimate should be halved and that for the South divided by three. Chused, "Married Women's Property Law," 1373–1374, studying an urban area—Baltimore County, Maryland—in the first half of the nineteenth century, found that male testation rates actually declined while female rates held steady. The evidence he presents, however, suggests that female probate participation did not really begin to *increase* substantially until after 1850.

35. Every study of probate records with which we are familiar found that the mean wealth of testates exceeded that of intestates.

36. The growth of joint tenancy has no doubt reduced the proportion of realty showing up at probate time, but it still cannot account for all the variation over time. In the 1890s joint tenancy was not a factor at all (see Chapter

Eight), and in the 1979 sample, half of all property held under joint tenancy was counted in the estate for tax purposes and, therefore, was included by us in the figures.
37. In their study of New York County and Kings County probate records in the period 1914–1929, Powell and Looker, "Decedents' Estates," 941, found that realty constituted 33 percent of probated wealth. "Recent Patterns of Testate Succession," Browder, 1319–1321, calculates that in Washtenaw County, Michigan in 1963 it was 25 percent; and in Cuyahoga County, Ohio, in 1964, Sussman, Cates, and Smith, *Family and Inheritance,* 74, cite it at 32 percent.

CHAPTER ONE: ENGLISH INHERITANCE LAW AND ITS TRANSFER TO THE COLONIES

1. Their land was held in knight service tenure. In exchange, the monarch demanded a certain number of men for military duty or the money to pay for the men. Feudal tenures of this type were formally abolished in the later seventeenth century.
2. William Blackstone, *Commentaries on the Laws of England* (Oxford: Clarendon, 1765–1769), 2:492–493; Charles Carlton, *The Court of Orphans* (Leicester: Leicester University Press, 1974).
3. Michael Sheehan, *The Will in Medieval England* (Toronto: Pontifical Institute of Mediaeval Studies and Texts, 1963), 303–306; and Elizabeth Levett, *Studies in Manorial History* (1938; reprint, New York: Barnes and Noble, 1963), 209.
4. The standard work on manorial customs in postconquest England is still George C. Homans, *English Villagers of the Thirteenth Century* (Cambridge, Mass.: Harvard University Press, 1941). Homans (109–219) associated impartible inheritance with grain cultivation in common fields, whereas partible inheritance, he felt, tended to be in woodland areas having less fertile land. Animal husbandry, therefore, played a larger role and holdings were individual farms. See Richard M. Smith, ed., *Land, Kinship and Life-Cycle* (Cambridge: Cambridge University Press, 1984), 14–16, 39–46, 135–139, for a summary of modifications to Homans' theories by scholars in the last few years. This newer scholarship stresses the role of demographic factors and land sales in altering inheritance customs. Margaret Spufford's book *Contrasting Communities: English Villagers in the Sixteenth and Seventeenth Centuries* (Cambridge: Cambridge University Press, 1974) provides a detailed analysis of how impartible and partible inheritance worked in the early modern period.
5. On the emergence of the patrilineage in the medieval period and the way it was superimposed on the older bilateral system of kinship, see David Herlihy, *Medieval Households* (Cambridge: Cambridge University Press, 1985), 82–83.

6. J. Z. Titow, "Some Differences between Manors and Their Effects on the Condition of the Peasant in the Thirteenth Century," *Agricultural History Review* 10 (1962): 6–11; and R. M. Smith, "Some Thoughts on 'Hereditary' and 'Proprietary' Rights in Land under Customary Law in Thirteenth and Early Fourteenth Century England," *Law and History Review* 1 (1983): 124–126. S. F. C. Milsom, "Inheritance by Women in the Twelfth and Early Thirteenth Centuries," in *On the Laws and Customs of England,* ed. Morris S. Arnold et al. (Chapel Hill: University of North Carolina Press, 1981), 60–89, reports that action of a widow to recover dower was one of the most frequent suits recorded in the early plea rolls. In contrast, curtesy was seldom a legal issue because the husband of a deceased heiress already had possession of the land. Power of the lord in the remarriage of widows is discussed in Eleanor Searle, "Seigneurial Control of Women's Marriage: The Antecedents and Function of Merchet in England," *Past and Present* 82 (1979): 3–43.

7. Levett, *Studies in Manorial History;* Homans, *English Villagers;* J. Ambrose Raftis, *Tenure and Mobility: Studies in the Social History of the Medieval English Village* (Toronto: Pontifical Institute of Medieval Studies and Texts, 1964); Cicely Howell, "Peasant Inheritance Customs in the Midlands, 1280–1700," in *Family and Inheritance: Rural Society in Western Europe 1200–1800,* ed. Jack Goody, Joan Thirsk, and E. P. Thompson (Cambridge: Cambridge University Press, 1976), 112–155.

8. R. M. Smith, " 'Hereditary' and 'Proprietary' Rights," 122.

9. Robert Gottfried, *Epidemic Disease in Fifteenth Century England: The Medical Response and the Demographic Consequences* (New Brunswick, N.J.: Rutgers University Press, 1978), 23–32.

10. *Statutes of the Realm,* 22–23 Car. 2, c. 10; 1 Jas. 2, c. 17.

11. Henrie Swinburne, *A Briefe Treatise of Testaments and Last Willes* (London, 1590), 105–106.

12. Blackstone, *Commentaries* 2:492–493. On the York practice see Ronald Marchant, *The Church under the Law: Justice, Administration, and Discipline in the Diocese of York 1560–1640* (Cambridge: Cambridge University Press, 1969), 91. Henry Horwitz, "Testamentary Practice, Family Strategies, and the Last Phases of the Custom of London, 1660–1725," *Law and History Review* 2 (1984): 223–239, finds that a majority of testators had been ignoring the custom or circumventing it in the sixty-five years before its demise.

13. On the corporate lineage in Europe see Andrejs Plakans, *Kinship in the Past: An Anthropology of European Family Life 1500–1900* (Oxford: Blackwell Publisher, 1984), 196–216; Bertha Phillpotts, *Kindred and Clan in the Middle Ages and After* (Cambridge: Cambridge University Press, 1913); and Lorraine Lancaster, "Kinship in Anglo-Saxon Society," *British Journal of Sociology* 9 (1958): 230–250. For a culture that had a clear corporate lineage system, see Hilary J. Beattie, *Land and Lineage in China* (Cambridge: Cambridge University Press, 1979) and Fu-mei Chang Chen and Ramon H. Myers, "Customary Law and the Economic

Growth of China during the Ch'ing Period," *Ch'ing-Shih wen-t'i* 10 (1978): 4–28. We owe these last two references to David Buck.

14. Charles Donahue, Jr., "What Causes Fundamental Legal Ideas? Marital Property in England and France in the Thirteenth Century," *Michigan Law Review* 78 (1979): 59–88. We owe this reference to James Brundage.

15. Howell, "Peasant Inheritance Customs," 140–141; and Keith Wrightson and David Levine, *Poverty and Piety in an English Village: Terling, 1525–1700* (New York: Academic, 1979), 92–93, find that among testators with children, legacies to collateral heirs are rare. Richard T. Vann, "Wills and the Family in an English Town: Banbury, 1500–1800," *Journal of Family History* 4 (1979): 346–367, charts the drop over the early modern period in bequests beyond the immediate family. Most researchers do agree that male testators felt a strong obligation to see that their widows were not left destitute. What some have also drawn attention to, however, is the degree to which propertied husbands increasingly pared down and restricted the inheritance rights of widows to aid their lineal heirs. See Barbara J. Todd, "The Remarrying Widow: A Stereotype Reconsidered," in *Women in English Society 1500–1800*, ed. Mary Prior (London: Methuen, 1985), 54–92; and Carole Shammas, "Women and Inheritance in the Age of Family Capitalism," paper delivered at the American Historical Association meeting in Washington, December 1980. Todd also identified a manor that, in the 1580s, changed a widow's free bench from "life" to "during widowhood only." B. A. Holderness, "Widows in Preindustrial Society: An Essay upon Their Economic Functions," in *Land, Kinship, and Life-Cycle*, ed. Richard M. Smith (Cambridge: Cambridge University Press, 1984), 433, also sees free bench deteriorating over the course of the early modern period. On the other hand, Nesta Evans, "Inheritance, Women, Religion, and Education in Early Modern Society as Revealed by Wills," in *Probate Records and the Local Community*, ed. Philip Riden (Gloucester, Mass.: Sutton; distributed by Humanities, Atlantic Highlands, N.J., 1985), 53–70, finds that in a group of medieval and early modern Suffolk communities, the pre-1540 testators were less likely to give widows absolute rights in realty than were those willing property in the subsequent one hundred years. There is of course the question of how much land was transferred in wills before the 1540 Statute of Wills formally allowed the practice. Evans also found, however, that the naming of wives as executrixes increased in the early modern period. On the decline in remarriage, see Roger Schofield and Edward A. Wrigley, "Remarriage Intervals and the Effect of Marriage Order on Fertility," *Marriage and Remarriage in Populations of the Past* ed. J. Dupaquier et al. (New York: Academic, 1981), 212.

16. Lawrence Stone, *Family, Sex, and Marriage in England 1500–1800* (New York: Harper and Row, 1977), 156.

17. Eileen Spring, "Law and the Theory of the Affective Family," *Albion* 16 (1984): 1–20, discusses the strict family settlement and marriage settlements at length and reinterprets some of the evidence on the subject con-

tained in Stone, *Family, Sex, and Marriage* and Lloyd Bonfield, *Marriage Settlements 1601–1740* (Cambridge: Cambridge University Press, 1983). As Bonfield points out demographic factors—specifically the death of the father before the majority of the son—could break the life tenancy cycle. Still, compared to most inheritance systems, that of the English aristocracy was a model of dynastic efficiency.

18. Lawrence Stone and Jeanne C. Fawtier Stone, *An Open Elite? England 1540–1880* (Oxford: Clarendon, 1984). Daniel Scott Smith draws an interesting contrast between the ability of the British aristocracy to maintain their position and that of the South Carolinian elite to perpetuate their kin in office generation after generation during the eighteenth and first half of the nineteenth century. The British were much more successful, and Smith attributes this partly to legal differences, including those related to inheritance. See his "Genealogy, Geography, and the Genesis of Social Structure: Household and Kinship in Early America" paper delivered at the conference Anglo-American Social History, Williamsburg, Vir., September 5–7, 1985, 37.

19. The various permutations of the law can be followed in Gail McKnight Beckman, comp., *The Statutes at Large of Pennsylvania in the Time of WIlliam Penn 1680 to 1700* (New York: Vantage, 1976); and James T. Mitchell and Henry Flanders, eds., *The Statutes at Large of Pennsylvania from 1682 to 1801,* 16 vols. (Harrisburg, 1896–1915), vols. 1–6. Before 1700 these laws applied to Delaware as well.

20. This includes the 1641 Massachusetts law, a 1647 act in Rhode Island, and a Connecticut statute published in 1656; see Thomas G. Barnes, ed., *The Book of the General Lawes and Libertyes* (San Marino: Huntington Library, 1975), 53–54; John D. Cushing, ed., *The Earliest Acts and Laws of the Colony of Rhode Island and Providence Plantations 1647–1719* (Wilmington, Del.: Glazier, 1977), 43; and idem, ed., *The Earliest Laws of the New Haven and Connecticut Colonies* (Wilmington, Del.: Glazier, 1977), 54–56.

21. Duke's Laws, "Roslyn Copy," Hempstead 1665, Microfilm Collection of Early State Records, B.1 New York, reel 1; "Concession and Agreements of the Proprietors, Freeholders, and Inhabitants of the Province of West New Jersey in America, 1676," ibid., B.1 New Jersey, reel 1. The printed laws of New Jersey in the period with which we are concerned have nothing on descent or distribution; see John D. Cushing, ed., *The Earliest Printed Laws of New Jersey 1703–1722* (Wilmington, Del.: Glazier, 1978).

22. Beckman, *Pennsylvania in the Time of William Penn,* 31.

23. Herbert Johnson, *Essays on New York Colonial Legal History* (Westport, Conn.: Greenwood, 1981), 201; see also David Evan Narrett, "Patterns of Inheritance in Colonial New York City 1664–1775: A Study in the History of the Family" (Ph.D. diss., Cornell University, 1981), 132–133, 221–222.

24. George L. Haskins, "The Beginnings of Partible Inheritance in the Ameri-

can Colonies," in *Essays in the History of Early American Law,* ed. David H. Flaherty (Chapel Hill: University of North Carolina Press, 1969), 204–244, reviews the possible reasons for the double share. On the debate in England and Europe on primogeniture, see Joan Thirsk, "The European Debate on Customs of Inheritance 1500–1700," in *Family and Inheritance,* ed. Jack Goody, Joan Thirsk, and E. P. Thompson (Cambridge: Cambridge University Press, 1976), 177–191.

25. This quotation was taken from the New Hampshire intestacy law passed in 1718, *Acts and Laws* (Boston, 1726), 102; but with minor differences all New England colonies had similar prefaces to their inheritance statutes.

26. Cushing, *New Haven and Connecticut,* 56.

27. Charles McLean Andrews, "The Influence of Colonial Conditions as Illustrated in the Connecticut Intestacy Law," in *History of Early American Law,* ed. Flaherty, 336–366.

28. C. Ray Keim, "Primogeniture and Entail in Colonial Virginia," *William and Mary Quarterly,* 3d ser., 25 (1968): 546.

29. The Massachusetts law dates back to 1647, but it was apparently changed in 1649 so that dower was only in lands; see John D. Cushing, ed., *The Laws and Liberties of Massachusetts 1641–1691* (Wilmington, Del.: Scholarly Resources, 1976), 1:23–24, 96. Connecticut dower in personalty ended in 1673; see Cushing, *New Haven and Connecticut,* 28–29, 95. In Pennsylvania and Delaware the act changing dower from both types of property to just realty was part of the 1706 law; see Mitchell and Flanders, *Statutes at Large of Pennsylvania,* 2:199–206.

30. Marylynn Salmon in Chapter Seven of her book *Women and the Law of Property in Early America* (Chapel Hill: University of North Carolina Press, 1986) has an extensive discussion of the dower law in the Chesapeake.

31. William Walter Hening, comp., *The Statutes at Large: Being a Collection of All the Laws of Virginia* (Philadelphia, 1823), 3:372.

32. Lorena S. Walsh, " 'Till Death Us Do Part' ": Marriage and Family in Seventeenth-Century Maryland," in *The Chesapeake in the Seventeenth Century,* ed. Thad W. Tate and David L. Ammerman (Chapel Hill: University of North Carolina Press, 1979), 126–152; and Darrett Rutman and Anita Rutman, " 'Now-Wives and Sons-in-Law': Parental Death in a Seventeenth-Century Virginia County," in *ibid.,* 153–182. The problems created by remarriages are reflected in the establishment of the Maryland Orphan's Court; see Lois Green Carr, "The Development of the Maryland Orphan's Court, 1654–1715," in *Law, Society, and Politics in Early Maryland,* ed. Aubrey C. Land, Lois Green Carr, and Edward C. Papenfuse (Baltimore: Johns Hopkins University Press, 1977).

33. John D. Cushing ed., *The Laws of the Province of Maryland* (Wilmington, Del.: Glazier, 1978), 155–56.

34. Salmon, *Women and the Law of Property,* devotes Chapters Five and Six to marriage settlements.

35. Blackstone, *Commentaries* 2:208–238.
36. *Statutes of the Realm,* 22–23 Car. 2, c. 10.
37. Blackstone, *Commentaries* 2:504–505, 515–516.
38. William Hand Browne, ed., *Proceedings and Acts of the General Assembly of Maryland 1638–1664* (Baltimore: Maryland Historical Society, 1883) 1:157; Dukes Laws, n.p.; and Beckman, comp., *The Statutes at Large of Pennsylvania in the Time of William Penn,* 224.
39. Mitchell and Flanders, eds., *Statutes at Large of Pennsylvania,* 12:556–566. We are indebted to Toby Ditz for pointing out an error in our interpretation of early American succession and escheat.
40. Massachusetts, *Acts and Laws of Her Majesties Province of the Massachusetts Bay* (Boston, 1714), 269; Hening, *Statutes at Large* 3:372.
41. A. G. Roeber, " 'We Hold These Truths . . .': German and Anglo-American Concepts of Property and Inheritance in the Eighteenth Century," copyrighted paper, 1985.

CHAPTER TWO: COLONIAL TESTAMENTARY PRACTICE AND FAMILY CAPITALISM

1. C. Ray Keim, "Primogeniture and Entail in Colonial Virginia," *William and Mary Quarterly,* 3d ser., 25 (1968): 545–586; Douglas Lamar Jones, *Village and Seaport: Migration and Society in Eighteenth Century Massachusetts* (Hanover, N.H.: University Press of New England, 1981), 97–102. The North-South convergence may account for the similarities in population growth rates found by Lee J. Alston and Morton Owen Schapiro, "Inheritance Laws across Colonies: Causes and Consequences," *Journal of Economic History* 44 (1984): 285–286, for primogeniture and multigeniture colonies. There has been an assumption that primogeniture depresses population growth because younger sons are forced to migrate. The theory ignores not only the way impartible and partible inheritance actually worked in colonial society but also the importance of personalty.
2. Given the shortage of specie and even paper money in the colonies, "cash" gifts probably materialized in the form of credits.
3. There were 350 testate estates that had information on gross personal wealth. The aggregate total of that wealth was 87,385 pounds Pennsylvania currency, of which 82,294 pounds belonged to 313 male testators, and 5,091 pounds came from the estates of 37 female willmakers. Mean wealth was 262.9 pounds and 137.6 pounds, respectively.
4. Obviously, fathers while living passed property to adult children. Evidence from wills and other sources, however, suggests that most kept legal control over the substance of their wealth until death. See John W. Adams and Alice Bee Kasakoff, "Migration and the Family in Colonial New England: The View from Genealogies," *Journal of Family History* 9

(1984): 30–31, on sons' postponement of migration until death of parents, a finding that implies postmortem distribution.

5. Land, and in some southern colonies, slaves, could be entailed, meaning that this property could never be sold but would have to descend to heirs of the body, or sometimes just male heirs of the body, forever. Life estates, which could pertain to any kind of property, could not be alienated by the heir but could be sold by whomever the testator named as the recipient after the death of the person receiving the life estate. The type of conditional fee of interest here is the one whereby an heir had to have a child in order to be granted the property forever instead of for life. Trusts were instruments that usually gave the income from some form of property to the heir for life or a term of years but put the actual control in someone else's (the trustee's) hands. Trusts—not well developed in Pennsylvania during the colonial period—could be of many types, but frequently the heir never received the principal (or corpus). It eventually passed to another heir, often a grandchild (the remainderman) named by the testator.

6. On the comparative insignificance of collateral kin in inheritance for another area of colonial America, see John E. Crowley, "The Importance of Kinship: Testamentary Evidence from South Carolina," *Journal of Interdisciplinary History* 16 (1986): 559–577.

7. Buying out other heirs, an option eldest sons had under the Pennsylvania intestacy law as well as through a provision of some wills, was seldom a one-shot affair accomplished immediately after the decease of a father. It usually took some years because the son lacked the capital to pay off everyone at once.

8. [Anonymous], *The Laws Respecting Women,* reprinted, with foreword by Shirley Raissi Bysiewicz (London, 1777; reprint, Dobbs Ferry, N.Y.: Oceana, 1974).

9. Married men were the main testators who used overseers; while they comprised two-thirds of the testators, they were 83 percent of those who appointed overseers. Lois Green Carr and Lorena S. Walsh, "The Planter's Wife: The Experience of White Women in Seventeenth-Century Maryland," *William and Mary Quarterly* 3d ser., 34 (1977): 542–571, find that nominating overseers began dying out as a practice in Maryland in the early eighteenth century. Their work is one of the few that mentions the role of the overseer in the colonies.

10. Evidence of land being divided among several sons and a consistently small percentage of testators giving land to daughters or a steady decline in the percentage of such legacies to daughters during the colonial period is found in Christopher M. Jedrey, *The World of John Cleaveland: Family and Community in Eighteenth-Century New England* (New York: Norton, 1979), 75; Toby Ditz, "Daughters and Inherited Property in Rural Connecticut, 1750–1820," paper delivered at the 1982 meeting of the Social Science History Association, Bloomington Ind.; Daniel Snydacker, "Kin-

ship and Community in Rural Pennsylvania, 1749–1820," *Journal of Interdisciplinary History,* 13 (1982): 46–52; Lois Green Carr and Lorena S. Walsh, "Woman's Role in the Eighteenth Century Chesapeake," paper delivered at the Conference on Women in Early America, Williamsburg, Vir., November 5–7, 1981; Lois Green Carr, "Inheritance in the Colonial Chesapeake," paper delivered at the U.S. Capitol Historical Society, Washington, D.C., March 28, 1985; Gail S. Terry, "Women, Property, and Authority in Colonial Baltimore County, Maryland: Evidence from the Probate Records, 1660–1759," paper presented at a conference, The Colonial Experience: The Eighteenth-Century Chesapeake, Peabody Library, Baltimore, September 1984; Jean Butenhoff Lee, "From Parent to Child: Descent of Land and Slaves in Charles County, Maryland 1732–1783," ibid.; James Deen, "Patterns of Testation: Four Tidewater Counties in Colonial Virginia," *American Journal of Legal History,* 16 (1972): 154–176; Daniel Blake Smith, *Inside the Great House: Planter Family Life in Eighteenth-Century Chesapeake Society* (Ithaca, N.Y.: Cornell University Press, 1980), 245; Linda E. Speth, "More Than Her 'Thirds': Wives and Widows in Colonial Virginia," in *Women, Family, and Community in Colonial America: Two Perspectives* (New York: Haworth, 1983), 16; Joan R. Gunderson and Gwen Victor Gampel, "Married Women's Legal Status in Eighteenth-Century New York and Virginia," *William and Mary Quarterly,* 3d ser., 39 (1982): 122–123; and John E. Crowley, "Family Relations and Inheritance in Early South Carolina," *Histoire sociale/Social History* 17 (1984): 47–50. Some of those whose studies continued past the Revolution found bequest patterns changing again, with less gender typing in gifts of property and more of a tendency toward equality. Terry, "Women, Property, and Authority," table 7, and Crowley, "Family Relations and Inheritance," 48, both present evidence that the total portions (personalty and realty) given daughters tended to be smaller than those awarded sons.

11. On the southern situation see Keim, "Primogeniture and Entail," 552–553, Deen, "Patterns of Testation," 170; Terry, "Women, Property, and Authority," table 4; and D. B. Smith, *Inside the Great House,* 244. On New England see John J. Waters, "Family, Inheritance, and Migration in Colonial New England: The Evidence from Guilford, Connecticut," *William and Mary Quarterly,* 3d ser., 29 (1982): 64–86; Linda Auwers, "Fathers, Sons, and Wealth in Colonial Windsor Connecticut," *Journal of Family History* 3 (1978): 144; and Daniel Scott Smith, "Population, Family, and Society in Hingham, Massachusetts 1635–1880" (Ph.D. diss., University of California at Berkeley, 1973), 160.

12. Snydacker, "Kinship and Community," 53.

13. Lee, "From Parent to Child," 16–17, 21, 23, 34; Crowley, "Family Relations and Inheritance," 50; Keim, "Primogeniture and Entail," 556–560.

14. Alston and Schapiro, "Inheritance Laws across Colonies," 281, draw attention to the different composition of wealth in the South.

15. Crowley, "Family Relations and Inheritance," 50.
16. David Evan Narrett, "Patterns of Inheritance in Colonial New York City 1664–1775: A Study in the History of the Family" (Ph.D. diss., Cornell University, 1981), chap. 4; Stephanie Grauman Wolf, *Urban Village: Population, Community, and Family Structure in Germantown Pennsylvania 1683–1800,* (Princeton, N.J.: Princeton University Press, 1976), 324–325; Suzanne Dee Lebsock, "Women and Economics in Virginia: Petersburg 1784–1820 (Ph.D. diss., University of Virginia, 1977), 84. Except for Narrett's study, the trend toward equal shares for daughters is either a late colonial or an early national trend.
17. Terry, "Women, Property, and Authority," 6; and Carr and Walsh, "Woman's Role," table 14 for Somerset County. Deen, D. B. Smith, Gunderson and Gampel, and Crowley all indicate southern husbands grew less generous to wives over the course of the colonial period. In the North the subject is less well studied. Narrett, Patterns of Inheritance, 141, sees a decline in New York City. Alexander Keyssar, "Widowhood in Eighteenth-Century Massachusetts: A Problem in the history of the Family," *Perspectives in American History* 8 (1974): 83–122, paints a grim picture of the dependency of widows, but the trend over time is unclear. The study by Kim Lacy Rogers, "Relicts of the New World: Conditions of Widowhood in Seventeenth Century New England," in *Woman's Being, Woman's Place: Female Identity and Vocation in American History,* ed. Mary Kelley (Boston: Hall, 1979), 26–52, stops at the end of the seventeenth century.
18. Such bequests are so numerous in New England and the Middle Colonies that historians have been able to use them for dietary estimates; see James T. Lemon, *The Best Poor Man's Country* (Baltimore: Johns Hopkins Press, 1976) and Sarah F. McMahon, "Provisions Laid Up for the Family': Toward a History of Diet in New England, 1650–1850," *Historical Methods* 14 (1981): 4–21. In the South, however, they are said to be rare: Terry, "Women, Property, and Authority," 27; and Crowley, "Family Relations and Inheritance," 50. Elizabeth A. Kessel in her study of Maryland German families, "The German Family in Frederick County, Maryland 1720–1790," paper presented at a conference, The Colonial Experience: The Eighteenth-Century Chesapeake, Peabody Library, Baltimore, September 1984, finds 16 percent of the wills contained lodging and food provisions for widows.
19. In Bucks County 22.6 percent of all married male testators specified provisions and lodging arrangements, while 29 percent of the affluent did so.
20. Work on colonial guardianship has been mainly confined to the Chesapeake, Gunderson and Gampel, "Married Women's Legal Status," 127–128, assert that almost none of the wills from New York or Virginia that they studied removed children from the guardianship of their mothers. Lois Green Carr, in work on Somerset County, Maryland, however, found increasing use of "outsiders" as guardians in the eighteenth century (per-

sonal communication, January 11, 1985). Carr examines the law of guardianship in Maryland in her article "The Development of the Maryland Orphan's Court, 1654–1715," in *Law, Society, and Politics in Early Maryland,* ed. Aubrey C. Land, Lois Green Carr, and Edward C. Papenfuse (Baltimore: Johns Hopkins University Press, 1977), 41–62. What Jean Butenhoff Lee, "The Social Order of a Revolutionary People: Charles County Maryland, 1733–86" (Ph.D. diss., University of Virginia, 1984, 136–140) has drawn attention to is the tendency of fathers and even widowers and widows to neglect naming anyone guardian. Suzanne Dee Lebsock, *The Free Women of Petersburg* (New York: Norton, 1984), 41, reports the same phenomenon occurring during the early national period in the Virginia town she studied.

21. In addition to the article by Alexander Keyssar, see Gary B. Nash, *The Urban Crucible: Social Change, Political Consciousness, and the Origins of the American Revolution* (Cambridge, Mass.: Harvard University Press, 1979); Susan Grigg, "Towards a Theory of Remarriage: Early Newburyport," *Journal of Interdisciplinary History* 8 (1977): 183–221; and Carole Shammas, "The Female Social Structure of Philadelphia in 1775," *Pennsylvania Magazine of History and Biography* 107 (1983): 69–83.

22. Carr, "Inheritance in the Colonial Chesapeake," table 7; and Terry, "Women, Property, and Authority," table 9.

CHAPTER THREE: TENSION IN THE SYSTEM

1. *The Laws of the Commonwealth of Massachusetts from November, 1780 . . . to February 28, 1807* (Boston, 1811), 1:111; New Hampshire, *Session Laws,* February 1789, 492; John D. Cushing, comp., *The First Laws of the State of Rhode Island* (Wilmington, Del.: Glazier, 1983), 2: 281–282.

2. Virgil Maxy, comp., *The Laws of Maryland* (Baltimore, 1811), 2:18; William Waller Hening, comp., *The Statutes at Large: Being a Collection of all the Laws of Virginia, from the First Session of the Legislature, to the Year 1819* (Richmond, Va., 1809–1823; reprint, Charlottesville, Va.: University Press of Virginia, 1969), 12:139; John D. Cushing, comp., *The First Laws of the State of South Carolina* (Wilmington, Del.: Glazier, 1981), pt. 1, 6–7.

3. On the relationship between legal reform and independence from England, see James W. Ely, Jr., "American Independence and the Law: A Study of Post-Revolutionary South Carolina Legislation," *Vanderbilt Law Review* 26 (1973): 939–971.

4. Thomas Cooper, ed., *The Statutes at Large of South Carolina* (hereafter cited as *South Carolina Statutes*) (Columbia, S.C., 1836–1839), 5:163.

5. Stanley N. Katz, "Republicanism and the Law of Inheritance in the American Revolutionary Era," *Michigan Law Review* 76 (1977–1978): 14.
6. Quoted in ibid., 17.
7. John D. Cushing, comp., *The First Laws of the State of Connecticut* (Wilmington, Del.: Glazier, 1982), 54; idem, comp., *The First Laws of the State of New Jersey* (Wilmington, Del.: Glazier, 1981), 125; North Carolina, *Session Laws,* April 1784, 32.
8. On the nature of the colonial land and capital market, see Winifred B. Rothenberg, "The Emergence of a Capital Market in Rural Massachusetts, 1730–1838," *Journal of Economic History* 45 (1985): 781–808.
9. See, for example, Bucks County Orphans Court Dockets, book 2 (1787–1801), 252, 261–262, 270 (1795) in the Bucks County Courthouse, Doylestown.
10. Bucks County Orphans Court Dockets, book 1 (1752–1765), book 2. In the earlier period, five younger sons and one daughter acquired their families' farms. For the years 1787–1801, seven younger sons and six daughters did so. Infrequently, an intestate had owned two or more parcels of land that could be allotted to various heirs. Unequal divisions of that nature occurred in five of the seventy-nine actions.
11. Cooper, *South Carolina Statutes,* 5:162; Hening, *Statutes at Large* 12:156–157; Maxy, *Laws of Maryland* 2:16; Charles Z. Lincoln, ed., *The Colonial Laws Of New York from the Year 1664 to the Revolution* (Albany: 1894), 1:9, 114; 5:616–617.
12. Cooper, *South Carolina Statutes* 5:164.
13. On the property rights of married women, see William Blackstone, *Commentaries on the Laws of England* (1765–1769), 1:430–432, 2:433–436; [Anonymous], *The Laws Respecting Women,* reprint ed. with a foreword by Shirley Raissi Bysiewicz (London, 1777; reprint, Dobbs Ferry, N.Y.: Oceana, 1974), 148–163; Tapping Reeve, *The Law of Baron and Feme, of Parent and Child, of Guardian and Ward, of Master and Servant, and of the Powers of Courts of Chancery* (New Haven, Conn., 1816), 1–8, 22–30, 60–63, 192–193; Zephaniah Swift, *A System of the Laws of the State of Connecticut: In Six Books* (New Haven, Conn., 1795–1796), 1:194–195; James Kent, *Commentaries on American Law* (New York, 1826–1830), 2:129–143.
14. Bucks County Orphans Court Dockets, book 2.
15. James T. Mitchell and Henry Flanders, comps., *The Statutes at Large of Pennsylvania from 1682 to 1801* (Philadelphia, 1896–1911).
16. Ibid., 341.
17. Beeson v. M'Nabb, 42 Pa. 106 (1833); see also Turner v. Hauser, 41 Pa. 420.
18. Gheen, Executor of Osborn v. Osborn, 17 Sergeant and Rawle 173 (1928).
19. Cooper, *South Carolina Statutes* 5:162. Cases establishing widows' rights to cash payments are Scott's Creditors v. Scott, 1 Bay's South Caro-

lina Reports 506 (1795); and Charlotte Heyward v. J. C. Cuthbert, Brevard's South Carolina Reports, pt. 2, 483 (1814).

20. John D. Cushing, comp., *The First Laws of the State of Georgia* (Wilmington, Del.: Glazier, 1981) pt. 1, 313.

21. In Pennsylvania, the rights of widows who renounced their husbands' wills continued to be governed by the common law rather than by statute. On the common law definition of dower, see Blackstone, *Commentaries* 2:129–139; *Laws Respecting Women,* 188–292; Reeve, *Baron and Feme,* 37–59.

22. Maxy, *Laws of Maryland* 2:490; Hening, *Statutes at Large* 12:145; North Carolina, *Session Laws,* April 1784, 34–35.

23. On the relationship between the value of slave property and widows' inheritance rights, see John E. Crowley, "Family Relations and Inheritance in Early South Carolina," *Histoire Sociale/Social History* 17 (1984): 35–57; and Marylynn Salmon, *Women and the Law of Property in Early America* (Chapel Hill: University of North Carolina Press, 1986), 147–156.

24. North Carolina, *Session Laws,* April 1784, 35.

25. The distinction between widows' shares of realty and personalty was not recognized by Linda K. Kerber, *Women of the Republic: Intellect and Ideology in Revolutionary America* (Chapel Hill: University of North Carolina Press, 1980), 146, in her discussion of a postrevolutionary decline in dower for North Carolina widows. This led her to exaggerate the loss.

26. Cushing, *State of Georgia,* pt. 1, 313–314.

27. Ibid., 313.

28. Cooper, *South Carolina Statutes* 5:162. On nineteenth-century developments, see the discussion in Chapter Four.

29. Hening, *Statutes at Large* 12:139.

30. Maxy, *Laws of Maryland* 2:485.

31. Ibid., 17; Hening, *Statutes at Large* 12:139.

32. Reeve, *Baron and Feme,* 274–275.

33. Pennsylvania, *Session Laws,* April 1855, 366.

34. Hening, *Statutes at Large* 12:139.

35. Ibid., 139–140; Maxy, *Laws of Maryland* 2:18.

36. Cushing, *State of South Carolina,* pt. 1, 6–7.

37. Reeve, *Baron and Feme,* 39, 52; Blackstone, *Commentaries* 2:130. Comparative law on this point is discussed in Salmon, *Women and the Law of Property,* 163–167.

38. Grace Scott v. Ezra Croasdale, 1 Yeates 75 (1791). The case is also reported in 2 Dallas 127.

39. Morris's Lessee v. Smith, 1 Yeates 243–244 (1792).

40. Pennsylvania, *Session Laws,* June 1887, 332.

41. Morton J. Horwitz, *The Transformation of American Law, 1780–1860* (Cambridge, Mass.: Harvard University Press, 1977), 56–58.

42. Salmon, *Women and the Law of Property,* 175–183.

43. Hastings v. Crunkleton, 3 Yeates 262 (1801).
44. Salmon, *Women and the Law of Property,* 16–37.
45. Lincoln, *Colonial Laws of New York* 5:202.
46. These words appeared in the South Carolina statute on private examinations (Cooper, *South Carolina Statutes* 5:302–303).
47. *Laws of the Commonwealth of Pennsylvania* (Philadelphia, 1810–1844), 1:307.
48. John M. Murrin, "Anglicizing an American Colony: The Transformation of Provincial Massachusetts" (Ph.D. diss., Yale University, 1966); and idem, "The Legal Transformation: The Bench and Bar of Eighteenth-Century Massachusetts," in Stanley N. Katz and John M. Murrin, eds., *Colonial America: Essays in Politics and Social Development* (New York: Knopf, 1983), 540–571.
49. Salmon, *Women and the Law of Property,* 32–37.
50. John D. Cushing, ed., *Massachusetts Province Laws, 1692–1699* (Wilmington, Del.: Glazier, 1978), 99; *Laws of the Commonwealth* 1:131; Theron Metcalf and Horace Mann, eds., *The Revised Statutes of the Commonwealth of Massachusetts* (Boston, 1836), 404.
51. Salmon, *Women and the Law of Property,* 102–103.
52. Rippon v. Dawding, Ambler 565 (1769); Walter White, Lessee of Earles Barnes v. Solomon Hart, 1 Yeates 221 (1793).
53. Marylynn Salmon, "Women and Property in South Carolina: The Evidence from Marriage Settlements, 1730–1830," *William and Mary Quarterly,* 3d ser., 39 (1982): 668–669.
54. The rise of the companionate ideal in American marriages is discussed in Mary Beth Norton, *Liberty's Daughters: The Revolutionary Experience of American Women, 1750–1800* (Boston: Little, Brown, 1980), especially in Chapter Eight.
55. Reeve, *Baron and Feme,* 165–166.
56. A comparison of the settlement terms of women remarrying and women marrying for the first time is included in Salmon, "Women and Property," 679–683.
57. On the rules respecting jointures, see Blackstone, *Commentaries* 2:137–139; *Laws Respecting Women,* 209–212; Reeve, *Baron and Feme,* 41–46.
58. Dinah Stone and John Stone, adm'rs of Elizabeth Stone (late Massey) unadministered by John Stone, deceased v. Charles Massey, 2 Yeates 363 (1798).
59. Ibid., 364–365.
60. Postell and wife and Smith and wife v. Executors of James Skirving, 1 Desaussure 158 (1789).
61. Helms v. Franciscus, 2 Bland 576 (1818).
62. Ibid.; Stephen Rogers et al. v. R. Curloss, Administrator of Bretton, Marlboro County Equity Decress, 30 (ca. 1825), South Carolina Department of History and Archives, Columbia; E. S. Kenny v. Udall and Kenny, 5 Johnson's Chancery Reports 464 (1821). Pennsylvania courts did not order the creation of separate estates for wives (see Jacob Yohe v.

William and John Barnet, Administrator of Henry Barnet, 1 Binney 358 [1808]; and Samuel Torbert and Beulah his Wife v. Jacob Twining and Thomas Story, 1 Yeates 432 [1795]).
63. Salmon, "Women and Property," 663.
64. Salmon, *Women and the Law of Property,* chap. 5.

CHAPTER FOUR: INHERITANCE LAW AND
THE RIGHTS OF WOMEN AND CHILDREN
IN THE NINETEENTH CENTURY

1. The four were California, Idaho, Nevada, and New Mexico. George McKay, *A Treatise on the Law of Community Property,* 2d ed. (Indianapolis: Bobbs-Merrill, 1925), 65, declared the rule that husbands, like wives, could only lay claim to one-half of community property upon the death of a spouse the most "glaring disadvantage of the system." "Its effect on a husband's business," he wrote, "may be disastrous." McKay applauded states that passed statutes giving all community property to surviving husbands and, thereby, denying testamentary rights over community property to wives.
2. The territories and their dates of admittance are California, 1850; Minnesota, 1858; Oregon, 1859; Kansas, 1861; Nevada, 1864; Nebraska, 1867; Colorado, 1876; North Dakota, 1889; South Dakota, 1889; Montana, 1889; Washington, 1889; Idaho, 1890; Wyoming, 1890; Utah, 1896; Oklahoma, 1907; New Mexico, 1912; Arizona, 1912; Alaska, 1959; and Hawaii, 1960: West Virginia entered in 1865, but it had been a part of Virginia, not a territory, and its inheritance laws were virtually identical to its parent state. It is not counted, therefore, among the post-1850 jurisdictions. Those states not admitted by 1890 nonetheless had territorial laws on inheritance, which appear in Appendix B. Bernard Farber, *Family and Kinship in Modern Society* (Glenview, Ill.: Scott, Foresman, 1973), 108–109, divides nineteenth-century state and territory jurisdictions east and west of the Mississippi in looking at inheritance laws and patterns of kinship. He, like many others who have studied the differences in family law, attributed them mainly to disparate ethnic and cultural traditions. Undoubtedly the introduction of the civil law by the Spanish and French colonial powers was a necessary precondition for the partial adoption of community property law by some of the states; it was hardly sufficient, however, because Anglos were firmly in control of most of the western state legislatures, and most of the law adopted was common law. A few states adopted the civil law but only in regard to family property. Louisiana is the exception that proves the rule; it was the only community property state before Texas's entry in 1845. It had a powerful ethnic minority and consequently founded its entire legal system on the civil code. With Texas and even more with the states enter-

ing from 1850 on, the debates on married women's property were what swung legislators over to acceptance of the community property system. On what happened in California, see Orrin K. McMurray, "The Beginnings of the Community Property System in California and the Adoption of the Common Law," *California Law Review* 3 (1915): 359–380. Other western states made different adjustments to the common law to take care of the problem.

3. Alaska and Hawaii, which had fairly traditional common law rules of inheritance, are further examples of the fact that an ethnically diverse population is of little importance if the ruling class is totally Anglo.

4. For a good example of the role the "woman question" played in the decision of some states to adopt the community property system, again see the account of the debate in California, McMurray, "Community Property System in California," 359–380.

5. Chester G. Vernier, *American Family Laws* (1935; reprint, Westport, Conn.: Greenwood, 1971), 3:629.

6. Norma Basch, *In the Eyes of the Law: Women, Marriage, and Property in Nineteenth-Century New York* (Ithaca, N.Y.: Cornell University Press, 1982), 113.

7. Elizabeth Bowles Warbasse, "The Changing Legal Rights of Married Women 1800–1861" (Ph.D. diss., Radcliffe College, 1960), was one of the first to point out the relationship between the financial crises of the 1830s and 1840s and the first married women's property legislation. Kathleen Elizabeth Lazarou, "Concealed under Petticoats: Married Women's Property and the Law of Texas 1840–1913" (Ph.D. diss., University of Texas, 1980), also stresses how the fears about women and children being left destitute led to passage of the acts. Peggy A. Rabkin, *Fathers to Daughters: The Legal Foundations of Female Emancipation* (Westport, Conn.: Greenwood, 1980), explores the role of the codification movement and the hostility toward what were believed to be the more feudal aspects of the English common law in the legislation. Richard H. Chused, "Married Women's Property Law: 1800–1850," *Georgetown Law Journal* 71 (1983): 1359–1425, and, especially, Basch, *Eyes of the Law,* chaps. 2–4, demonstrate the importance of the women's rights movement and its allies in the evolution of the laws.

8. Basch, *Eyes of the Law,* chap. 5, has some good examples of the opposition of common law defenders and self-appointed pro-family spokesmen toward married women's property acts.

9. See Louis Hartz, *Economic Policy and Democratic Thought, Pennsylvania, 1776–1860* (Cambridge, Mass.: Harvard University Press, 1948), chap. 2, on the situation in Pennsylvania. For the later period in the United States generally, see Stephen Skowronek, *Building a New American State: The Expansion of National Administrative Capacities, 1877–1920* (Cambridge: Cambridge University Press, 1982), chap. 5.

10. Isidor Loeb, *The Legal Property Relations of Married Parties* (New York: Columbia University Press, 1900), 138.

11. According to Warbasse, "Legal Rights of Married Women," 236, the

married women's property act passed the assembly as a rider to another bill. The act was entitled "A Supplement to an act entitled 'An Act relative to the Le Raysville Phalanx,' passed March Anno Domini one thousand eight hundred and forty-seven, and relative to obligors and obligees, to secure the right of married women, in relation to defalcation, and to extend the boundaries of the borough of Ligonier" (see *Laws of Pennsylvania*, April 11, 1848, 536).

12. "An Act securing to married women their separate earnings," Pennsylvania, *Session Laws*, April 3, 1872, 35.
13. Lawrence M. Friedman, "The Dynastic Trust," *Yale Law Journal* 73 (1964): 547–592. For a contemporary account of women's property law and trust law in Pennsylvania, see Clement M. Husbands, *The Law of Married Women in Pennsylvania* (Philadelphia: Johnson, 1878).
14. Nissely v. Heisey, 70 Pa. 420 (1875); Gutshall v. Goodyear, 107 Pa. 131 (1884).
15. Pennsylvania, *Session Laws*, March 29, 1832, 201.
16. Yohe v. Barnet, 1 Binney 358 (1808).
17. Ibid., 364–365.
18. Beyer v. Reesor, 5 Watts and Sergeant 502–503 (1843); Ferree v. Elliott, 8 Sergeant and Rawle 315.
19. Pennsylvania, *Session Laws*, March 29, 1832, 205.
20. "An Act for the Better Settling of Intestates' Estates," (1705–1706) and "An Act for Amending the Laws Relating to the Partition and Distribution of Intestates' Estates," (1748–1749) in James T. Mitchell and Henry Flanders, comps., *The Statutes at Large of Pennsylvania from 1682 to 1801* (Philadelphia, 1896–1911), 2:205, 5:63–64.
21. The common law offered much less protection for the matrilineage than did the civil law of Continental Europe. The mid-nineteenth-century concern, therefore, was something new. It seemed a sort of compromise by those who wanted to improve the lot of wives but could not advocate a shift from a lineal to a conjugal orientation in inheritance.
22. Pennsylvania, *Session Laws*, March 29, 1832, 205. The procedure was the same as that enforced in conveyances of realty. The woman had to testify that she acted of her own free will and not as a result of her husband's coercion. In *Gutshall v. Goodyear*, the supreme court upheld a husband's claim to his deceased wife's inheritance because she had relinquished it to him pursuant to the procedures outlined in the 1832 law (see 107 Pa. 123 [1884]).
23. The statute read, "A married woman may, under a power legally created for the purpose, dispose of her real or personal estate by will or appointment, in nature of a will, and that any married woman may, with the assent or license of her husband, dispose of her personal estate by will" (see *Laws of Pennsylvania*, April 8, 1833, 249). On the earlier equity and common law court rulings, see Marylynn Salmon, *Women and the Law of Property in Early America* (Chapel Hill: University of North Carolina Press, 1986), 15, 100–104, 112–113.
24. "An Act Relating to the Descent and Distribution of the Estates of Intes-

tates," *Laws of Pennsylvania*, April 8, 1833, 317, was the new law. The previous legislation was "An Act Directing the Descent of Intestates' Real Estate, and Distribution of their Personal Estates, and for Other Purposes Therein Mentioned," in Mitchell and Flanders, *Statutes at Large of Pennsylvania* 15: 84–85.

25. The state supreme court upheld this statute in 1870; see Gillan's Executors v. Dixon, 65 Pa. 395 (1870).

26. *Laws of Pennsylvania*, April 11, 1848, 536.

27. Ibid.

28. See, for example, Peck v. Ward, 18 Pa. 506.

29. Appeal of Lee, 16 A. 514 (1889).

30. *Laws of Pennsylvania*, April 27, 1855, 368.

31. Ibid., May 4, 1855, 430–431.

32. "An Act To Enable Mothers in Certain Cases to Appoint Testamentary Guardians," ibid., June 10, 1881, 96. Case law also developed that defined when a husband's behavior disqualified him from being able to elect against the will of his wife; see Appeal of Knox, 18A. 1021 (1890) and In re White's Estate, 41 A. 742 (1898).

33. "An Act To Amend Certain Defects of the Law for the More Just and Safe Transmission and Secure Enjoyment of Real and Personal Estate," *Laws of Pennsylvania*, April 27, 1855, 366–369. See decisions Appeal of Miller, 52 Pa. 113 (1866); Appeal of Johnson, 88 Pa. 346 (1879); Seitzinger's Estate, 32 A. 1097 (1895); Turner's Estate, 5 Dist. 36 (1896).

34. "An Act Relating to Certain Duties and Rights of Husband and Wife, and Parents and Children," *Laws of Pennsylvania*, May 4, 1855, 431–432. The failure to grant illegitimate children this right may go back to a concern expressed by Tapping Reeve, *The Law of Baron and Feme, of Parent and Child, of Guardian and Ward, of Master and Servant, and of the Powers of Courts of Chancery* (New Haven, Conn., 1816), 274–275, that they were a source of "domestic uneasiness." The uneasiness was presumably the fear that they might be heir to wealth that did not come from either their matrilineage or patrilineage.

35. Basch, *Eyes of the Law*, 114–122; Charles H. Dahlinger, "The Dawn of the Woman's Movement: An Account of the Origin and History of the Pennsylvania Married Woman's Property Law of 1848," *Western Historical Magazine* 1 (April 1918): 74–78.

36. *Laws of Pennsylvania*, April 11, 1848, 537.

37. Note, for example, the attitude expressed in Diver v. Diver, 56 Pa. 109–110 (1867). This is seen in the title of the statute as well as in judicial interpretations. According to the title, the act was designed "to secure the right of married women, in relation to defalcation" (see *Laws of Pennsylvania*, April 11, 1848, 536).

38. "An Act Relating to Certain Duties and Rights of Husband and Wife, and Parents and Children," *Laws of Pennsylvania*, May 4, 1855, 430.

39. "An Act Securing to Married Women Their Separate Earnings," Pennsylvania, *Session Laws*, April 3, 1872, 35.

40. *Laws of Pennsylvania,* May 4, 1855, 430.
41. In re Seltzer's Estate, 42 A. 290 (1899); see also Appeal of Lee, 16 A. 514 (1889).
42. Cases discussing instances when widows were forced to rely on heirs or purchasers for payment of their shares include Beeson v. McNabb, 42 Pa. 106 (1833); Turner v. Hauser, 41 Pa. 420 (1833); McCall's Appeal, 56 Pa. 363 (1867); Gheen V. Osborn, 17 Sargeant and Rawle 171 (1828).
43. Whereas with personalty the widow received one-half if there were no children, one-third if there were, widowers received all a wife's separate personalty if there were no children, one-half if one child, one-third if two children, one-fourth if three, and so on.
45. Commonwealth v. Stauffer, 10 Pa. 354–355 (1849). For other judgments on cases involving realty given for widowhood only, see Cornell et ux. v. Lovett's Executor, 35 Pa. 103–106 (1860); Hotz's Estate, 38 Pa. 423–424 (1861); Appeal of McGuire 11 A. 72 (1887); In re Bruch's Estate, 39 A. 814 (1898); In re Holbrook's Estate 62 A. 368 (1905); and Huber v. Hamilton 60 A. 789 (1905). The courts refused, however, to enforce restraints on remarriage when the legacy was in personalty.
45. McCurdy and Stevenson v. Canning, 64 Pa. 39 (1870).
46. Diver v. Diver, 56 Pa. 109–110 (1867). Other cases demonstrating judicial support of the right to hold as tenants of the entirety include Auman v. Auman, 21 Pa. 343 (1853); Stuckey v. Keefe's Executors, 26 Pa. 399 (1856); Bates v. Seely, 46 Pa. 249 (1863); Gillan's Executors v. Dixon et al., 65 Pa. 398 (1870); In re Bramberry's Estate, 27 A. 407 (1893); and Dexter v. Billings, 1 A. 184 (1885).
47. In the 1790s only three New England states had "intent" laws. By 1890 the twenty jurisdictions were in all parts of the United States. See Chapter Three and Appendix B.
48. The intestacy laws of only ten out of fifty jurisdictions in the 1890s gave the entire estate to the spouse when no children survived.

CHAPTER FIVE: TESTAMENTARY BEHAVIOR IN THE 1790s AND 1890s

1. On the changing nature of corporations see Peter Dobkin Hall, *The Organization of American Culture, 1700–1900* (New York, New York University Press, 1982), chaps. 2–6; and Hendrik Hartog, *Public Property and Private Power: The Corporation of the City of New York* (Chapel Hill: University of North Carolina Press, 1983).
2. Table I.4 breaks down the composition of probated wealth into realty, tangible, and intangible personalty. The great increase in the nineteenth century cannot be attributed solely to the fact that there were more elderly testators in the 1890s sample because, when only testators with all adult children are considered, there is still a gap of comparable size. In the

1790s intangible wealth made up 24.6 percent of total wealth for testators with all adult children, and in the 1890s it was 62.7 percent of total wealth for that subgroup.

3. On the land availability thesis see Richard A. Easterlin, "Population Change and Farm Settlement in the Northern United States," *Journal of Economic History* 36 (1976): 45–75. Put in its simplest terms, the causal problem is, did fathers (and mothers?) curtail fertility during the child-bearing years knowing the approximate number of children for whom they would be able to provide, or did they adjust their inheritance strategies to the number of children with which they ended up, or did they do both?

4. Lawrence M. Friedman, "Patterns of Testation in the Nineteenth Century: A Study of Essex County (New Jersey) Wills," *American Journal of Legal History* 8 (1964): 47, shows that throughout the nineteenth century in the area he studied, charitable gifts were not common either. Fewer than 10 percent of all testators made such bequests.

5. Mark W. Friedberger, "Handing Down the Home Place: Farm Inheritance Strategies in Iowa 1870–1945," *Annals of Iowa* 47 (1984): 518–536.

6. In an inheritance study of York County, Pennsylvania, that goes up to 1820, Daniel Snydacker, "Kinship and Community in Rural Pennsylvania, 1749–1820," *Journal of Interdisciplinary History* 13 (1982), 47, finds that one-third of the testators with farms liquidated their holdings. Toby Ditz reports in her work on a group of Connecticut towns, "Daughters and Inherited Property in Rural Connecticut, 1750–1820" (Paper delivered at the 1982 Social Science History Association Meeting, Bloomington, Ind.), a tendency in the early nineteenth century for testators in what she identifies as the most commercialized community to be less concerned about viable farms and to hand out parcels that would most certainly have had to be converted into cash by heirs.

7. Originally we thought it would be interesting to split the 1791–1801 sample into pre–April 1794 and post–April 1794, the latter being the period after the intestacy law removed the eldest son's right to a double share. We found, however, that the nature of the discrimination among sons, daughters, and wives was such that even though the intestacy standard changed, the assignment of portions to the "more," "same," or "less" than intestacy categories did not alter very much. Testators both before and after the 1794 law usually gave sons as a group more than their cumulative double and single shares. As far as the "same as intestacy" category is concerned, generally testators with only one child fell into this group or post-1794 testators who gave equal portions to all children. The double portion to eldest sons was almost never seen either before or after 1794. Thus it did not seem worth splitting the sample in the tables.

8. In the 1890s, 18 percent of testators gave realty as part of their legacy to male heirs, while 19 percent gave land to female heirs.

9. For this argument see Gloria Main, "Rural Widows in Pre-Revolutionary

Massachusetts" (Paper delivered at the U.S. Capitol Historical Society, Washington, March 26–28, 1985).

10. The notion of hard times brought on by the disappearance of available land has been argued most forcefully by Kenneth Lockridge in "Social Change and the Meaning of the American Revolution," *Journal of Social History* 6 (1973): 403–439.

11. In comparing the results of specifications with "presence of adult sons" versus "number of adult sons" and "presence of adult daughters" versus "number of adult daughters," it became clear that widows' portions declined sharply even if there was only one son, whereas if widows' portions shrank as a result of having daughters, it happened when there were a number of daughters to take care of.

12. When taken at the mean, personal wealth reduced the predicted value of the dependent variable "generosity of male testators" by -1.127 in the colonial period, by -2.232 in the 1790s, and by -0.771 in the 1890s.

13. John W. Adams and Alice Bee Kasakoff, "Migration and the Family in Colonial New England: The View from Genealogies," *Journal of Family History* 9 (1984): 28. They note that the town studies of Linda Auwers, Kenneth Lockridge, Timothy Breen, and Stephen Foster found the same pattern of first-comers being more mobile in searching for a place to settle.

14. For a more extensive discussion of women as wealthholders, see Carole Shammas, "Early American Women and Control over Capital" (Paper delivered at the U.S. Capitol Historical Society, Washington, D.C., March 28, 1985).

15. Stuart M. Blumin, "The Hypothesis of Middle-Class Formation in Nineteenth-Century America: A Critique and Some Proposals," *American Historical Review* 90 (1985): 299–338, discusses the characteristics of this middle class and contrasts it with both the upper class and the working class.

16. Mary P. Ryan, *Cradle of the Middle Class: The Family in Oneida County, New York, 1790–1865* (New York: Cambridge University Press, 1981), table B.2; William H. Newell, "Through the Eyes of Dying Men: Attitudes towards Women in the Wills of Butler County, Ohio 1803–1865" (Paper delivered at the 1982 Social Science History Association Meeting, Bloomington, Ind.); and Ditz, "Daughters and Inherited Property." For information on intervivos transfers see Friedberger, "Handing Down the Home Place."

17. Ryan, *Cradle of the Middle Class,* table B.1; and Newell, "Through the Eyes of Dying Men."

18. Friedman, "Patterns of Testation," 52; and Daniel Scott Smith, "Inheritance and the Position and Orientation of Colonial Women" (Paper presented at the Second Berkshire Conference on the History of Women, Cambridge, Mass., 1974), table 1.

CHAPTER SIX: THE FEDERAL ESTATE TAX AND INHERITANCE

1. The close relationship between war and inheritance taxes has been noted by Randolph E. Paul, *Federal Estate and Gift Taxation* (Boston: Little, Brown, 1942), 6; and Louis Eisenstein, "The Rise and Decline of the Estate Tax," *Tax Law Review* 11 (1955–1956): 223–259.
2. Harlan Eugene Read, *The Abolition of Inheritance* (New York: Macmillan, 1918); William J. Shultz, *The Taxation of Inheritance* (Boston: Houghton Mifflin, 1926), 98; and Ronald Frederick King, "From Redistributive to Hegemonic Logic: The Transformation of American Tax Politics, 1894–1963," *Politics and Society* 12 (1983): 1–52, show that progressive thinking on tax policy was widespread. In most cases, however, advocates of using progressive tax rates to control vast fortunes hoped thereby to restore the "free" market.
3. Richard D. Wagner, *Inheritance and the State: Tax Principles for a Free and Prosperous Commonwealth* (Washington: American Enterprise Institute, 1977); C. Lowell Harriss, "Revising Estate Taxation," *Tax Review* 32 (1971): 13–16; and Dan Throop Smith, "Impact of Federal Estate and Gift Taxes," *Tax Review* 37 (1976): 17–20. None of these treatments contain any substantive analysis of data.
4. Lloyd Leva Plaine and Winifred Ann Sutton, "Changes in Estate and Gift Tax Law Made by the Economic Recovery Tax Act of 1981," *Women Lawyer's Journal* 68 (1982): 141–149, contains one of the clearest explanations of how the act changed estate and gift tax law. The top marginal rate was 77 percent until 1977, when it dropped to 70 percent.
5. Eisenstein, "Estate Tax." On the general decline in the progressivity of progressive taxation, see Randolph E. Paul, "Erosion of the Tax Base and Rate Structure," *Tax Law Review* 11 (1955–1956): 203–222.
6. Carl S. Shoup, *Federal Estate and Gift Taxes* (Washington: Brookings Institution, 1966) and Gerald R. Jantscher, *Trusts and Estate Taxation* (Washington: Brookings Institution, 1967) are two of the studies that came out of the investigation of estates and trusts. Janet M. Meiburger, "Current Suggestions for Gift and Estate Tax Legislation," *Tax Law Review* 30 (1975): 451–464, reviews the various changes put forward in the two decades before the 1976 act on estate and gift taxation.
7. Lester G. Thurow, *Generating Inequality: Mechanisms of Distribution in the United States Economy* (New York: Basic Books, 1975), 197. John Brittain, *Inheritance and the Inequality of Material Wealth* (Washington: Brookings Institution, 1978), 94, expresses similar sentiments.
8. Paul L. Menchik and Martin David, "Income Distribution, Lifetime Savings, and Bequests," *American Economic Review* 73 (1983): 672–690, mention that the Treasury Department is now embarked on a new study trying to link income and estate returns.
9. If 1938 is taken as the base year, then the deflator for 1955 is 2.07, and for 1977, 4.27. Price deflators appearing in Bureau of the Census, *His-*

torical Statistics of the United States, Colonial Times to 1970 (Washington: Government Printing Office, 1975), 197, were readjusted to make 1938 the base year. Post-1970 deflators were obtained from idem, *Statistical Abstracts of the United States* (Washington: Government Printing Office). Generally, in this book, we use 1958 as the base year, but for Tables 6.3 and 6.4, it seemed the most straightforward approach was to use 1938.

10. George Cooper, *A Voluntary Tax? New Perspectives on Sophisticated Estate Tax Avoidance* (Washington: Brookings Institution, 1979), 59–61.

11. Those for a limit include Stephen K. McNees, "Deductibility of Charitable Bequests," *National Tax Journal* 26 (1973): 79–98; and David Westfall, "Proposed Limitations on the Estate Tax Deduction for Charitable Transfers," in *Research Papers,* ed. Commission on Private Philanthropy and Public Needs (Washington: Department of Treasury, 1977), 4:2353–2359. Among those against any limits are John Holt Myers, "Estate Tax Deduction for Charitable Benefits: Proposed Limitations," ibid., 2299–2318; Richard E. Wagner, "Death, Taxes, and Charitable Bequests: A Survey of Issues and Options," ibid., 2337–2352; Michael J. Boskin, "Estate Taxation and Charitable Bequests," ibid., 3:1453–1484; Chairman and Staff, Council on Foundations, "Private Foundations and the 1969 Tax Reform Act," ibid., 1557–1661; and Smith, "Estate and Gift Taxes," 20.

12. McNees, "Deductibility of Charitable Bequests"; Boskin, "Estate Taxation and Charitable Bequests"; Martin S. Feldstein, "Charitable Bequests, Estate Taxation, and Intergenerational Wealth Transfers," in *Research Papers,* ed. Commission on Private Philanthropy and Public Needs (Washington: Department of Treasury, 1977), 4:1485–1500; Thommas Barthold and Robert Plotnick, "Estate Taxation and Other Determinants of Charitable Bequests," *National Taxation Journal* 37 (1984): 225–237; Charles T. Clotfelter, *Federal Tax Policy and Charitable Giving* (Chicago: University of Chicago Press, 1985), 222–252; and especially, Paul Leonard Menchik, "A Study of Inheritance and Death Taxation: A Microeconomic Approach" (Ph.D. diss., University of Pennsylvania, 1976). The equation results for multimillion-dollar estates in these studies are either inconclusive on the price elasticity of bequests because of large standard errors or have an elasticity below unity. That is, the price of making bequests (calculated as 1 minus the marginal estate tax rate) goes down faster than charitable bequests increase. Thus the charitable bequests generated by the deduction are insufficient to cover the loss in taxes. The results are particularly amusing because a couple of the investigators, Boskin and Feldstein, clearly hoped to justify the charitable deduction with the equations. They find some comfort in the fact that the less affluent estates have elasticities over unity. As most of charitable giving, however, occurs among the multimillionaire group, it seems the main thrust of their findings, whether they admit it or not, is that the charitable deduction does result in fewer dollars in the public coffers. In addition to

the contrary results, there are questions about the legitimacy of measuring the price elasticity of bequests in this manner. To gauge the effect of the price of bequests on the value of bequests, it is necessary to hold estate wealth constant. With estate wealth in the regression, however, there is severe collinearity between it and price of bequests because the latter is measured by the marginal tax rate. Indeed, the Barthold and Plotnick study found the effect of the price of bequests to be statistically insignificant. The problem is that people may give to charity because of tax breaks, but they may also make bequests because they are rich and have extra money to give to philanthropy. Because of the intercorrelation of the independent variables, it is highly questionable whether the effects of wealth and the marginal tax rate can be separated.

13. Emil M. Sunley, Jr., "Dimensions of Charitable Giving Reported on Federal Estate, Gift, and Fiduciary Tax Returns," in *Research Papers,* ed. Commission on Private Philanthropy and Public Needs (Washington: Department of the Treasury, 1977), 2325.

14. American Association of Fund Raising Counsel, *Giving USA* (New York: American Association of Fund Raising Counsel, 1974), 28.

15. The Treasury reports on foundations are Department of the Treasury, *Report on Private Foundations* (Washington: Government Printing Office, 1965); IRS, *Statistics of Income 1974–1978, Private Foundations* (Washington: Government Printing Office, 1981); and Thomas B. Petska, "An Examination of Private Foundations for 1979," *Statistics of Income Bulletin* 2 (1982): 9–29. Thomas B. Petska and Daniel Skelly, "Private Foundations, Federal Tax Law, and Philanthropic Activity: An IRS Perspective," in *Statistics of Income and Related Administrative Record Research,* ed. Internal Revenue Service (Washington: Government Printing Office, 1982), 171–183, compares figures from the 1962–1978 period.

16. Joseph A. Pechman, *Federal Tax Policy,* 4th ed., (Washington: Brookings Institution, 1983), 241; Joseph C. Goulden, *The Money Givers* (New York: Random House, 1971), 43. Waldemar A. Nielsen, *The Big Foundations* (New York: Columbia University Press, 1972), gives additional examples of how foundations have been used to further family and trustee interests.

17. For example, see Jeffrey Hart, "Foundations and Social Activism: A Critical View," in *The Future of Foundations,* ed. Fritz Heimann (Englewood Cliffs, N.J.: Prentice-Hall, 1973), 43–57.

18. R. D. Wagner, *Inheritance and the State,* 5.

19. Robin Barlow, Harvey E. Brazer, and James N. Morgan, *Economic Behavior of the Affluent* (Washington: Brookings Institution, 1966), 97–112; Shoup, *Federal Estate and Gift Taxes,* 17; Thurow, *Generating Inequality,* 140–141.

20. Paul L. Menchik, "The Importance of Material Inheritance," in *Modeling the Distribution and Intergenerational Transmission of Wealth,* ed. James D. Smith (Chicago: University of Chicago Press, 1980), 159–185. He studied the heirs of more than one thousand Connecticut residents

who died in the 1930s and 1940s leaving estates of over forty thousand dollars.

21. Brittain, *Inequality of Material Wealth*, 6, uses some data from the Securities and Exchange Commission on bank-administered trusts and estates and compares it with information about wealthholders in 1969. He finds that in the five million dollar and over bracket, there is a one to four ratio. That is, there are 2,412 trusts in that category and 9,330 wealthholders.

22. Joseph A. Pechman, "Analysis of Matched Estate and Gift Tax Returns," *National Tax Journal* 5 (1950): 153–164; Shoup, *Federal Estate and Gift Taxes,* 216. James D. Adams, "Equalization of True Gift and Estate Tax Rates," *Journal of Public Economics* 9 (1978): 59–71, has argued that the decision not to make gifts before death is rational economically, largely because with estates there was no payment of capital gains on appreciated capital. The fact that no such tax was levied on gifts either, if the assets were not sold, and the possible advantages of dividing up an estate seem to undercut the advantage Adams sees in keeping an estate intact until death.

23. Jantscher, *Trusts and Estate Taxation,* 10–13, implies that trusts should increase because of estate planning, but he also shows the small percentage of total wealth that the very rich put in trusts.

24. Lawrence M. Friedman, "The Dynastic Trust," *Yale Law Journal* 73 (1964): 548–592; William H. Wicker, "Spendthrift Trusts," *Gonzaga Law Review* 10 (1974): 1–18; Shoup, *Federal Estate and Gift Taxes,* 94.

25. Thurow, *Generating Inequality,* 140–141.

26. Menchik, "Importance of Material Inheritance," 175.

27. Minturn T. Wright III, "Termination of Trusts in Pennsylvania: Some Current Trends," *University of Pennsylvania Law Review* 115 (1966–1967): 917–934.

CHAPTER SEVEN: DEMOGRAPHIC CHANGE, OLD-AGE POLICY, AND THE FAMILY

1. Lawrence M. Friedman, "Patterns of Testation in the Nineteenth Century: A Study of Essex County (New Jersey) Wills," *American Journal of Legal History* 8 (1964): 34–53.

2. Ibid., 37–38.

3. Peter Uhlenberg, "A Study of Cohort Life Cycles: Cohorts of Native Born Massachusetts Women, 1830–1920," *Population Studies* 23 (1969): 414.

4. Holger R. Stub, *The Social Consequences of Long Life* (Springfield, Il.: Thomas, 1982), 131.

5. Friedman, "Patterns of Testation," 44, found testator age at death in the 1950s to be the late sixties or early seventies.

6. William Graebner, *A History of Retirement: The Meaning and Function of an American Institution, 1885–1978* (New Haven, Conn.: Yale University Press, 1980), and W. Andrew Achenbaum, *Shades of Gray: Old Age, American Values, and Federal Policies since 1920* (Boston: Little, Brown, 1983) are exceptions.

7. Alicia Haydock Munnell, *The Effect of Social Security on Personal Savings* (Cambridge, Mass.: Ballinger, 1974), 12.

8. For a discussion of this issue, see Michel R. Dahlin, "From Poorhouse to Pension: The Changing View of Old Age in America, 1890–1920" (Ph.D. diss., Stanford University, 1982).

9. Ibid., 23–24.

10. Munnell, *Social Security*, 12; see also Graebner, *History of Retirement*, chap. 10.

11. William C. Greenough and Francis P. King, *Pension Plans and Public Policy* (New York: Columbia University Press, 1976), 234.

12. Daphne T. Greenwood, "Age, Income, and Household Size: Their Relation to Wealth Distribution in the United States," in *International Comparisons of the Distribution of Household Wealth* ed. Edward Wolff (New York: Oxford University Press, forthcoming). On nineteenth century wealth inequality see Jeffrey G. Williamson and Peter H. Lindert, "Long-Term Trends in American Wealth Inequality," in *Modeling the Distribution and Intergenerational Transmission of Wealth,* ed. James D. Smith (Chicago: University of Chicago Press, 1980), 9–94.

13. A random sample of one community in the 1970s found that only 4 percent of the adults over fifty had participated in or had access to an organized or sponsored retirement-planning program. Robert C. Atchley, "What Happened to Retirement Planning in the 1970s?" in *Aging and Retirement: Prospects, Planning, and Policy* ed. Neil G. McCluskey and Edgar F. Borgatta (Beverly Hills, Calif.: Sage, 1981), 80.

14. While four-fifths of aged respondents to a 1968 social security survey reported having some liquid assets, primarily in bank and savings accounts, only those in higher income brackets had sufficient assets to generate much additional income. Over 70 percent of all elderly couples, both poor and not poor, owned a home. See Lenore E. Bixby et al., *Demographic and Economic Characteristics of the Aged: 1968 Social Security Survey* (Washington: Department of Health, Education, and Welfare, 1971), 124.

15. Munnell, *Social Security*, 73.

16. Greenough and King, *Pension Plans and Public Policy*, 111–114, 137; Graebner, *History of Retirement*, chap. 8.

17. Munnell, *Social Security*, 25–26. The number of monthly beneficiaries of private pension and deferred profit-sharing plans has risen. In 1930 there were 100,000 beneficiaries; in 1940, 160,000; in 1950, 450,000; in 1960, 1,780,000; and in 1970, 4,720,000. Bureau of the Census, *Historical Statistics of the United States, Colonial Times to 1970* (Washington: Government Printing Office, 1975) 354, table H 287–304.

18. American Council of Life Insurance, *Life Insurance Fact Book 1984* (Washington: American Council of Life Insurance, 1984), 37.

19. Munnell, *Social Security,* 25.

20. Thad W. Mirer, "The Wealth–Age Relation among the Aged," *American Economic Review* 69 (1979): 435. Of affluent testators in a 1964 Brookings survey, 23 percent listed making a bequest as one motive for saving. See Robin Barlow, Harvey E. Brazer, and James N. Morgan, *Economic Behavior of the Affluent* (Washington: Brookings Institution, 1966), 198.

21. Munnell, *Social Security,* 23–25.

22. Ibid., 32–35.

23. James B. Davies, "Uncertain Lifetime, Consumption, and Dissaving in Retirement," *Journal of Political Economy* 89 (1981): 561–577.

24. These definitions of life-cycle and capital wealth are from Edward N. Wolff, "The Size Distribution of Household Disposable Wealth in the United States," *Review of Income and Wealth* 29 (1983): 124–146.

25. Ibid., 142.

26. Williamson and Lindert, "Inequality," 62.

27. Dahlin, "From Poorhouse to Pension," 199–203.

28. Beth B. Hess, "America's Aged Revisited: Who, What, When, and Why?" in *Growing Old in America,* 2d ed., ed. Beth B. Hess (New Brunswick, N.J.: Rutgers University Press, 1980), 9.

29. Carole Haber, *Beyond Sixty-Five: The Dilemma of Old Age in America's Past* (Cambridge: Cambridge University Press, 1983), 95–107.

30. Florence E. Parker, Estelle M. Stewart, and Mary Conymgton, *Care of Aged Persons in the United States* (1929; reprint, New York, Arno, 1976) 3, 20–21, 29.

31. Michael E. Hunt et al., *Retirement Communities: An American Original* (New York: Haworth, 1984), 1–2.

32. Ibid., chap. 1.

33. Burton Kavis Dunlop, *The Growth of Nursing Home Care* (Lexington, Mass.: Heath, 1979), 1.

34. Ibid., 29, 47. Adult children of the old were unable or unwilling to care for the aged in their homes for a number of reasons. Some of them were retired themselves and found the physical, emotional, and economic burden of home care too great. Also women are usually the care-givers for aged family members. As more and more women work, they are not available to give daily care to aged relatives. See Judith Treas, "Family Support Systems for the Aged: Some Social and Demographic Considerations," *Gerontologist* 17 (1979): 488.

35. Dunlop, *Growth of Nursing Home Care,* 1; *Historical Statistics of the United States,* 73. The 1976 figure is from Frank E. Moss and Val Halamandaris, *Too Old, Too Sick, Too Bad: Nursing Homes in America* (Germantown, Pa.: Aspen Systems Corp., 1977), 21.

36. Francis Kobrin, "The Fall in Household Size and the Rise of the Primary Individual in the United States," *Demography* 13 (1976): 127–138.

37. Daniel Scott Smith, "Historical Change in the Household Structure of the

Elderly in Economically Developed Societies," in *Aging: Stability and Change in the Family,* ed. Robert W. Fogel et al. (New York: Academic, 1981), 109.

38. Jeffrey P. Rosenfeld, *The Legacy of Aging: Inheritance and Disinheritance in Social Perspective* (Norwood, N.J.: Abalex, 1979), 29. More on Rosenfeld's findings in Chapter Nine.

39. "Continuing-Care Communities for the Elderly: Potential Pitfalls and Proposed Legislation," *University of Pennsylvania Law Review* 128 (1980): 886–887 and n. 14. Similar estimates are found in Hunt et al., *Retirement Communities,* 262.

40. "Continuing-Care Communities for the Elderly," 888.

41. Phyllis Seligson Schacht, "Protection for the Elderly Person and His Estate: Regulating and Enforcing Life-Care Contracts," *Probate Law Journal* 4 (1982–1983): 107–110. The five states that regulate life care contracts are Florida, Colorado, California, Michigan, and Arizona. Regulations are primarily concerned with the financial stability of the life care provider institution (108–110). The author discusses the ambiguities of the Pennsylvania law (108).

42. Richard M. Garvin and Robert E. Burger, *Where They Go to Die: The Tragedy of America's Aged* (New York: Dial, 1968), 80, 90–93; "Continuing-Care Communities for the Elderly," 903–909; and Schacht, "Protection for the Elderly," 120.

43. *Senior Living: Bucks County Housing Guide for Older Adults* (Buck County Commissioners and the Area Agency on Aging, n.d., 34–35; Pennsylvania Department of Health, *Natality and Mortality Statistics, 1979* (Harrisburg, Pa.: Health Data Center, 1980); Ethel Shanas and Marvin B. Sussman, "The Family in Later Life: Social Structure and Social Policy," in Fogel et al., *Aging,* 215. Rosenfeld, *Legacy of Aging,* 103, found that 6 percent of the estates of institutionalized elderly in his study escheated to the state; that is, the estates reverted to the state for lack of heirs. These people without close kin tended not to write wills, so there were no designated heirs to take the place of the family.

44. Beth J. Soldo, "America's Elderly in the 1980s," *Population Bulletin* 35 (1980): 23.

45. Ibid., 24.

46. Stub, *Social Consequences of Long Life,* 151; Rosenfeld, *Legacy of Aging,* 73. See also, for example, Rene A. Wormser, "How to Save Money by Giving It Away," *U.S. News and World Report,* December 28, 1956, 134.

47. Stub, *Social Consequences of Long Life,* 192.

48. Helen Heusinkveld and Noverre Musson, *1001 Places to Live When You Retire* (Chicago: Dartnell Corp., 1964), 19. See also George Byron Gordon, *You, Your Heirs and Your Estate: An Approach to Estate Planning,* rev. ed. (Rockville Centre, N.Y.: Farnsworth, 1973), 23.

49. Rita J. Simon, William Rav, and Mary Louise Fellows, "Public versus Statutory Choice of Heirs: A Study of Public Attitudes about Property

Distribution at Death," *Social Forces* 58 (1980): 1263; Marvin B. Sussman, Judith N. Cates, and David T. Smith, *The Family and Inheritance* (New York: Russell Sage, 1970), 89; Rosenfeld, *Legacy of Aging*, 27; and Carol A. Engler-Bowles, and Cary S. Kart, "Intergeneration Relations and Testamentary Patterns: An Exploration," *Gerontologist* 23 (1983): 171. The Engler-Bowles and Kart article uses nineteenth-century data as well as twentieth; it was only a pilot study, however, so there are very small numbers of observations reported.

50. Dahlin, "From Poorhouse to Pension," 198–199.
51. Smith, "Household Structure of the Elderly," 109.
52. Ethel Shanas, "Social Myth as Hypothesis: The Care of the Family Relations of Old People," *Gerontologist* 19 (1979): 8.
53. Tamara K. Hareven, "Historical Changes in the Timing of Family Transitions: Their Impact on Generational Relations," in *Aging*, Fogel et al., 162.
54. Gunhild O. Hagestad, "Problems and Promises in the Social Psychology of Intergenerational Relations," in ibid., 24.

CHAPTER EIGHT: INHERITANCE LAW AND THE UNFINISHED REVOLUTION

1. Leo Kanowitz, *Women and the Law: The Unfinished Revolution* (Albuquerque: University of New Mexico Press, 1969).
2. Homer H. Clark, Jr., *The Law of Domestic Relations in the United States* (St. Paul, Minn.: West, 1968), 223–224; and Caleb Foote, Robert J. Levey, and Frank E. A. Sander, *Cases and Materials on Family Law* (Boston: Little, Brown, 1966), 319. See also Association of American Law Schools, *Selected Essays on Family Law* (Brooklyn: Foundation Press, 1950), 531.
3. See, particularly, John D. Johnston, Jr., "Sex and Property: The Common Law Tradition, the Law School Curriculum, and Developments toward Equality," *New York University Law Review* 47 (1972): 1034–1072.
4. Chester G. Vernier, *American Family Laws*, 5 vols. (1935; reprint, Westport, Conn.: Greenwood, 1971).
5. In community property states, widows automatically received half of the community property when their husbands died. In addition, if the men died intestate, they received one-half of the husband's share regardless of the number of children. The share of the husband's separate estate a widow could claim varied from jurisdiction to jurisdiction, but the most common proportion was one-third. While community property state widows did not do as well as widowers, they, in almost all intestacy situations, received more than their counterparts in common law jurisdictions.
6. On inheritance law trends in the United States and Western Europe, see Mary Ann Glendon, *State Law and the Family: Family Law in Transition*

in the United States and Western Europe (Amsterdam: New Holland, 1977), 279–289.

7. Under the common law, the dower to which a widow was entitled at the death of her husband was the income from one-third of all real property he had held during his lifetime unless she had renounced her dower claim when he alienated the land. Actuarial tables were published during the nineteenth and early twentieth centuries that estimated the "present value" of dower and curtesy at the time of the spouse's death and projections before that death. See, for example, Florien Giauque and Henry B. McClure, comp., *Tables for Ascertaining the Present Value of Vested and Contingent Rights of Dower, Curtesy, Annuities,* 4th ed. (Cincinnati: Robert Clarke, 1904).

8. See Carl N. Degler, *At Odds: Women and the Family in America from the Revolution to the Present* (New York: Oxford University Press, 1980), 328–331 on this debate.

9. Leila J. Rupp, "The Survival of American Feminism: The Women's Movement in the Postwar Period," in *Reshaping America: Society and Institutions, 1945–1960,* ed. Robert H. Bremner and Gary W. Reichard (Columbus: Ohio State University Press, 1982), 33–65; Ethel Klein, *Gender Politics: From Consciousness to Mass Politics* (Cambridge, Mass.: Harvard University Press, 1984), chap. 1; Nancy F. Cott, "Feminist Politics in the 1920s: The National Woman's Party," *Journal of American History* 71 (1984): 43–68; and Leila J. Rupp, "The Women's Community in the National Woman's Party, 1945 to the 1960s," *Signs* 10 (1985): 715–740.

10. Klein, *Gender Politics,* 12, 17–21.

11. Jo Freeman, *The Politics of Women's Liberation* (New York: McKay, 1975), 44–70; Sara Evans, *Personal Politics: The Roots of Women's Liberation in the Civil Rights Movement and the New Left* (New York: Random House, 1979).

12. Klein, *Gender Politics,* 22.

13. Ibid.

14. Barbara A. Brown et al., *Women's Rights and the Law: The Impact of the ERA on State Laws* (New York: Praeger, 1927), 19–32.

15. For the clearest description of the property law problems women faced in both common law and community property states, see Anne K. Bingaman, "The Impact of the ERA on Marital Economics," in *Impact ERA: Limitations and Possibilities,* ed. Equal Rights Amendment Project of the California Commission on the Status of Women (Millbrae, Calif.: Femmes, 1976), 116–126.

16. Ibid., 117.

17. For the old arguments see Association of American Law Schools, *Selected Essays on Family Law,* 525–549, and for a more recent dismissal see Roxanne Barton Conlin, "Equal Protection versus Equal Rights Amendment: Where Are We Now?" *Drake Law Review* 24 (1975): 277.

18. Opposition to Wisconsin's adoption of the community property system surfaced again in the 1984–1985 legislative session when a bill to clarify

portions of the act was blocked. In 1986, the Republican gubernatorial candidate, who subsequently defeated the incumbent, pledged to repeal the legislation.

19. Commonwealth of Pennsylvania, *Report of the Commission to Codify and Revise the Law of Decedent's Estates* (Philadelphia: Allen, Lane, Scott, 1917), 5, 7, 19.

20. In Pennsylvania, real estate held in the name of a husband and wife creates, unless contrary intention be clear, a tenancy by entireties. Like joint tenancy, the survivor takes all. Unlike joint tenancy, during lifetime neither party can alienate the property without the agreement of the other. Because most states have married couples use joint tenancy rather than tenancy by the entireties, and as at death they both operate in the same way, we refer in the text to couples buying jointly. On tenancy by entireties, see Oval A. Phipps, "Tenancy by Entireties," *Temple Law Quarterly* 25 (1951): 24–57. Tenants in common is yet another form of holding property. Such tenants do not acquire ownership of the whole when the other tenant dies. They only have a right to the share of the property they initially purchased.

21. Article I, Section 28, Pennsylvania Constitution.

22. Pennsylvania Commission for Women, *The Impact of the State Equal Rights Amendment in Pennsylvania Since 1971* (Harrisburg, Pa.: Pennsylvania Commission for Women, 1976), 6.

23. Homemaker's Committee, National Commission on the Observation of International Women's Year, *The Legal Status of Homemakers in Pennsylvania* (Washington: Government Printing Office, 1977), 37.

24. Pennsylvania Commission for Women, *Equal Rights Amendment in Pennsylvania*, 2.

25. DiFlorido v. DiFlorido, 459 Pa. 650 (1975).

26. When California adopted the community property system in 1850, the state followed civil law custom and did not allow either spouse testamentary power over his or her half of community property. Then in 1860 husbands obtained the right to will their half, *West's Annotated California Codes, Probate Code Sections 1 to 399* (St. Paul, Minn.: West, 1956), 399.

27. California Commission on the Status of Women, *ERA Conformance: An Analysis of the California State Codes* (Sacramento: Documents Section, 1975). The commission received funding from the Rockefeller Foundation for a national study of the societal impact of conformance of laws to the ERA, and several publications followed from that study. See Equal Rights Amendment Project, California Commission on the Status of Women, ed., *Impact ERA: Limitations and Possibilities*, ix.

28. California Commission on the Status of Women, *ERA Conformance*, 184.

29. *West's California Codes, Probate Code 1985 Compact Edition* (St. Paul, Minn.: 1985), 463–465.

30. The pro- and anti-ERA categories for states are based on the list in Janet K.

Boles, *The Politics of the Equal Rights Amendment* (New York: Long-man, 1979), 2–3. The inheritance laws are those for 1982 in our Appendix C. All fifty states are included, both common law and community property.

31. Marvin Sussman, Judith N. Cates, and David T. Smith, *The Family and Inheritance* (New York: Russell Sage, 1970), 89; and Rita J. Simon, William Rav, and Mary Louise Fellows, "Public versus Statutory Choice of Heirs: A Study of Public Attitudes about Property Distribution at Death," *Social Forces* 58 (1980): 1265–1267.

32. For an argument that the law of the family has been weakening the relationship between husband and wife as well as that between family and child, see Mary Ann Glendon, *The New Family and the New Property* (Scarborough, Ont.: Butterworth, 1981).

CHAPTER NINE: TESTAMENTARY BEHAVIOR IN THE LATE TWENTIETH CENTURY

1. Taking out life insurance with an heir named as beneficiary is a fourth way of avoiding estate taxes. Because such insurance is not part of a probated estate, however, there is no way to tell how much life insurance the testators in our sample held. We do know from other studies, such as those of Carl S. Shoup, *Federal Estate and Gift Taxes* (Washington: Brookings Institution, 1966), 67; Robin Barlow, Harvey E. Brazer, James N. Morgan, *Economic Behavior of the Affluent* (Washington: Brookings Institution, 1966), 55–59, 111; and Marvin Sussman, Judith N. Cates, and David T. Smith, *The Family and Inheritance* (New York: Russell Sage, 1970), 178–180; that life insurance policies are owned by most testators, but the affluent do not increase the amount held as income rises. Life insurance holding predated the imposition of a federal estate tax, and the motives for taking out policies seem to be related more to concerns about security than schemes to avoid taxes.

2. The 1976 estate tax reform substituted a unified (gift and estate) tax credit for the specific exemption of 60,000 dollars. Beginning with decedents dying in 1977, the tax credit amounted to approximately a 120,000-dollar exemption that gradually increased to 175,000 dollars by the early 1980s, when it was completely phased in. Because it was a unified tax credit, however, intervivos gifts had to be subtracted from the amount an estate could claim under the credit. Considering this and the fact many of the testators in the 1979 Bucks and 1980 Los Angeles samples died in the previous year or even before, it seemed that 120,000 dollars was good cut-off point separating those at risk to pay estate taxes from those who almost surely were not.

3. Carter P. Pomeroy, *The Codes and Statutes of California . . . 1901* (San Francisco: Bancroft Whitney, 1892). Lawrence M. Friedman, "Patterns

of Testation in the Nineteenth Century: A Study of Essex County [New Jersey] Wills," *American Journal of Legal History* 8 (1964): 47, found in samples of New Jersey wills between 1850 and 1900 that under 10 percent left bequests to charity.

4. Sussman, Cates, and Smith, *Family and Inheritance,* 114, report in their study of Cuyahoga County, Ohio, wills in the mid-1960s that, out of the total 3.5 million dollars given to charity by the four hundred or more testators, all but 70,000 dollars of it came from one estate. Shoup, *Federal Estate and Gift Taxes,* 216, shows that among millionaires whose estate tax returns in 1945, 1957, and 1959 were linked to earlier gift tax returns, over half *never* made either an intervivos taxable gift or a bequest to charity.

5. Lawrence M. Friedman, "The Dynastic Trust," *Yale Law Journal* 73 (1964): 547–592. One of the biggest debates surrounding trusts is whether state law should specify the kinds of investments trustees may make with the money under their control or whether a "prudent man" test in court is sufficient. For more recent information on this subject, see Robin Pruitt Seifel, "The Changing Landscape of Professional Trustee Investment Standards," *Probate Law Journal* 4 (1982–1983): 31–54.

6. Also, at least half of these generation-skipping arrangements were not of the children-to-grandchildren variety but involved collateral kin instead. Guardianship also seemed in some cases to be as strong a motive as the tax saving.

7. See Chapter Six on gifts and Joseph A. Pechman, "Analysis of Matched Estate and Gift Tax Returns," *National Tax Journal* 5 (1950): 153–164; Shoup, *Federal Estate and Gift Taxes,* 216; and James D. Adams, "Equalization of True Gift and Estate Tax Rates," *Journal of Public Economics* 9 (1978): 59–71.

8. Edward H. Ward and J. H. Beuscher, "The Inheritance Process in Wisconsin," *Wisconsin Law Review* 1950 (1950): 415, report that in their samples of Dane County wills from 1929 to 1944, "trust estates at most (in 1929) comprised 20% of all estates with a will; the smallest proportion was 6.7% (for 1934), and the average for all years was 13.2%." Most trusts were for middle-income estates (those valued at under twenty thousand dollars), suggesting they were primarily for guardianship purposes and for spouses. Sussman, Cates, and Smith, *Family and Inheritance,* 189, found in their 1960s study that only 14.5 percent of those testators at risk to pay estate taxes (i.e., having an estate over sixty thousand dollars) made trusts, and almost all were for spouses. Of those 2 percent of estates under sixty thousand dollars that involved trusts, three-fourths were guardianship trusts. E. G. Horsman, "Inheritance in England and Wales: The Evidence Provided by Wills," *Oxford Economic Papers,* new ser., 30 (1978): 419, finds a much higher percentage (77 percent) of affluent (fifty thousand pounds and above in 1973) estates in England using trusts, but most involved life estates for spouses and did not include generation skipping.

9. Mark W. Friedberger, "Handing Down the Home Place: Farm Inheritance Strategies in Iowa," *Annals of Iowa* 47 (1984): 539. For additional information on the role of ethnicity in twentieth-century farm inheritance, especially in relation to German groups, see Edward V. Carroll and Sonya Salmon, "Inheritance Patterns in Two Illinois Farm Communities" (Paper presented at the 1985 Social Science History Association Meeting, Chicago).

10. Daniel Scott Smith, "Historical Change in the Household Structure of the Elderly in Economically Developed Societies," in *Aging: Stability and Change in the Family,* ed. Robert W. Fogel et al. (New York: Academic, 1981), 110.

11. Jeffrey P. Rosenfeld, *The Legacy of Aging: Inheritance and Disinheritance in Social Perspective* (Norwood, N.J.: Ablex, 1979).

12. Smith summarizes the debate in "Change in the Household Structure," 109.

13. For similar findings on the predominance of professionals over friends as executors, see Sussman, Cates, and Smith, *Family and Inheritance,* 232.

14. Allison Dunham, "The Method, Process and Frequency of Wealth Transmission at Death," *University of Chicago Law Review* 30 (1962–1963): 260, discovered in a late-1950s survey of Cook County, Illinois, residents that only 4 percent of testators liked the intestacy laws, while 54 percent wished to give all to the spouse. Of those with small estates, 85 percent wanted to leave their entire estate to a husband or wife. Also if children were adults with their own families, a testator was more inclined to want to leave more to the spouse. Sussman, Cates, and Smith, *Family and Inheritance,* 89, show that in the mid-1960s in Cuyahoga County, 85 percent of those with children still left all to the spouse. Again, it was the smaller estate holders who were most likely to make this choice. John R. Price, "The Transmission of Wealth at Death in a Community Property Jurisdiction," *Washington Law Review* 50 (1975): 277–340, found that in 1969, fourteen out of seventeen (76.4 percent) of Washington state married male testators left everything to the spouse, while three out of five of the married women did likewise. But in addition, thirty-one married people made community property contracts that gave their entire estate to a spouse. In a more recent five-state survey, Rita J. Simon, William Rav, and Mary Louise Fellows, "Public versus Statutory Choice of Heirs: A Study of Public Attitudes about Property Distribution at Death," *Social Forces* 58 (1980): 1265–1267, found that 68 percent of men and 57 percent of women favored leaving everything to the spouse. Existence and age of children did not make a great deal of difference in the percentage they wished the spouse to have.

15. If separate marriage settlements were made, we coded the cases missing. Only 2–3 percent of the cases in the samples were thus affected. Also there were not enough cases known to involve remarried testators to justify a separate category. Presumably the size of this group will increase in future.

16. About the only change was that a wife could inherit her husband's entire estate if there were no heirs. Dower rights had also changed. See Chapters One and Three.

17. For Pennsylvania intestates dying after June 1978, one-half of the estate went to the spouse if there were children regardless of number. It turned out that all of the wills of married people with children, save one, were written before 1978, and thus we had to use the older law for comparison.

18. Olin L. Browder, Jr., "Recent Patterns of Testate Succession in the United States and England," *Michigan Law Review* 67 (1968–1969): 1303–1360, also found in a study of testates in Washtenaw County, Michigan, that there was an inverse relationship between the size of an estate and the giving of all of it to the spouse.

19. Friedman, "Patterns of Testation," 43; Carol A. Engler-Bowles and Cary S. Kart, "Intergenerational Relations and Testamentary Patterns: An Exploration," *Gerontologist* 23 (1983): 169; and Browder, "Recent Patterns of Testate Succession," 1307.

20. Mortality in Los Angeles at the end of the nineteenth century was higher than in more mature, less urban areas, although it was improving. Life expectancy at birth in 1880 has been estimated at thirty-six years and at forty-two years in 1900. See Maxine Weinstein, Karen Oppenheim Mason, and Barbara Laslett, "Social and Demographic Components of Change in Household Composition in Late Nineteenth-Century, Los Angeles" (Paper presented at the 1985 meeting of the Social Science History Association, Chicago). The city's mortality profile, according to the authors, ressembles that of an urban tubercular population. Also see Eileen M. Crimmins and Gretchen A. Condran, "Mortality Variation in U.S. Cities in 1900," *Social Science History* 7 (1983), 31–60.

21. John Brittain, *Inheritance and the Inequality of Material Wealth* (Washington: Brookings Institution, 1978), 45–46.

22. Karen Oppenheim Mason and Barbara Laslett, "Women's Work in the American West: Los Angeles, 1880–1900 and Its Contrast with Essex County, Massachusetts in 1880," *Research Reports, Population Studies Center, University of Michigan* (Ann Arbor: Population Studies Center, 1983), 38.

APPENDIX A: SAMPLES OF PROBATE RECORDS FROM BUCKS COUNTY, PENNSYLVANIA, AND LOS ANGELES COUNTY, CALIFORNIA

1. Evarts B. Greene and Virginia D. Harrington, *The American Population before the Federal Census of 1790* (Gloucester, Mass.: 1932; reprint, Peter Smith, 1966), 117.

2. Ansley J. Coale and Paul Demeny with Barbara Vaughan, *Regional Model Life Tables and Stable Populations,* 2d ed. (New York: Academic, 1983),

63, 113. Given the high level of immigration into Pennsylvania during the eighteenth century, it is difficult to choose the proper life table. In making our choice we found helpful Daniel Scott Smith, "The Demographic History of New England," *Journal of Economic History* 32 (1972): 165–183; idem, "A Malthusian-Frontier Interpretation of United States Demographic History before c. 1815," in *Urbanization in the Americas: The Background in Comparative Perspective,* ed. Woodrow Borah, Jorge Hardoy, and Gilbert A. Stelter, (Ottawa: National Museum of Man, 1980), 15–22; Maris A. Vinovskis, "Mortality Rates and Trends in Massachusetts before 1860," *Journal of Economic History* 32 (1972): 184–213; and Robert Higgs, "Mortality in Rural America 1870–1920," *Explorations in Economic History* 10 (1973), 177–195.

3. Greene and Harrington, *Population before the Federal Census,* 120.
4. Bucks County Death Registers, 1893–1906, 3 vols, Bucks County Court House, Doylestown.
5. Commonwealth of Pennsylvania, Department of Health, *Natality and Mortality Statistics Annual Report, 1978* (Harrisburg, Pa.: Health Data Center, 1979); and State of California, *Vital Statistics of California, 1978* (Sacramento: State Printing Office, 1981).
6. Alice Hanson Jones, *Wealth of a Nation to Be* (New York: Columbia University Press, 1980), 98, 129; James Lemon, *Best Poor Man's Country: A Case Study of Early Southeastern Pennsylvania* (Baltimore: Johns Hopkins University Press, 1972), 88; and Gary B. Nash, *The Urban Crucible* (Cambridge, Mass.: Harvard University Press, 1979), 399–400.
7. Lee Soltow, "Male Inheritance Expectations in the United States in 1870," *Review of Economics and Statistics* 64 (1982): 258.

Index

Page numbers for tables are in boldface type.